THE CRITIQUE OF DIGITAL CAPITALISM

THE
CRITIQUE
OF
DIGITAL
CAPITALISM

AN ANALYSIS OF THE POLITICAL ECONOMY OF
DIGITAL CULTURE AND TECHNOLOGY

Michael Betancourt

punctum books ⓟ brooklyn, ny

THE CRITIQUE OF DIGITAL CAPITALISM: AN ANALYSIS OF
THE POLITICAL ECONOMY OF DIGITAL CULTURE AND
TECHNOLOGY
© Michael Betancourt, 2015.

First published in 2015 by
punctum books
Brooklyn, New York
http://punctumbooks.com

punctum books is an independent, open-access pub-
lisher dedicated to radically creative modes of intellectual inquiry and writing across a whimsical para-
humanities assemblage. We solicit and pimp quixotic,
sagely mad engagements with textual thought-bodies,
and provide shelters for intellectual vagabonds.

Cover Artwork: Michael Betancourt, 2014_023 (0;01;
07;15), July 18, 2014.png. Book design by Jake Valente.

ISBN-13: 978-0692598443
ISBN-10: 0692598448

Facing-page illustration by Heather Masciandaro.

for Leah

TABLE OF CONTENTS

ACKNOWLEDGMENTS

Essays revised for publication in this book were previously published by the journals *CTheory, Hz* and *Vague Terrain*. Portions of revisions/expansions to these articles were originally published in a different form on my blog, *cinegraphic. net*.

Introduction included material from "The Birth of Sampling" in *Vague Terrain,* May 2011.

Chapter 1: adapted from "Labor/Commodity/Automation," Event–Scene: e133, *CTheory,* September 15, 2004.

Chapter 2: "Automated Labor: The 'New Aesthetic' and Immaterial Physicality," Theory Beyond the Codes: 048 *CTheory,* February 5, 2013.

Chapter 3: "The Aura of the Digital," 1,000 Days of Theory: td041, *CTheory*, September 5, 2006.

Chapter 4: "Bitcoin," Theory Beyond the Codes: tbc053, *CTheory,* June 18, 2013.

Chapter 5: "The Valorization of the Author," *Hz* 10, (Summer 2007).

Chapter 6: "Serial Form as Entertainment and Interpretative Framework: Probability and the 'Black Box' of Past Experience," *Semiotica: Journal of the International Association for Semiotic Studies* 157.1-4 (2005): 315–324.

Chapter 7: "The State of Information," Resetting Theory: rt007, *CTheory,* August 28, 2009.

Chapter 8: "The Demands of Agnotology::Surveillance," Theory Beyond the Codes: 058, *CTheory*, July 17, 2014.

Chapter 9: "Immaterial Value and Scarcity in Digital Capitalism," Theory Beyond the Codes: 002, *CTheory,* June 10, 2010.

Chapter 10: adapted from a talk given at *Digital Inflections: CTheory Global Online Seminar on Critical Digital Studies,* 1 pm PDT, June 17, 2010.

Introduction

This book is a revised compilation of essays previously published in a number of academic journals over roughly the first decade of the twenty-first century. Collectively they have been concerned with the elaboration and development of a critique of capitalism as it has been adapted/transformed by the invention of digital technologies, most especially the new forms of production specific to the automated and autonomous systems that technology makes possible. It is a critique that began with a materialist examination of the ways that digital technology has "magical" properties, seemingly allowing production without consumption of resources: the aura of the digital provided an entry point for what had grown into an examination of the frameworks of authority, production and domination specific to the digital at the end of the twentieth and beginning of the twenty-first centuries.

These essays, with appropriate revisions and expansions, present a single coherent critique of how digital technology dominates the horizons of possibility. Central to this consideration is the illusion of production-without-consumption enabled by digital technology and automation. It enables a colonization of social relationships—a valorization of social activity and human behavior—as well as the substitution of immaterial production based in semiosis for productive activity based in facture. Apparent in the breach that now lies between the virtual domain of the digital and the reality of physicality is the *ideology of automation,* the *aura of the digital,* the *aura of information,* an *aspiration to the state of information,* and finally *digital capitalism* itself. All these developments have a common basis in an immaterialism-without-limits that stands apart from, and superior to, the physical; however, this lacuna is an illusion. The digital is not a realm without boundaries: capital scarcity sets the limits for the immaterial production characteristic of digital capitalism, a point of extension beyond which the political economy must inevitably collapse.

The 'authorship' phenomenon common to social media and digital commerce is a symptom of this colonization of social relations by digital technology. In the process, it reveals an aspiration to achieve a *complete* awareness of all informational possibilities (the aspiration to the 'state of information') in a specific transformation of previously non-commercial activities that might produce a commercial action (such as browsing in a store), into a commodity in themselves. It is a dramatic change, drawing continuous surveillance and perfect recall together into a new, *immaterial commodity* that comes into being as surveillance—the totalizing description of human action. This transformation of activity to commodity depends on the semiotic, recombinative power of digital technology. Immaterial production is characteristic of digital capitalism, and (equally characteristically) presents itself as something *other* than a commodity form: the impact of the *aura of information.* This aspiration is digital capitalism's attempt to create a complete description of all *information as instrumentality* (data) where the disconnected, contextless dimensions of *all* activities performed within the digital realm become equally valid, and *valuable,* to immaterial production as commodities. This 'material' (data) is the 'value' contained by social networks, and is the reason these companies are perceived to be valuable even when they produce no revenue.

Immaterial commodities, via the *digital aura,* enable the oxymoronic claim of a manifest immateriality—of the state of information being realized in a direct, tangible form—via a digital instrumentality. The contemporary application of digital computers to information gathering, storage, and processing necessitates considering a novel theory of knowledge that, through reification, gains agency as the *aura of information.* It is inherently immanent in the interlocking conditions that are digital capitalism. By being a reification of the capitalist acquisitive demand for continuous growth, while at the same time being an imagined end to "scarcity," it reveals a utopian impulse where the aura of the digital stands as proof of an immaterial order, suggesting both the triumph, and the dissolution, of capitalism itself. These dualities are paradoxical; contradictory impulses emerge in digital capitalism as a central part of its expansive procedure: demanding, and then justifying the general deployment of immaterial, semiotic production as the primary method for wealth generation.

The foundations of the aura of information lie, like the digital aura, in the nature of computer technology itself. Crucial to their function is the fragmentation of the continuous, physical world into discrete blocks of data—samples—whose storage, manipulation, and recombination follows a semiotic procedure governed by 'rules' that constrain the digital computer to a strict instrumentalist function, separate from the meaning and/or historical context of the materials being accessed, sorted, combined. This reification transforms digital technology into the embodiment of an immaterial realm where production is a *recombinant* procedure—fundamentally a semiotic function—that creates an immaterial "product."

The technical capabilities of this computer technology obscure the nexus of capital, human agency, social reproduction, and physical production; thus, the denial of physicality that is specific to the aura of the digital, and apparent in the evolution from hand-labor to the automation characteristic of 'digital capitalism,'[1] is inherent in how this technology has been deployed. The nineteenth century "protestant work ethic" is the conceptual starting point for this development, merging the 'ideology of autonomous achievement' with digital technology to create a new 'ideology of automation.' It appears in the social realm through fantasies of autonomy—the "self-made man"—independent of the social reproduction that makes their success and survival possible. This imaginary autonomy elides human labor from production, apparently rendering human agency *obsolete* in the digital information economy, and authorizing the valorization of social behavior. The active principle for these transformations is the 'aura of the digital,' which reifies capitalist ideology by masking the role and importance of an underlying physical reality. In its place is a corrosive fantasy that digitality has opened up a magical realm beyond physical constraints, where the duality of production/consumption is resolved to allow growth without limit—the continual expansion of wealth—beyond the constraints of production, materiality, and labor.

Due to the steady development and expansion of digital technology over the course of the twentieth century, sampling has achieved a central, even dominant position both culturally and technologically. The sample is as necessary for digital technology as it is for celluloid motion pictures—making it a fundamental technique of contemporary mediated cultures. However, it is clearly on view in a much older, historical device called the "cat organ" (also known by the Spanish term "katzenkavalier," German "katzenklaver," or "cat piano"), a *musical instrument* described in Juan Christoval Calvète's 1552 book chronicling King Felipe II of Spain's

[1] The term 'digital capitalism' was first posed by Dan Schiller in his 1999 book of the same title. While his description proceeds from the same technical basis as my own, they are an example of convergent thinking based in similar initial premises; the current discussion and theorization is independent of his earlier conception even though they both proceed from similar observations.

travels in Europe.[2] A consideration of this early example of semiotic reassembly offers insight into contemporary ethical questions that could be asked about digital capitalism. The operation of the cat organ was summarized by French writer and critic Jean-Baptiste Weckerlin in his 1877 book *Musiciana, extraits d'ouvrages rare ou bizarre* (*Musiciana, excerpts from rare or bizarre books*):

> When the King of Spain, Felipe II was in Brussels in 1549 visiting his father the Emperor Charles V, each saw the other rejoicing at the sight of a completely singular procession. At the head marched an enormous bull with a little devil sitting between his horns juggling fire. Prancing in front of the bull was a young boy sewn into a bear skin riding on a horse whose ears and tail were cut off. Then came the archangel Saint Michael in bright clothing, and carrying a balance in his hand.
>
> The strangest part was a cart that carried the most singular music imaginable. It held a bear that played the organ: instead of pipes, some twenty boxes, each containing a cat whose narrow tail came out the bottom and was connected to the keyboard by a string, so that when a key was pressed, the corresponding tail would be pulled hard, and would produce a lamentable meow. The historian Juan Christoval Calvète, noted the cats were arranged properly to produce a succession of notes from the octave ...(chromatically, I think).
>
> This abominable orchestra arranged itself inside a theater where monkeys, wolves, deer and other animals danced to the sounds of this infernal music.[3]

---

[2] Juan Christóbal Calvete de Estrella, *El Felicísimo Viaje del Muy Alto y Muy Poderoso Príncipe Don Felipe* (Madrid: La Sociedad de Bibliófilos Españoles, 1930), 73–77.

[3] Jean-Baptiste Weckerlin, *Musiciana; extraits d'ouvrages rares ou bizarres, anecdotes, lettres, etc. concernant la musique et les musiciens* (Paris: Garnier Frères, 1877), 349. For further reading about the relation of this precession, see Claude-François Ménestrier, *Des Représentations en musique anciennes et modernes* (Paris: Chez R.

Cat lovers might wish the cat organ was a fictional horror, much like Arthur Ewing's "mouse organ" on *Monty Python's Flying Circus*.[4] It produces *katzenmusic* by torturing live animals as a productive means, causing them to mew on demand: literally *cat-calls* that are not merely cat-calls, but something more—a form of music semiotically reassembled from the distinct voices controlled by the device. As Weckerlin's description of the procession shows, the cat organ functions symbolically, based on the association of cats with devils and an immaterial, supernatural order where normally antithetical animals come together in a peaceable kingdom: the harbinger of an immaterial realm.[5]

The cat organ produces a magical transformation of animal noise into harmonious order; and the procession dramatizes an immaterialist theory. It is a demonstration of 'Godly might and universal design,' thus forcing immaterial forces into an immanent presence, presented through technical instrumentality: the angel Michael imposes a heavenly order that drives demonic forces before it. Enacting this order requires a systematic denial of the actual physicality of its means: the live animals encased in the katzenkavalier. The specific subordination enacted by the cat organ is at one and the same time an expulsion from consciousness, it is an earlier form of the same blindness which is the aura of the digital, stripping concerns with physicality from consideration. This separation of *source* (material basis) from *meaning* reflects the action of a *semiotic* process.

To Weckerlin and contemporary audiences, the horror of this machine lies with the fact that individual animals are significant to the device only in so far as they stand-in for the specific pitch they produce—in effect, they are living samples

Guinard, 1681), and Samuel Bauer, *Denkwürdigkeiten*, Vol. XI (1830).

[4] "Arthur Ewing and His Musical Mice," *Monty Python's Flying Circus*, BBC, October 12, 1969, written by John Cleese, Graham Chapman, Terry Jones, Eric Idle, et al.

[5] Lance Bertlesten, "Journalism, Carnival, and Jubilate Agno," *ELH* 59.2 (Summer 1992): 375 [357–384].

of abstract musical tones. This transfer is significant to understanding the device's relevance to contemporary technology: the cat organ finds its parallel in the software application *AutoTune* where any voice can be correctly tuned to be perfectly in pitch, a transubstantiation of ordinary voices into pure musicality. In arranging live cats so the timbre of their voices would at one and the same time become the various pitches of a musical composition, the cat organ implicitly reifies an understanding of physical reality analogous to contemporary digital sampling and fragmentation; it reflects a specifically *digital* conception of physicality: the operative procedure is semiotic, the results dependent upon the reorganization of a collection of data samples. The *katzenkavalier* is thus an early symptom of the digital both conceptually and in approach: *sampling*, via the fragmentation of physical reality into discrete packets (the individual cats), for semiotic reassembly and manipulation as a new product: *(katzen)music*, an immaterial form whose existence only comes into being through a mechanical apparatus of performance-torture that renders the semiotic transformation of cat's mewing into abstract musical form.

The cat organ reappears (quite literally) in the 1990s as a pair of Christmas albums released by the group *Jingle Cats*. They were a popular sensation—their first album, *Meowy Christmas,* was completely sold out at Christmas in 1993, and followed in 1994 with *Here Comes Santa Claws:* both albums feature music "sung" by cats' meowing on key. As the "Jingle Cats" website notes,[6] in a disturbing reflection of the original cat organ's basis, the music was created using real cats. This transformation-without-torture was possible because of digital synthesizer technology that could sample actual cat's mews and then adjust them to be on key, thus allowing the use of real cats in the performance. These albums converge upon the semiotic procedure built-in to the cat organ. Both are symptomatic of the ability of digital technology to fragment a continuous physical reality, disassociating it from its

[6] See www.jinglecats.com.

source. This disassembly into component elements enables their reassembly from/into a new form—*data*. Semiosis enables and proceeds autonomously without concern for the physicality of the material translated to digital form.

Apparent even in the historical cat organ, is the concept of the "aura of the digital." This neutral protocol so clearly on view in the cat organ is also a cybernetic (machinic) one that incorporates the living into the non-living: cats encased in the instrument of their torture-performance. This cybernetic dimension is an analogue to the digital transferal (and surrender) of human agency to the automated and digital computer where particular human concerns become data in the reconfiguration of social space to reflect the immaterial valorization of digital capitalism.

In contemporary digital capitalism, this process strips concerns with immanent physicality (and the very real limitations of the physical world) from consciousness, replacing it with an illusory abundance—the idea that digital technology "ends scarcity" through the purely semiotic process of digital replication (an unintelligent, autonomous protocol of transfer and reproduction). It is the apparent "truth" that all digital copies are equally good which supports the aura of the digital's a/effects. In considering the digital aura, several features immediately emerge: the effective immortality of digital media, their potential for endless, perfect replication, and the ways that the immaterial is always already limited by the scarcity of capital. The *ethical* dimension posed by the sampling process arises because the digital, in particular, proceeds by separating means from meaning (its unintelligent nature).

It is the limiting factor imposed by the scarcity of capital which makes a critique of the political economy not only a potential aspect of examinations of the digital, it is also an explanation for the various economic crises that have arisen both in the United States and elsewhere. It challenges the notion that "this time is different" through a continual return to the disassociative production method: *semiosis,* where a fragmented source is reconfigured for a purpose independent from its material basis: human life, agency and social reproduction as commodities, rather than as essential factors for the production-consumption relationship. It is this issue—the ethical dilemma posed by immaterialism—that haunts these essays: each focuses on a single conceptual feature and explores it in detail, in the process identifying discrete areas that serve as signifiers for the digital's colonization—as reified capitalist ideology—of what were previously social activities as new forms of economic production, while at the same time offering a glimpse of a digital capitalism severed from physical production and the consumption of physical material, labor and capital. It is this apparent (and illusory) production *ex nihilo* via technologies of surveillance and automated semiosis (financialization using High Frequency Trading algorithms is the most obvious example) that has come to define the contemporary political economy where the social reproduction of labor is not of concern to capitalism.

Torture is at the foundation of the cat organ: it is symptomatic of the disassociation common to the aura of the digital. To be without concern for the physical impacts denied through the shift to immaterialism is to create the potential for abuses of that physical domain. The cat organ's sampling process—where the animals become insignificant to its meaning and purpose, but essential to its form—is inherently contained within the foundational procedure of the digital, reflecting the same stripping of physicality from conscious awareness that is *essentially* the aura of the digital; this development is an ideological force operative within the sociopolitical economy of the United States, guiding the implementation of so-called "social media" and automated production.

The transformation of social activity into commodity emerges from the illusion that digital production creates value without expenditure—the illusion of capital production without its necessary consumption. It is symptom of the structure of a pathological capitalist ideology becoming realized in the fantasy of digital technology. Simultaneously, this aura of the digital threatens the status quo because the illusion of profit without expenditure suggests the possibility that the digital could enable an end to capitalism itself (ignoring the reality of limited resources, time, expense, etc. that otherwise govern all forms of value and production). It is this second aspect of the digital that poses a utopian potential—the transcendence of the limitations imposed by physical reality.

Material limitations are countered in the semiotic process of isolation, fragmentation and reassembly that provides the technical basis for digital technology. The immaterialist basis is an eruption whose foundations are semiotic. It is the ability of the technology to fragment and proceed through an autonomous protocol that breaks the continuous physical reality into discrete packets of relevant data that enables the neutrality of the digital in relation to that which it conveys: there is no concern for the physicality of the material translated to digital form. Thus the torture that is at the foundation of the technical apparatus of the cat organ is inherently the sampling procedure of the digital, and reflects the same stripping of physicality from conscious awareness that is essential for the aura of the digital. The terror posed by sampling (revealed by the katzenkavalier) emerges in the horror-fantasies of science-fiction in the form of the A.I., the robot, the intelligent machine or the cyborg focused on the enslavement-destruction of humanity.

That there is an ethical concern in relation to this historical infernal device's use of sampling—the necessary foundation for the digital semiosis—implies a similar ethical dimension and critique may be relatable to the aura of the digital's occlusion of physicality from consciousness. These ethical questions are emerging, however, not from the manipulation of sampled animal voices, but in the aftermath of the "Housing Bubble" of 2008 where the sampled and semiotically manipulated materials were at once both less tangible (securitized debt) and immanently visible dispossessed humanity. The ideology reified in digital technology suggests the financialization and the economic collapses of the Dot.

Com Bubble and the Housing Bubble, et al., were not only inevitable, but are a structural effect of the transition to immaterial production, and the human collateral damage a sign of its productive action. These economic upheavals are direct evidence for the impact of immaterial production through the digital manipulation of finance as a semiotic system. Understanding the origins of this social dilemma is the underlying purpose of this examination.

Chapter One

The Ideology of Automation

Intellectual labor produces fundamentally immaterial commodities. These products of human thought always already have a reflexive, indexical link to the cultures where they are produced: both a producer of ideological forms, and a reflection of those same forms—either in a positive sense, where it is clearly shaped by a particular ideological construction, or in the negative sense, where it works "against the grain" of the ideological structures it necessarily originates within. Made visible only through its tangible products—written or verbal texts, the various categories of design or art—the *labor* element of this construct must necessarily remain intangible, a mental working until given physical form. The nineteenth century "Protestant work ethic" is the conceptual starting point for the development of a new 'ideology of automation' that merges the nineteenth century 'ideology of autonomous achievement' with digital technology to eliminate human labor from production, apparently rendering human agency irrelevant (effectively obsolete) for the generation of value in the digital information economy.

Perhaps the paradigmatic example of immaterial production, *education,* has been subjected to a transformation during the twentieth century that critic Dion Dennis has described as the "neo-liberal political redefinition of higher education as a private rather than a public good."[1] This contemporary transformation of "intellectual labor" away from something of benefit to society as a whole offers a reflection of what immaterial labor becomes under digital capitalism: a modular commodity that can (and will) be valorized, then automated. The current transformation of immaterial labor is a direct indicator that multinational corporations engaged in 'off-shoring' immaterial production are in the process of exceeding the ability of national governments, such as the United States, to regulate and control their activity through existing law. It is part of a long-term trend where businesses transcend the limitations of the countries that (temporarily) contain them.

This shift in the *meaning* of education is at once both a reorganization of academic institutions to reflect an *individualist* model of society, and a basic change in the conception of intellectual labor itself to become a commodity form. This new configuration has its origins in the nineteenth century ideology of "autonomous achievement" described by T. Jackson Lears in his study *No Place of Grace,* an ideology used to justify the economic exploitation of labor and the social position of the economically powerful upper classes during that century. The proposition that increased, automated production does not displace human labor—what is sometimes termed the "Luddite fallacy"[2]—is a reflection of the ideology of automation in action: that increased mechanical productivity inherently increases worker productivity thus lowering costs of production and product. The shifting of labor to exploit lower costs was common within the United States in the nineteenth century; contemporary off-shoring is inevitable in this construct. At the same time, the emergent ideology of automation is revealed by a transformation of labor to au-

---

[1] Dion Dennis, "The Digital Death Rattle of the American Middle Class: A Cautionary Tale," *CTheory*, November 18, 2003, a136, www.ctheory.net/articles.aspx?id=402.

[2] Martin R Ford, *The Lights in the Tunnel: Automation, Accelerating Technology and the Economy of the Future* (New York: Acculant Publishing, 2009).

tonomous production, displacing human labor entirely, a shift from production to consumption.

However, off-shoring labor is only a symptom of these transformations: by separating human agency from production, the progression from direct hand-working to machine tools reaches its apogee with the Fordist assembly line where production is subject to a semiotic fragmentation into discrete units, independent of each other The assembly line makes the role of human action clear, since even in the separation of productive tasks from both the unifying design conception and each other, the need for human engagement in the production itself remains. This manual element, the action, cannot be fully converted to commodity because of the need to employ human labor (with all the direct limitations labor entails). Automation offers an illusory elision of the limits posed by human labor: with automation, the necessary link between the 'intention' and the labor which realizes that 'intent' in production is apparently severed; this is the ideology of automation—the breach between human intention and its active engagement in/as production. The expansion of this automation to non-physical production is implicit in how digital technology has been deployed.

The shift of intellectual labor to commodity as immaterial production—including both "education" and "creativity"—reveals the ideology of automation in action. This transformation comes as a result of the same computer technologies that make the off-shoring of "knowledge worker's labor" economically viable: the movement of immaterial labor follows the established, globalized paradigm that shifted physical production from the United States to countries where wages are lower as improved, low-cost communications technologies become commonplace.[3] Automation of intellectual labor depends on digital technologies. Their relationship is circular: without digital communications technology, the emergence of immaterial production would be prevented by an inherent latency in communication—the manual aspects

---

[3] Dennis, "The Digital Death Rattle."

of human facture impose a lapse in production inherent to the breakdown of the process into component parts performed as individual actions by discrete individuals—the *human* part of labor. As technologies improve due to the success of immaterial labor, it becomes easier to shift the site where labor is performed on a global scale. Improved technologies imply an increased instability and uncertainty for labor (both physical and immaterial), demonstrating the incompatibility between the values produced by immaterial and physical production. The extractive, semiotic nature of immaterial production reflects the movement from the social production of human society to autonomous production. It is a productive metaphor: that intellectual action can be physically contained, compartmentally broken into modular pieces, and thus (via automation) made subject to a replacement with digital technology without consequent *human* social displacements and impacts—the ideology of automation in action.

§1.1

Historian T.J. Jackson Lears, writing in *No Place of Grace: Anti-Modernism and the Transformation of American Culture,* discusses how the ideology of the "Protestant Work Ethic" developed in the nineteenth century. His analysis presents the origins of off-shoring as a side-effect of the ideology of "autonomous achievement": in the nineteenth century, the upper classes used the model of the "Protestant Work Ethic," combined with Thomas Robert Malthus' linkage of economic gain with moral restraint in *An Essay on the Principle of Population,* and Adam Smith's capitalist theory about "free markets" in *An Inquiry into the Nature and Causes of the Wealth of Nations,* to construct a liberal ethical model where economic success—the American "self-made man"—would stand as evidence of would stand as evidence of spiritual and moral success as well. Achieving this success was a *personal* act of *will.* Spiritually and morally superior individuals would be rewarded economically for adhering to their higher ethical standards. Those who were poor or unsuccessful economically were thus morally inferior as well, thus twice justifying their position in society:

> For decades the task [of justifying an ethos of autono-
> mous achievement] fell to moral philosophers.…A man's
> conscience informed him about the moral universe; since
> ethical truth was knowable, the problem of morality was
> simply a matter of will: one chose one's duty or shirked it.
> And duty, in every case, involved autonomous achieve-
> ment. The disciplined pursuit of individual self-interest
> was a moral imperative; prosperity was dependent on vir-
> tue.[4]

"Autonomous achievement" allows a redefinition of education as a private rather than a public good. The central thrust
of this ideology is that the individual, through *personal* labor,
achieves success without the assistance of government,
friends, family, inherited position, or any other *outside* agency. It ignores many of the advantages those whom it serves
had before they started, as well as excuses how they achieved
their success by exploiting the labor of others. This pretense
justifies the off-shoring of all jobs except the highest level of
management—the CEO and board of directors—all of whom
are members of the economically privileged upper classes.
The parallels between off-shoring physical production and
off-shoring immaterial production (and services) may be
signs that the automation of immaterial activities, as with
earlier physical labor, may be forthcoming.

As Dion Dennis has noted, with the direct and immediate
economic gains made available through higher education
subsidized by the United States government, the waves of
college graduates between 1950 and 1980 were able to dramatically improve their standard of living.[5] This change in
social position feeds the ideology of "autonomous achieve-

---

[4] T.J. Jackson Lears, *No Place of Grace: Anti-Modernism and the
Transformation of American Culture, 1880-1920* (New York: Pantheon, 1981), 19–20.
[5] Dennis, "The Digital Death Rattle."

ment" through a myopic denial of the governmental role in this social uplift, producing a situation where the shift from public good to private improvement mirrors the self-serving ideology employed by the nineteenth century upper class: it enacts the premise that success was produced through *individual* labor without assistance.

The shift of responsibility for education onto the individual shows that the middle and lower classes who aspire to change social position have adopted the ideology of "autonomous achievement." Dennis has connected this shift to the dominance of neo-liberal capitalism:

> Neo-liberal discourse promoted a marketplace framework where risk was redistributed from the collective to the individual. Government was no longer to be the guarantor of security. It was redefined as a partner in individual risk assessment and management. Within this econometric universe, people succeed or fail based solely on their own assessments of risk, and level of personal responsibility and merit. With its atomistic presuppositions, and its denial of large-scale social or structural phenomena, action to influence structural changes in national and global economies was limited to the dispensing of individualistic prescriptions for life-long learning and retraining. Notions of collective action, in support of the public commons or a public good became stigmatized, and discredited as a dishonest, mystifying set of rhetorical tricks deployed by an anti-American intellectual elite. With its individualistic focus, this is an atomistic ideology with a deep elective affinity for the mass export of jobs, the escalation of CEOs salaries, and the wholesale restratification of the American class system.[6]

By rejecting the government's role in their elevation, the middle class collectively participated in the dismantling of those factors which would have protected them against their

---

[6] Dennis, "The Digital Death Rattle."

economic and political liquidation by the upper classes. At the same time, the belief that any form of government involvement is necessarily bad served to enable the deregulation of corporate activity beginning in the 1980s (this is the period when off-shoring began). Rejecting the government's ability to govern is built-in to the ideology of "autonomous achievement." It is what makes "autonomous achievement" *autonomous.* Privatization is thus a fundamental component of this ideology. It entails a belief in the superiority of markets over *all* other values. The rise of automation is its logical implementation as industrial procedure; the expansion to immaterial production follows from the inherent potentials of digital automation.

In a study on the privatization of public art museums, arts funding, and cultural institutions in the US and UK, historian Chin-Tao Wu notes about the period following World War II that US tax brackets were dramatically revised downward, as Table 1.1 shows (see p. 19). The increased taxation of the middle classes as a result of higher pay levels was a contributing factor to the embrace of neo-liberal, anti-taxation/regulation policies. The rising number of middle class income earners who were suddenly subject to greater taxation, but were accustomed to a low tax rate (because they had previously occupied a much lower income bracket), enabled the steady lowering of taxes at all income levels. Thus taxation provides a way to track the emergence and consolidation of power by the upper classes that Dennis has described. As Table 1.2 shows (see p. 20),[7] there is a correlation between the first generation of government-subsidized college graduate's *children* (i.e., the second generation college graduates who were between 45 and 59 in 2003) leaving college, and the beginning decline in tax rate. The steady lowering from the tax rate at its highest point in the 1950s begins when an increased number of college-trained workers would be assuming higher-paying middle management positions, *and* would have more available income since their children

[7] See the US Census Bureau website: www.census.gov/population/ www/socdemo/education/cps2003.html.

have now graduated college and entered the work force. While the level of taxation for the upper classes has not dropped to the levels at the start of the twentieth century, it is possible to see the trend moving in that direction.

Table 1.2 shows the educational attainment figures provided by the US Census Bureau. Dennis' "educational boom" peaks with the children of World War II veterans (the largest numbers of these children being those born between 1949 and 1953) entering college between 1967 and 1971 (avoiding the Vietnam draft through the educational exemption)—the specific group that moves into the work force during the 1970s. This group, the generation known as "yuppies"— young, upwardly mobile professionals—is the one that most completely embraces the ideology of "autonomous achievement."

The evolution towards higher education as a prerequisite for employment noted by Dennis could be called a side effect of a "will to autonomy" that the middle classes have embraced. The steady shift towards lower tax rates begins in 1964, at exactly the same moment that the surge in college-level attainment begins: the children born in 1942 entering the work force. These would predominately be the "war babies" born in the year following their father's enlistment, while the peak years 1949-1953 would be those born following their father's return. This first group would then be graduating college and entering the professional, "white collar" work force starting in 1962 or 1963. These demographic correlations match changes in taxation for the rich and educational advancement among the middle classes.

While the tax rate for the upper classes—the richest portion of the United States, those who own and direct the labor of others, both "white collar" and, by extension, "blue collar" workers—has fluctuated over the course of the twentieth century, there is another historical correlation worth noting: the historical dominance of corporate power over economic and political life, and the lowest levels of taxes for the richest citizens. Beginning with Teddy Roosevelt's active enforcement of the Sherman Anti-Trust Law at the start of the twentieth century, and its amendment by The Clayton Act in 1914, the Unites States government began to regulate the economic actions of the upper classes indirectly through their ownership of large corporations. Taxes began a steady ascent during this period. Within four years of the creation of the Federal Trade Commission,[8] the highest tax bracket climbed from 7% to 77%, corresponding to both an actively engaged military (World War I), and increased scrutiny and oversight by the new agency.

The trend in taxation reverses during the 1960s. A dramatic reduction in taxes occurred between 1964 and 1988, dropping from 77% to 33% for the highest income bracket. This change corresponds to both the emergence of "autonomous achievement" as an active ideology for the middle class, and the gradual off-shoring of physical labor, joined at the turn of the millennium by the off-shoring of knowledge workers and "support" jobs for the information economy.

§1.2

The ideology of personal responsibility for education coupled with an increase in the number of highly skilled, college educated workers both inside and outside the United States has helped create the current liquidity of immaterial labor. Central to the ability of corporations to off-shore that labor is the appearance of global, digital communications networks that enable oversight-at-a-distance. Without this communications network, there could be no off-shoring of immaterial labor. The development and dominance of the ideology called "globalization" that Dennis tracks follows this historical arc, visible in lowered taxes for the wealthy CEOs who head corporations.

The role of government in corporate oversight has declined over this period. Globalization attacks public institu-

---

[8] The Federal Trade Commission Act, establishing the FTC as an oversight agency whose mandate was to investigate and bring suit against unfair business practices, became law on September 26, 1914.

tions and replaces them with private interests as both Dennis and Wu have shown. The groups effected by this transformation of government are the historically "lower" ("blue collar") classes—those who could be termed "proletarian." These workers survive based on their own labor rather than through the direction of other's labor. In this regard, the middle class ("white collar") labor is no different that that of the "blue collar" workers: both groups are directed by the upper classes who employ them. The immaterial labor performed by the "white collar" employees now being off-shored is only different in kind from their "blue collar" brethren who work in manufacturing. The ideology of "autonomous achievement" these workers—both "white color" and "blue collar"—adopted is a result of their position as the "petit" bourgeoisie who aspire to become fully bourgeois by emulating the beliefs, customs, and culture of the upper class.[9] This aspiration has resulted in their jobs being subject to off-shoring because they have dismantled (or disabled) the governmental oversight in business that protected them.

The logical extension of this off-shoring is readily apparent: all labor becomes a commodity. As with manufacturing, immaterial labor will be shifted from country to country in order to exploit the differences in labor costs, much as a corporation will shift purchasing raw materials for manufacturing. What this development reflects is a commoditization of creativity and the immaterial labor that goes with it. This paradigm shift comes at a moment when other forms of immaterial production begin to become commodities. Technologist Dave Stutz describes this process in the software industry:

> The word commodity is used today to represent fodder for industrial processes: things or substances that are found to be valuable as basic building blocks for many different purposes. Because of their very general value,

[9] Clement Greenberg, *The Collected Essays and Criticism, Volume 1*, ed. John O'Brian (Chicago: University of Chicago Press, 1986), 5–11.

they are typically used in large quantities and in many different ways. Commodities are always sourced by more than one producer, and consumers may substitute one producer's product for another's with impunity. Because commodities are fungible in this way, they are defined by uniform quality standards to which they must conform. These quality standards help to avoid adulteration, and also facilitate quick and easy valuation, which in turn fosters productivity gains.[10]

Stutz is writing about computer programs, an immaterial product, and one of the most visible areas whose development has been off-shored. This type of 'production' is a result of 'creativity'—intellectual action (an immaterial production)—rather than of physical manufacturing. This transformation of creativity into a commodity is a new phase of industrial production contained in the idea of an "information economy"—that the manipulation of old data and creation of new data, parallel to manufacturing, becomes a portable "industrial process" with the data in itself becoming an "object" (intellectual property) that parallels the role of raw materials used in other kinds of manufacturing.[11] This transformative, immaterial production is only possible with digital technology. 'Autonomous achievement' finds a link to digital technology through this emergent "information economy" where education becomes the "knowledge industry" in a reification of the 'productive' metaphor used in the transformation of intellectual labor to immaterial commodity.

§1.3

A paradigm shift in the conception of immaterial labor—from human activity to modular commodity—is demonstrated by corporations off-shoring immaterial labor. This trans-

---

[10] Dave Stutz, "Some Implications of Software Commodification," 2004, http://www.synthesist.net/writing/commodity_software.html.
[11] It is easy to understand the concern of intellectual property rights when viewed from inside this commodity-driven framework.

fer is based in a paradigm of digitality that is—especially at a technological level—a reification of the modernist grid; this link between modularity and grid constructions is not accidental or trivial. It reflects a fundamental process of segmentation that is essential to the 'productive' metaphor. Its contents are essentially identical, divorced from the physical variability inherent to other material constructs by the unrelenting oppositions of binary code whose meaning stand apart from the form of the work once it has been rendered into an unstable, human-readable form.

For silicon—the material of both quartz crystals and glass—to become digital is to literally become opaque, the process of sight no longer being a matter of seeing-through, but of seeing-within: insight, transcendent vision, an ideological transfer that implies both an internalization of comprehension/ production and a divestiture of physical constraints; this transition is the aura of the digital. The ideology it creates takes science-fiction author Arthur C. Clark's observation about advanced technology being identical to magic and turns it from imaginary future to the lived experience of the present, in the process filling the space of the digital with imaginary, instrumental forms of "life," (from computer viruses, to worms, spiders, bots and spyware), whose function is parasitic. At the same time, the lifeworld becomes machinic: "lifehacking," and DNA as a variety of digital code, manipulated and modeled within the digital technology that enables its transformation into factory—the 'productive' metaphor as living instrumentality. The threat of "human resources" becomes reified as the biological world is translated into a valorized field of products (genes) awaiting commercial development based in their conception as a "semiotic code" akin to the digital codes of computers themselves.

It is this convergence of machinic, semiotic, and biologic that the paradigm of the digital intersects with the political economy and the *problema* posed by human agency in relation to the autonomous aspects of the digital realm. The political-economy becomes not simply a matter of economic or class structure, but of machinic relations within the realm of greater and lesser control produced, maintained, and reified by *how* digital capitalism and the ideology of the digital reinforce each other through technology.

Within this space the Modernist grid lies as the enabling paradigm for the structure and organization of elements that can and cannot otherwise be reconciled, controlled, valorized. It is in this breaking into samples that the potential for quantization and value extraction-exchange becomes possible. The technology of sampling is a fundamental aspect of the capitalist productive procedure (the assembly line) as much as it is innate to the semiotic process of immaterial production. Digital technology necessarily forces all things into the uniformity of the grid (and in the process the 'sample') producing the expansion of digital capitalism. Those 'ways of being' formerly not valorizable become the new domain of valorization: indexes of happiness, demographics tailored to unique individuals—the affective domains—whose action is to distract from the adjustment of life to the demands made by an ever more extensive, comprehensive grid of data whose goal is the complete accounting of the lifeworld (the aspiration to the state of information). The claim that this digital grid is capable of achieving what mathematics calls "completeness"—a logical accounting for all potentials—is the aura of information in action. Douglas Hofstadter, professor of Cognitive Science and Computer Science at Indiana University, explains *completeness* as a corollary to the idea of mathematical consistency in *Gödel, Escher, Bach,* his book concerned with the limits on knowledge imposed by paradox:

> Where consistency is the property that "Everything produced by the system is true", completeness is the other way round: "Every true statement is produced by the system."[12]

While Hofstadter is careful to note that mathematical com-

[12] Douglas R Hofstadter, *Gödel, Escher, Bach: An Eternal Golden Braid* (New York: Basic Books, 1979), 100–101.

pleteness refers only to the theorems produced in a logical system, and not every system in the world, the digital aspiration in the aura of information to literally implement information as instrumentality means precisely that: to construct an information storage and retrieval system that *does* contain everything that is (both true and false) in the world—this aspiration is the aura of the digital in operation. It is made possible by digital automation's potential to act without human intervention—thus engaging in the same affect apparent in the "disinterested observation" or "objectivity" of photographs. The digital aura acts to detach the inbuilt biases and concerns of autonomous production from consciousness, severing labor and production from human agency. The nineteenth century Arts and Crafts movement's famous aphorism "by hammer and by hand do all things stand"—with its implicit recognition that human agency was needed for any and all production—ceases to be true.

§1.4

The treatment and handling of labor as a commodity is missing from the conceptual landscape of the twentieth century in the United States specifically because the conversion of labor-as-commodity has been blocked by *The Clayton Act, Title 15 U.S.C. §§ 13*, passed into law in 1914. Without the vastly improved shipping and communications technologies put in place since the 1960s, the off-shoring of labor (both physical and immaterial) would be cost-prohibitive. These new technologies—including shipping containers, communications satellites, and the Internet—now enable labor-as-commodity. The ability to shift between differentially priced labor markets gives corporations an absolute advantage in their manufacturing costs since they can now reduce the otherwise fixed costs of labor. The Clayton Act identifies and forbids this exploitation of labor-as-commodity by creating a uniform minimum wage—but only inside the United States:

(d) Payment for services or facilities for processing or sale

It shall be unlawful for any person engaged in commerce to pay or contract for the payment of anything of value to or for the benefit of a customer of such person in the course of such commerce as compensation or in consideration for any services or facilities furnished by or through such customer in connection with the processing, handling, sale, or offering for sale of any products or commodities manufactured, sold, or offered for sale by such person, unless such payment or consideration is available on proportionally equal terms to all other customers competing in the distribution of such products or commodities.

Establishing a uniform minimum wage postponed the conversion of labor into a commodity until off-shoring began accelerating during the 1970s and 1980s, transferring manufacturing jobs from the United States to countries with lower prevailing wages. The advent of off-shoring enables the transformation of labor into a commodity precisely because it falls outside the jurisdiction of the Clayton Act. The potential of labor to become a commodity is therefore implicit in labor itself, but it is a potential that has been suppressed in the United States through legislation.

Yet, the Clayton Act was primarily created to address physical labor, not its immaterial or automated varieties. The consideration of creative work as a modular component in a larger construction is a fundamental change in how we view "white collar" intellectual labor. The general commoditization of labor—both physical and intellectual—demonstrates that the globalized corporation, even if located within the United States, is functioning (at least to some extent) outside the framework of United States anti-trust law. The Clayton Act's provision for uniform minimum wages is also the reason for the contemporary conversion to commodity since corporations justify their off-shoring as taking advantage of lower wages elsewhere in the world—i.e. as a result of the Clayton Act's constraints *inside* the United States. This avoidance of the Clayton Act is the true meaning of 'off-

shoring.' It is an exploitation of differences in local economies and variances in currency valuation between the United
States (the global reserve currency during this period) and
whatever local currency where the wages were paid.

As automation replaces human intellectual labor there
will logically be additional waves of 'off-shoring' as workers
and globalized corporations again 'need' to cut costs through
reduced labor expenses, both directly in the form of salaries
and indirectly through the collateral costs of "benefits" such
as health care and pensions. What began with the off-shoring
of physical production in the 1980s, continues with the off-
shoring of immaterial labor, presenting the possibility for a
cycle of downsizing within the United States that periodically
will remove the lowest level of employment from the US labor market in preparation for those tasks being automated.
Harvey Cohen, writing for *Strategy Analysis,* describes the
possibility for creating "smart systems" that automate immaterial labor previously performed by human action. This
change would repeat the displacements produced by automation of physical labor, but on a global scale:

> Embedded intelligence within an increasing number of
> devices and applications is creating smart systems that are
> becoming more and more efficient and cost-effective in
> replacing humans who perform narrowly focused and
> somewhat low-skilled tasks such as customer and help-
> desk support, directory assistance, advisory functions,
> reference and interactive assistance. Intelligent capital—
> and the idea of replacing human cogitation and action
> with machine reasoning and decision-making—is becom-
> ing more compelling, in the long run, than the idea of
> outsourcing such work to lower-cost economies to take
> advantage of short-term labor-rate arbitrage. In the long
> run, for simple tasks, smart machines will replace the
> most cost-effective humans.[13]

---

[13] Cohen, *The Threat of Intelligent Capital.*

Immaterial labor is inventing its own obsolescence through "smart" digital automation for tasks previously requiring human thought *and* oversight. Such a development suggests the gains to be made by 'third world' countries through off-shoring may be brief. It is the next stage of the separation of immaterial activity from human agency. This separation, both in the United States and elsewhere, comes as the result of globalization's colonial demands on third world economies and on the economy of the United States itself. Both are shaped to service the immediate needs of the corporation, and adapt themselves over time to those needs. The shifts from a local (or national labor market) to globalization has produced the current phase of off-shoring.

§1.5

Autonomous labor—that performed by machines, whether through automated processes algorithmically driven (as with High Frequency Trading software), through generative systems, or physically in the robot assembly line—posing unanswered questions about the historical categories of labor, value, and production—is inherently disruptive: the social reproduction costs of automation are vastly different in degree and character than those of living, human social reproduction. The problem posed by the labor of machines is entangled with cultural, historical, and aesthetic assessments in which the machine does not fit established (traditional) conceptual mappings of human society. Thus, this newly autonomous non-human labor results in peculiar appropriations and transfigurations of the machine in relation to human society. A central issue to this entanglement is the inability of Marxian theory to accommodate the meaning of machine labor within conventional analytics, a problematic issue resting on the differences in industrialization and the concept of 'machine' that lie between the nineteenth and the twenty-first centuries.

The earlier ability to consider machine labor as an extension of human action—as the mechanical amplification of human labor—is replaced by models where the machine does not augment but supplant, in the process apparently removing the human intermediary that historically lies between the work of designer-engineers and the human production required in the fabrication of their plans. This transition point marks a shift from the fragmentation of the assembly-line where tasks are organized around the repetitive action of masses of human labor (itself an organization that implies semiotic disassembly and standardization) to the automated fabrication where the design is generated on digital machines and then implemented by other digital machines with only a minimal role of human labor in the facture process. In such a transformed factory, there is only a limited role for humans and it necessarily renders large sections of the "human resource" idle as their manual functions in production are now automated. The ideology of automation emerged via the transformation, already in progress for material production, of intellectual labor to automated, immaterial production. While HFT systems are specialized examples, the automation of routine tasks (tax accounting software such as *TurboTax* automates the specialized knowledge and expertise formerly the exclusive domain of accountants) reveals this same procedure in action in a much broader context and impacting a larger segment of intellectual labor.

Table 1.1. The Top Federal Personal Income Tax Rate in the
US, 1913 to 1988[14]

Year	Tax Rate
1913-15	7
1916	15
1917	7
1918	77
1919-1921	73
1922-1923	58
1925-1931	25
1932-1935	63
1936-1940	79
1941	81
1942-1943	88
1944-1945	94
1946-1951	91
1952-1953	92
1954-1963	91
1964	77
1965-1981	70
1982-1986	50
1987	38
1988	33

[14] Chin-tao Wu, *Privatizing Culture* (New York: Verso, 2002), 5.

Table 1.2. Percent of College Graduates (as of 2003)

All Races and Both Sexes (by age)	Total (numbers in thousands)	Educational Attainment		
		Total	Less than Bachelor's degree	Bachelor's degree or higher
		Percent	Percent	Percent
15 years and over	225,250	100.0	76.6	23.4
15 to 17 years	12,628	100.0	99.9	0.1
18 to 19 years	7,554	100.0	99.9	0.1
20 to 24 years	19,884	100.0	88.8	11.2
25 to 29 years	18,721	100.0	71.6	28.4
30 to 34 years	20,521	100.0	68.5	31.5
35 to 39 years	21,284	100.0	70.2	29.8
40 to 44 years	22,790	100.0	70.9	29.1
45 to 49 years	21,420	100.0	70.1	29.9
50 to 54 years	18,814	100.0	68.9	31.1
55 to 59 years	15,470	100.0	71.0	29.0
60 to 64 years	11,930	100.0	75.5	24.5
65 to 69 years	9,438	100.0	80.4	19.6
70 to 74 years	8,673	100.0	81.5	18.5
75 years and over	16,123	100.0	84.6	15.4
15 to 17 years	12,628	100.0	99.9	0.1
18 years and over	212,622	100.0	75.3	24.7
15 to 24 years	40,066	100.0	94.4	5.6
25 years and over	185,183	100.0	72.8	27.2
15 to 64 years	191,016	100.0	75.6	24.4
65 years and over	34,234	100.0	82.6	17.4

Source: U.S. Census Bureau; Release Date: June 29, 2004

Chapter Two

The Emergence of Immaterial Physicality

In *The Fragment on Machines*, Karl Marx laid out a series of logical propositions about machine-enabled labor that appears to suggest the elimination of the living labor (human agency) required by these machines; however, this interpretation is obviously incorrect when the assumptions and context that produced his theorization are taken into consideration. Automated labor is a fundamental shift in the nature of value production, one that is potentially destabilizing to the entire capitalist productive system, revealing the inherent incompatibility between digital capitalism and social reproduction, not simply a matter of economic or class structure, but of *machinic* relations orchestrated by the different degrees of human agency required—greater and lesser control produced, maintained, and reified by *how* digital capitalism and the ideology of the digital reinforce each other through technology.

§2.1

James Bridle's 'new aesthetic,' presented as an online research project in 2011 and 2012,[1] suggests a physicalization of what was/is more commonly purely digital—a realization of immateriality as physicality. It (re)traces similar aesthetic developments as earlier exhibitions such as *Post-Digital Painting* did in 2002.[2] Bridle's 'new aesthetic' collects examples where automated production becomes a tangible dimension of human society, ranging from the autonomous action of *Google Street View's* face-blurring algorithm to the translation of bitmaps into decorative textile patterns. The particular sense this collection documents is a concerted effort at realizing and acknowledging the digital nature not only of the immaterial 'space' produced by computers and algorithmic systems (the results of digital automation), but the transfer of these autonomously produced artifacts into the physical realm. The automated machine labor revealed by this project is a symptom of the emergent autonomous production it documents, revealing the paradox of automation, labor, and value production: the cultural, historical, and aesthetic ruptures between automation and the (traditional) conceptual mappings of human society.

Within Bridle's archive there are several overlapping categories of material: (1) autonomously generated images that contain markers of the digital such as glitches of various types (encoding errors, algorithmic misidentifications of faces, pixilation/scan lines/digital noise, etc.); (2) physical constructions employing signifiers of digital forms (blocky pixel-imitating construction, scanlines, etc.); (3) translations of digital forms into a visual style (QR codes, low resolution bitmaps, etc.); (4) dynamic, interactive data visualizations (art installations such as *Pixels Per Person* by Carina Ow that visualizes wifi usage, biometric scanners, and augmented

---

[1] "The New Aesthetic" was the title of the blog James Bridle used to collect his materials: new-aesthetic.tumblr.com; he started posting on May 6, 2011 and noted on May 12, 2012 that "The New Aesthetic" tumblr was closed at that time. Bridle then resumed posting new materials on August 20, 2012.

[2] Joe Houston, *Post-Digital Painting* (Bloomfield Hills: Cranbrook, 2002).

reality—the *Google Glass* project is another prime example). These groupings are neither exhaustive nor mutually exclusive. While there are points of contact and degrees of overlap between them, they articulate general tendencies in the formal appearance of digital technology, and document an apparent paradox: immaterial physicality.

Bridle's 'new aesthetic' also contains examples of camouflage used to 'hide' from digital military systems. These images demonstrate a reorientation of physical structures towards their engagement with digital technology, specifically designed to resemble the artifacts and forms of digital imaging. Unlike earlier approaches that addressed specifically *human* recognition and capabilities, contemporary camouflage mimics the pixilation of digital imagery—it is addressing not human sight, but the automated recognition systems of machines and the digital cameras that accompany them. This shift from a primary concern with human recognition to the disruption of machine vision is a transformation of degree and locus of address, mirroring the shifts posed by the 'new aesthetic' generally.

The importance of primitive accumulation to capitalist expansion—the annexing of domains without required payments commonly given to labor—assumes a consumptive dimension in the latter half of the twentieth century as the technologies employed in war become increasingly expensive and (self)destructive; thus, war as a productive stimulus for capitalist expansion both through productive demand and through primitive accumulation (which the Iraq War under President George W. Bush so clearly demonstrated).[3]

All these works appear to render the aura of information tangible, physically present, but at the same time withdrawn from immediate engagement: the 'new aesthetic' offers itself as proof that the digital aspiration to the state of information is immanent—the translation of information to pure instrumentality—emanating directly from how the digital reifies

[3] James A. Baker III and Lee H. Hamilton, co chairs, *The Iraq Study Group Report* (New York: Vintage, 2006).

the capitalist ideology of accumulation in autonomous production. The technical aspects of digital technology become *style*—thus *new* aesthetic—a transfer instantiating the immaterial in a physical form, a "print-out" whose tangibility then becomes the operative dimension in asserting the presence of an immaterial, digital 'information space.' This physicality proffers the realization of information as instrumentality. Objects collected by Bridle reflect digitally-derived features displaying the existing capacities (both current and historical) of digital technology: the illusion they produce is one where what was immaterial, penumbral, crystalizes from the air into solid, tangible form: reification becomes realization—immaterial physicality.

§2.2

Capitalism is the transformation of labor into a commodity—the worker's externalization of their productive capacity as a *thing* to be exchanged. The historical machine is the crystallization of this externalized labor-commodity as a physical productive force, itself valuable, but at the same time dependent upon the very human labor it encapsulates. The categorical divisions Marx proposed—*material of labor:* those physical commodities transformed by the labor process, including but not limited to raw material; *means of labor:* the tools, machinery, and buildings utilized by labor; and finally what he terms *living labor:* the workers who run the machines and enable the production to proceed—reveal how the automated system can be recognized as the logical extension of the *means of labor,* an ultimate rendering of human *living labor* unnecessary to the completion of production.

This trajectory is inherent in the machine itself as an apparatus magnifying and supplanting human action. The evolution of the technical requirements to print a single sheet on a printing press is an example of this process: the earliest European printing press with moveable type built by Johannes Guttenberg around 1439 required human labor to set the type, wipe ink on the plates, situate the paper, and remove each sheet; a modern computer printer does all these actions autonomously, faster, and with much greater precision—in the process transforming the earlier printing press into a machine that only requires limited human involvement in its actual functioning (a human needs to load its paper reservoir). All the productive functions that required several people and both extended time and labor in 1439 are now entirely autonomous.

However, when Marx wrote *The Fragment on Machines*, the role of human agency in industrial production was not in doubt; his series of propositions concerned the relationships between capital, fixed capital (the investments made in machinery and buildings to house them) and labor (necessary to operate the machines). The trajectory of mechanization had not passed beyond being an enhancement to human productive capacity: first the development of hand tools, which enabled an absolute distinction between labor requiring manual capacities and that requiring intellectual labor, visible in the distinction between the stylus used in cuneiform writing and the plow used in cultivating crops. The emergence of mechanical and machine tools prior to and including the industrial revolution all serve to magnify human action and improve productive capabilities, but remain limited by the abilities of the machine operators. Production in the nineteenth century, even when employing mechanization, remained dependent on the agency of human labor both to keep the machines running and to guide their use in facture itself—for these machines, however much they streamlined the manufacturing process, human labor was essential. This assumption that machines require human participation for their productive action, still true with physical manufacturing, is entirely false within the realm of immaterial production. Marx's minimal discussion of the role of machines in production makes the observation that mechanization (and automation) requires labor for its action:

Transposition of powers of labor into powers of capital both in fixed and in circulating capital.—To what extent fixed capital (machine) creates value.—Lauderdale. Machine presupposes a mass of workers. [...] As such a means of production, its use value can be that it is merely the technological condition for the occurrence of the process (the site where the production process proceeds), as with buildings etc., or that it is a direct condition of the action of the means of production proper, like all *matières instrumentales*. Both are in turn only the material presuppositions for the production process generally, or for the employment and maintenance of the means of labor.[4]

The role of industrial machinery within this theoretical framework is marginal because the transformation of labor into commodity retains an implicit understanding that production requires human action, a "mass of workers," and even the term '*manu*facture' literally references this handwork aspect of production. Thus machinery appears as an addendum to the costs of production as an expense—the purchase of "tools" employed in manufacturing—but is not a substitute for labor, nor its replacement. Within this construction, the machine functions as a crystallization of capital expenditure in a form that is simultaneously a commodity— the machinery—and a generator of value as it is put in motion by human labor, itself alienated by the protocols of mechanization:

As long as the means of labor remains a means of labor in the proper sense of the term, such as it is directly, historically, adopted by capital and included in its realization process, it undergoes a merely formal modification, by appearing now as a means of labor not only in regard to its material side, but also at the same time as a particular mode of the presence of capital, determined by its total process—as *fixed capital*. But, once adopted into the pro-

[4] Karl Marx, *The Grundrisse (The Fragment on Machines)* (London: Penguin Classics, 1993), 690–691.

duction process of capital, the means of labor passes through different metamorphoses, whose culmination is the *machine,* or rather, an *automatic system of machinery* (system of machinery: the *automatic* one is merely its most complete, most adequate form, and alone transforms machinery into a system), set in motion by an automaton, a moving power that moves itself; this automaton consisting of numerous mechanical and intellectual organs, so that the workers themselves are cast merely as its conscious linkages.[5]

While Marx's description seems to invoke a contemporary, cybernetic understanding where human labor merges with mechanical procedures, this "automation" is not the automation of the digital system. While the agency of these human workers is severely constrained by machine technology, it is human labor's conscious action (what he calls "intellectual organs") that enables production. Labor was the fundamental 'component' of these technological innovations that gave rise to industrial production. It took an alienated form because of the demands production placed on labor as an intelligent, highly complex "cog" within an otherwise regimented activity—Marx's "intellectual organs" (agency)—the allowed actions within the mechanized factory are limited to and contained by the requirements of the device.

The *assumption* that machines require human agency only emerges as the complexity of those machines reaches a transition point, and parts of their operation requiring human action (but not agency) are replaced by automatic functions. This *necessary* labor, in which the machine's role is to magnify and aid human production, was a factual part of the available machinery during the nineteenth century when Marx was alive; the emergence of the factory robot and computer-driven autonomous production line was more than a century away. Factories were adopting the 'labor-saving' efficiency of mechanizing repetitive processes—those proce-

[5] Marx, *The Grundrisse,* 692.

dures that do not require intelligent guidance (agency), and are instead functions of fragmented and compartmentalized procedures such as those performed by a clockwork mechanism, much like the *Rathaus-Glockenspiel* clock in Munich, where the device follows an elaborate series of automated actions through careful gearing and organization of the mechanism itself. Human agency remains an essential, guiding part of the machine, but at the same time, there is an absolute distinction between the mechanical and the human, a division mandated by the nature of the technical apparatus itself, even, and especially when, the orchestration of these devices is designed to create the appearance of self-awareness. It is these increasingly complex machines of the industrial revolution powered by steam or electricity that perform calculations and other precise, highly specialized kinds of *intellectual activity* that place the role of human agency in doubt.

The nature of mechanized production in the nineteenth century is fundamentally different than autonomous, immaterial production: digital systems have enabled machines where human labor has been minimized or entirely eliminated, and production proceeds without human control, guidance, or interaction; High Frequency Trading (HFT) is a typical example of this automation of the decision process through algorithmic rules. The shifts apparent in the printing press are common features of how automated production replaces necessarily dehumanized labor. Autonomous production that began as a 'labor-saving' procedure now saves *all* human labor in/as the productive machine: it is this specific dimension of automated (immaterial) labor using digital technology that reflects an ideology of production-without-consumption.

Digitally-enabled automation makes the human labor previously rendered subservient within the productive system itself uncertain, posing a fundamental challenge to capitalism as historically defined through the transformation of *human* labor into a commodity—the use of human intelligence, skill, and labor time as a specific form of productive value. The potential for *full automation* emerges with the development of digital automation, one where human labor—human agency—becomes a wasted value, and which the 'new aesthetic' documents.

§2.3

The industrial revolution's innate challenges to traditional social structures apparent in the de-skilling of those trades replaced by industrial production resulted in the emergence of design reform movements throughout industrial Europe at the end of the nineteenth century under the influence of John Ruskin via William Morris (*Arts and Crafts* in the UK, *Art Nouveau* in France and Belgium, and both the *Secession* and *Jugendstyl* movements in Germany and Austria). These movements created classic examples of *ressentiment*—an anti-industrial aesthetic of hand-working.[6] *The Fragment on Machines* was written in the same period and addressed these same issues of industrial production as Ruskin; however, Marx's analysis emerged from economics rather than considering industrialization as an aesthetic problem.

In contrast to mechanized production's impact on the skilled trades, automation initially impacted *intellectual (immaterial) labor* rather than *physical (manual) labor*— from the *Antikythera Mechanism* produced around 100 BCE, to the *Prague Orloj* clock from 1410, to the *Rathaus-Glockenspiel* in 1907—automation and automated systems have principally been concerned not with manual production, but with the elimination of intelligent labor. This separation of the intellectual potential of labor from its actions quickly became apparent during the nineteenth century in the regimentation of intelligent tasks limited by machinery. But while the role of human agency is reduced by early calculating machines, they remained within the realm of labor-saving devices, replicating complex computations with only

[6] Nickolaus Pevsner, *Pioneers of Modern Design: From William Morris to Walter Gropius* (Bath: Palazzo Editions, 2011).

limited use value, and whose production required specialized intellectual labor: these are devices outside the realm of material production. Yet, following the same set of concerns with mechanical production as Ruskin, Marx is not addressing these devices.

The 'new aesthetic' emerges as the antipode to the Ruskin/Morris hand-worked aesthetic, as a parallel to the early twentieth century's "machine style": the Modernist, Art Deco style where human handiwork was systematically elided in favor of the glittering chrome and smooth surfaces now synonymous with industrial production on a mass scale. However, these Modernist designs remained unquestionably a product of human action—both intellectual and physical; it is the role of human agency that comes into question with the 'new aesthetic': the necessity not only for human labor in the production of the work, but the requirement of human agency (following the aura of the digital) as a productive and organizational principle. The immaterial physicality of the 'new aesthetic' presents a convergence of these machinic, semiotic, and biologic productions, revealing a fundamental contradiction posed by human agency in relation to autonomous production.

Autonomy from human production and the elision of human agency emerges as the intermediary between designer-engineer and final result becomes simply the action of the tool which exactly executes the planned work. The various artifacts brought together as the 'new aesthetic' are united by their orientation not towards human observation or functional utility, but rather by their invocation of productive values without human action—the aura of the digital's separation of *product* from all that is required to produce it: labor, capital, resources. This transition point marks a shift from the fragmentation of the assembly-line where tasks are organized around the repetitive action of masses of human labor (itself an organization that implies semiotic disassembly and standardization) to an automated fabrication where the design is generated on digital machines and then implemented by other digital machines without human labor in the facture process; the necessity of human-as-designer thus comes into question as it is the only aspect of non-machine agency remaining, an element whose necessity is challenged by evolutionary algorithms and automated design.

What the 'new aesthetic' documents is the shift from earlier considerations of machine labor as an amplifier and extension of human action—as an augmentation of human labor—to its replacement by models where the machine does not augment but supplant, in the process apparently removing the human intermediary that is the labor which historically lies between the work of human designer-engineers and fabrication following their plans. The 'new aesthetic' figures in this cycle as a symptom of a reorientation already underway, rather than its outcome, as human agency becomes insignificant to these modes of production, and automation usurps its position (agency) in the system as a whole.

The shift from immaterial values generated by automation (semiosis) to material values generated by automation (facture) signals a fundamental shift in the nature of capitalist production, one where human labor is of lesser significance to that of automation. It is through this convergence that problems posed by autonomous production are elided following the aura of the digital's stripping of physical considerations and limitations from consciousness: the emergence of production without human labor, of commodity and exchange values (both physical and immaterial) generated without the action of human agency. The fundamental condition of Marx's capitalism (labor-as-commodity) returns to a central position through the transformation of labor to automation and the inherent commodity nature of machines: the *definitional* condition of capitalism becomes the *literal* condition of production under automation. In the autofactory, there is no role for humans; unlike human labor which is entangled with the minimum dimensions of society (Agamben's "bare life"), the autonomous machine is pure commodity, non-life. Large bodies of the "human resource" fall idle as their manual functions in production are now automated, their own commoditization of their human labor becomes superfluous to the productive capitalism of automation—this is the ideology of automation that follows one fundamental law:

Anything that can be automated, will be.

The autonomous labor performed by machines—whether through automated processes algorithmically driven (as with High Frequency Trading software), through generative systems, or physically in the robot assembly line—is a crystallization of labor-as-commodity without requiring living labor's social reproduction costs: automation does not require a wage, does not impose social demands on its owners, and when it is expended, it can be discarded to be replaced by newer technology.

§2.4

The paradox of automated labor and capitalism arises directly from the limiting role that scarcity of capital poses to this productive system: the automated production of values can only continue if it is possible to *exchange* those values for other values. The aura of the digital, when instantiated through automated production, necessarily creates a paradox where instead of an exponential escalation in value production, it generates surplus values for which there is exponentially decreasing opportunity for exchange: the immaterial physicality that automation brings into existence (and which is documented by the 'new aesthetic') is one where the elimination of human labor also serves to undermine the concept of 'exchange value' itself, as Marx noted:

> Exchange-value appears first of all as the quantitative relation, the proportion, in which use-values of one kind exchange for use-values of another kind. This relation changes constantly with time and place. Hence exchange-value appears to be something accidental and purely relative, and consequently an intrinsic value, i.e., an exchange-value that is inseparably connected with the com-

modity, inherent in it, seems a contradiction in terms.[7]

The paradox appears precisely because exchange value emerges from the relationship between one commodity and another—from the *exchange of a commodity for the acquisition of another*; in capitalism this exchange devolves fundamentally to transfers of labor between different social strata where higher level values derive from the action of labor at lower levels in that same society. Thus the elimination of the lowest levels of human labor from the production process destabilizes the upper levels in a cascading fashion. This proposition is not an "end of capitalism" fantasy where automation ends the scarcity of both capital and physical limitations, but a structural contradiction in the nature of value itself when decoupled from human labor. By replacing the lowest levels of human labor with automation, greater efficiencies in production emerge, but at the same time that human labor is displaced; some of it occupies (is absorbed by its society into) higher-skilled (greater degree of intelligent agency) positions supported by those automated procedures; however, as that higher-skilled labor is also automated, society's ability to absorb this displaced labor necessarily creates a new problematic not specifically recognizable as the issue of class struggle described by Marx—a shift from conflict between those who labor and those who do not, to conflict between those controlling the production of exchange values and those excluded from exchange entirely: the human labor whose labor-as-commodity no longer possesses any utility, hence is *not* an exchange value.

The disappearance of the historical Luddites from contemporary digital production reflects the aura of the digital encroaching and conditioning consciousness. The view that machines, including computers, are not a challenge to human labor has become an *axiomatic* belief about machinery (The Luddite Fallacy). Instead, it is the cybernetic under-

---

[7] Karl Marx, *Capital: Volume 1* (London: Penguin Classics, 1990), 126.

standing implicit in misreading the *Fragment on Machines*—
a worry that machines will colonize the living, human body—
that had a currency at the end of the twentieth century, both
in popular entertainment (the "Borg" of *Star Trek*) and in the
Critical Art Ensemble's comments from *Electronic Civil Disobedience* published in 1996:

> Although technological development causes many people
> fear and anxiety, fewer and fewer believe that technology
> will replace them. In fact, the fear is really quite the oppo-
> site. As technology attaches itself to the body, the rela-
> tionship between the body and technology becomes
> increasingly symbiotic.[8]

In the general failure to acknowledge the potential of digital
computers to automate cognitive tasks, (a fact evident from
the earliest surviving calculation device, the *Antikythera
Mechanism* to the most contemporary digital computer: any
intellectual activity that can be reduced to particular rules
can be rendered autonomous)—the threat posed by automation to *human exceptionalism* is sublimated as fears about
digital technology colonizing the organic, human realm: the
idea that humanity must merge with computers to enable
them to *begin* thinking. If computers do not need to merge
with humanity in such a fashion, then humanity is not exceptional—opening the possibility for (at least some portions of)
human intellectual labor to be rendered obsolete, as HFT
does with the decision making process for stock and commodity trades in the financial markets.

A herald of the ideology of automation's expanding force
is apparent in the intersection of automated immaterial labor
with the formerly intellectual labor of human agents, and is a
literal realization of the bifurcation between design and facture, one where the devaluation of human labor reaches its
apogee: rendered obsolete by the machine, there is no longer

[8] Critical Art Ensemble, *Electronic Civil Disobedience and Other
Unpopular Ideas* (Brooklyn: Autonomedia, 1996), 59.

any *need* for human agency once the autonomous factory has been built except to switch it on. This situation is the implicit horror/terror common to computer technology (and its earlier realization as the golem or homunculus) as an actor in society. The ideology of automation reveals its close relationship to the earlier ideology of the *self-made man* whose success is not a product of family, investment, or privileged position in society—shorn of the requirement for a network of human actors working in concert to produce wealth (material or immaterial), the automated system enables an ideology where the productive human population appears obsolete, parasitic, on the "designers" whose plans they formerly executed—this is the ideology of automation embraced by the middle classes.

Ironically, by working to create computer systems that emulate or replace both human labor and human agency, the United States' middle class belief in the *self-made man,* in "autonomous achievement," becomes the reality of "automated achievement" for the upper classes, leaving the remainder of society to 'work' as consumers/debt generators, automation effectively eliminating them from the production process. HFT is one sign of this ideology of automation coming into action—a procedure that removes human agency from its historical role in immaterial production: the response time of the computer system is such that only machines can compete in a market where price fluctuations determined in microseconds make the difference between profit and loss. It is reified in the digital, reflecting a denial of the physical realm and the necessary role of human agency in creating and sustaining the social structures which enable the ideology of automation's fantasy of "freedom" from social (re)production and the constraints required by human society. This complex of relationships reflects the underlying bias of digital capitalism against the social.

Chapter Three

The Aura of the Digital

By dividing the interpretation of art work into several distinct "levels" it becomes possible to recognize a fundamental distinction between digital and non-digital art works, as well as recognize an underlying belief in the illusion of infinite resources: it replicates the underlying ideology of capitalism itself—that there is an infinite amount of wealth that can be extracted from a finite resource. It is an illusion that emerges in fantasies that digital technology ends scarcity by aspiring to the state of information. The digital presents the illusion of a self-productive domain, infinite, capable of creating value without expenditure, unlike the reality of limited resources, time, expense, etc. that otherwise govern all forms of value and production. The rise of automated, immaterial production reflects this process in action.

Digital forms also exhibit what could be called the "aura of information"—the separation of the meaning present in a work from the physical representation of that work. As digital works, via the "aura of information," imply a transformation of objects to information, understanding the specific structure of digital art makes the form of the "digital aura" much more explicit. This clarity allows a consideration of the differences between the scarcity of material production in physical real-world fabrication versus the scarcity of capital in digital reproduction: the necessity for control over immaterial commodities (intellectual property) in the virtuality of digital reproduction. Because capital is a finite resource itself subject to scarcity, yet also caught in the capitalist paradox of escalating value—in the dual forms of interest and profit on capital expenditures—there is the constant demand to create more commodity value in order to extract more wealth from society in order to maintain the equilibrium of the system: digital capitalism necessarily moves between "boom and bust" because of this inherent imbalance.

Understanding this "aura of information" requires an acknowledgement about the nature of the digital object: it is composed from both the physical media that transmit, store and present the digital work to an audience; the digital work itself is actually composed of both a machine-generated and a human-readable work created by the computer from a digital file (itself actually stored in some type of physical media). This "digital object" is the actual form of the digital work—a series of binary signals recorded by a machine and requiring a computer to render this unseen "code" readable by humans. The "digital object" becomes the human-readable forms of image, movie, text, sound, etc. only through the conventionalized actions of a machine that interprets the binary signals of the digital object and follows the built-in interpretative paradigm that renders this binary code into a human-readable form and thus superficially distinct works. All 'digital objects' have this singular underlying form— binary code—a fact that makes the digital object fundamentally different from any type of *physical object* precisely because it lacks the unique characteristic of specific form that defines the differences between paintings, drawings, books, sounds, or any other physical object or phenomenon. Unlike physical objects, digital objects are all basically the same, whatever their apparent form once they are interpreted by a machine. This transfer from instrumental code to human-readable object happens autonomously—no human agency is required to set the translation in motion; the illusion created by the ideology of automation proceeds from an extension of this active element in digital technology beyond these generative dimensions of digital reproduction's display of (art) works.

§3.1

Walter Benjamin's 1936 essay, "The work of art in the age of mechanical reproduction" initiated the critical discussion of the idea that artworks have "aura," and proposed that this "aura" is destroyed by the process of mechanical reproduction. His notion of "aura" quickly expands to include more than just art—anything that is reproducible is folded into his construction. While this description of Benjamin's article is highly reductive, it captures his essential thesis that inherently suggests a historical loss brought about by technological change. Following Benjamin's argument it is logical to suppose that art would be without "aura" once mechanical reproduction gives way to digital reproduction. As Dutch artist/economist Hans Abbing has noted in his study *Why are Artists Poor?*:

> Walter Benjamin predicted that the technical reproduction of art would lead to a breaking of art's spell ('Entzauberung'). Art became less obscure, more accessible and thus less magical because of technical reproduction. ... Benjamin's prediction is not difficult to grasp. Technical (re)production enables a massive production of artworks at low prices. It would be very strange indeed if this didn't reduce the exclusive and glamorous allure of art products. ... But thus far, this hasn't happened; [the composer] Bach and his oeuvre maintain their aura. In general, if one observes the high, if not augmented status and worship of art since Benjamin's essay first appeared, his prediction was either wrong or it is going to take longer before his

predictions are borne out.[1]

Abbing's observations about Benjamin's thesis that technological reproduction and mass availability result in dimin-
ished "aura" suggest that instead of diminishing the "aura" of
art, reproduction helps to extend the aura of the works reproduced instead of destroying that aura. This inverted interpretation of "aura" produced by the readily accessible and
available art work shifts the emphasis in Benjamin's article
from the traditional 'cult' value of art objects to what he
terms their commercial 'exchange' value. This emphasis on
what Benjamin supposes to be the traditional role of art
works in religious practices appears in his concept of aura as
the physicality of the art object, what he refers to as "authenticity":

> The authenticity of a thing is the essence of all that is
> transmissible from its beginning, ranging from its sub-
> stantive duration to its testimony to the history it has ex-
> perienced.[2]

As Abbing's proposition implies, Benjamin's idea of "authenticity" only becomes a meaningful value once there are reproductions of an art work, similar in appearance, but not
ident-ical to their source. Thus, the more widely promoted
an art work through reproduction, it is possible to suppose
that its "aura" would logically then increase as well; there is
an inversion of Benjamin's thesis. What Abbing suggests is
that "aura" is not as Benjamin proposed it, but is instead a
function of the reproductive process itself. This shift in conception of Benjamin's "aura" suggests that art objects have a
dual character. Their "aura" is both the physical traces of the

[1] Hans Abbing, *Why are Artists Poor? The Exceptional Economy of
the Arts* (Amsterdam: Amsterdam University Press, 2004), 307.
[2] Walter Benjamin, "The Work of Art in the Age of Mechanical
Reproduction," in *Illuminations: Essays and Reflections*, ed. Hannah
Arendt, trans. Harry Zohn (New York: Schocken Books, 1969), 221.

particular history that an object has experienced, and the relationship of that object to the tradition that produced it. These are two distinct values: one resides in the physical object, the other lies in the spectator's knowledge (and past experience) of the object's relationship to other, similar objects. If the first value is a "historical testimony," the second value can be called a "symbolic relationship." Even though the relationship to tradition is an independent value, separate from the physical properties forming the "historical testimony," it cannot be reduced to a set of physically present characteristics because it depends upon conceptual relationships produced in the minds of the human audience—functionally a semiotic 'reading' of a work guided by past experience with similar works. Separating these two values results in a new conception of "aura" independent of Benjamin's initial proposition that is specifically applicable to digital technology: the idea of "aura" results from the role the work plays for its audience sociologically (how they employ the work in their society.) This conception, as related to the audience's access to that art work, makes conflicts over "intellectual property" an inevitable consequence of the emergence of digital technology.

Mechanically or manually (re)produced objects always have an implicit limit on their availability (thus their accessibility); digital objects do not have a limit of this type—in principle an infinite number of any digital work could be produced without a change or loss, or even deviation between any of the works.[3] This distinction between all physical objects and digital objects reveals a fundamental similarity between the original art work and its mechanical reproductions; such similarity does not conflate the older relationships of copy with original: instead it reveals the basic difference between the digital and the physical. Every digital reproduction is identical to every other; digital objects are stored as a

---

[3] It is "in principle" only because *infinite* reproduction is a *literal impossibility;* however, an unlimited quantity of copies *can* be produced without deviation.

form of information, rather than limited as physical objects inherently are; thus, the digital state can be understood as a form of instrumental language—instructions for executing the "retrieval" that is a specific digital (art) work.

With physical objects each *object* is in fact unique, even when it is an identical example of a given type: while two sheets of white paper may be apparently identical in every way, each sheet is a unique example, physically discrete and independent of all others. Digital reproductions are all the same, rather than being unique examples of a given type (as with sheets of paper), each is an identical execution of uniform, constant instructions, a "copy." Information theory describes works of this kind as exhibiting *zero* information-theoretic entropy: because the execution of the instrumental data of digital objects (the electronic file stored by a computer) is an entirely *predictable* process within the framework of a given digital system, no information is required to produce a digital work from a digital object (electronic file).[4] Digital reproduction is therefore fundamentally different from any kind of reproduction previous to it, and the digital objects subject to this type of reproduction can be seen to constitute a new class of object.

Digital (art) works retain their initial form over time without degradation because there is no physical object that is subject to the decay of time. They can be edited, compiled, combined, and distributed without any change in any subsequent reproduction; "copies" can then be reproduced further, infinitely, without ever being subject to the necessary loss inherent to physical media. One "copy" is not only equivalent in content, it is identical to its source. The concept of a digital "original" disappears because all versions are all identical "originals," or are all identical "copies."

Contemporary language lacks the terms needed to describe the relationship between distinct instances of an iden-

[4] See Ralph Abraham, Peter Broadwell, and Ami Radunskaya, "MIMI and the Illuminati," *Pomona College* [Faculty Pages], December 16, 1996, pages.pomona.edu/~aer04747/mimi/miminotes.html.

tical digital object: "copy" assumes the traditional mode of originals and replicas; "clone" introduces a biological analogy that nevertheless suggests some anterior original source that (at least) potentially exists as the source. Because the data comprising the digital work itself remains constant, digital objects are indistinguishable; the distinction between any two iterations of a singular digital work is not an issue of content or form because the digitized information remains constant; it is an issue of location and physical presentation—where a specific version is located on (or in) the physical media that carries its imprint and/or displays it in a human-readable form.

§3.2

The distinction between physical objects and digital objects is absolute. These distinctions are related to a duality between symbolic meaning and physicality that begins with the earliest forms of mass reproduction: minting currency. The stamping of emblems on coins renders each token valuable by dual means: though its material (precious metals), and symbolically identified as authentic (that its value is real) by the markings emblazoned on its surfaces (its symbolic content). Authenticity is an interpretation based upon a second order of interpretation, derived from a decision about the symbolic content of an object. The digital object, lacking a physical component, exists as symbolic content that becomes a physically accessible form only when presented through a technological intermediary, (for example, a video on a computer monitor) or transformed into a physical object (such as a paper printout).

The separate valences of material and symbol can be understood as existing at different levels of interpretation: the physical provides the first level, with all the conclusions about the object's age, etc. forming a first order; the symbolic content, including its connection to traditions, similarity or difference with other objects, the interpreter's relationship to the particular object, etc. all form a second order of interpretation. While the second, symbolic order does require the first order (some type of physical presence) for its presentation, the interpreted content exists as an excess to the first order. It is information provided and created by the interpreter using past experience with interpreting the form and character of the first order that produces the second order.

The dualism of "aura" in physical objects appears as a function of both the material object and its symbolic content. That the dualism of "aura" is connected to the invention of exchange value (currency) is not accidental. Exchange value depends on human agency in social and political ways to achieve its meaning and maintain its value. It is precisely in the establishment of value through recourse to a particular scheme of many different objects governed by human agency that "value" emerges at all. Awareness of the symbolic relationship between one object and another is an interpreted result of human agency, and does not inhere in the object itself. Aura for digital works retains this dualism while shedding the literal constraint of specific physicality. The encounter with a digital object remains a material engagement, but one where the physical form is separate from the digital work, serving as a presentation of that work—i.e., what is seen and heard watching a video clip on a computer.

The separation of the specific presentation of a digital work from our conception of that work literally inscribes the Modernist desire to isolate the art work from the context that produces it[5] into our consciousness and our interpretation of the digital (art) object: instead of requiring the sanitized, clean white gallery space to eliminate external context from the interpretations of art, with digital works this eliding of the specifics of location, presentation, context, etc. happens in the mind of the spectator. This effect derives from the digital aspiration to the state of information. It reflects the aura of information.

[5] Brian O'Doherty, *Inside the White Cube: The Ideology of the Gallery Space*, rev. edn. (Berkeley: The University of California Press, 2000).

Because the material aspects of digital works are ephemeral, lasting no longer than the phenomenological encounter with the presentation of the digital object, (typically on a screen of some type), the "aura of information" suggests that the digital itself transcends physical form. This illusion defines the "aura of information." Because digital works emerge from a second-order interpretation, they belong to the same category of objects as music encoded for playback by a machine, as with the player-piano scroll. Digital objects are not readily human-readable, and only become sensible as works when processed by machine. Like the music encoded on the player-piano scroll, the digital object is separate from its physical embodiment, often produced in ways and with technologies (like language) that are independent of digital forms, but are readily reproducible without loss and totally dependent on the specific technologies of their performance or presentation.

As digital objects do not degrade with time; they will not disappear over time. The limit for a digital work is not based on its physical demise, but rather on its availability within contemporary technology. Older digital works are only "lost" because the technological support for accessing them vanishes: the digital work, theoretically, endures and can be retrieved at some future time. Digital reproduction then becomes not only an inherent characteristic of digital objects, it is also their means to effective immortality. The digital reproduction and transfer of files from older technology to new technology enables the continuation (perpetual maintenance) of digital works regardless of what technology they may have begun within; early computer programs, such as 8-bit arcade games that originally existed as ROM chips in, for example, the Atari 2600 Home Entertainment System game cartridges, are still accessible because contemporary technology is able to emulate these discarded, obsolete systems, thus enabling otherwise inaccessible digital works to be read with equipment vastly more powerful and otherwise incompatible with the older digital files. In the case of the digital works contained by the Atari 2600 computer game system there is a large, although limited, number of functional Atari Home Entertainment Systems, and when the last system irreparably breaks down, access to the original versions of the files on those ROM cartridges by their original hardware systems will be lost. Such a loss constitutes the historical testimony of this technology and the digital works accessible to it. However, the historical testimony these systems have is completely separate from the files contained by these ROMs, and the survival of the data on them is of a different nature than the survival of the original, physical system itself. (This reading is a result of a newer system emulating an earlier digital systems' function.)

The ability to separate the digital file from the hardware dramatizes the aura of digital objects: the digital work as immortal, transient, adaptable to any new presentation technology that comes along. It also connects the aura of digital objects to the aura of information since information is a function of interpretation and so can theoretically be transferred from one representational system to another, as when ancient, "dead" languages such as ancient Greek or Egyptian hieroglyphs are translated into contemporary languages such as English. Theoretically, the content of the earlier language remains constant; with digital objects this theoretical aspect of human language and meaning becomes actual fact because of the distinction between the machine language of binary code that is prescriptive, and human language that is descriptive and denotative. Because the binary machine language is a set of commands, the transfer and conservation of information held within that language is not subject to the semiotic "drift" of meaning that affects all human language. Thus the contents of even "dead" digital systems can be recovered, assuring the immortality of any digital object.

Yet, the immortality of digital files also leads to an accumulation of works whose management and accessibility inevitably will begin to become an issue in itself, beyond simply the question of being able to access antiquated files constructed and used with hardware that is obsolete and irreplaceable.

Once the immortality of digital works is understood to mean these works will accumulate and be immanently present indefinitely into the future, a Malthusian problem emerges. As more and more materials accumulate in digital form they will become increasingly difficult to organize, access, and use. The quantity of information will impede its ability to be used or evaluated. The "aura of information" implies that this continual databasing of information is a positive value in itself, separating information from the ability to use it or determine its significance. The "aura of information" gains its apparent value from information-poor predigital societies where access to and possession of information was a positive value because the volume of information even *potentially* available was limited both physically to specific objects, and by the ability to reproduce that information. In such an info-poor society, stockpiled information has value in itself because the amount of information remains limited. For digital technologies, the creation, storage, and distribution of information are not limited in the ways they are for traditional societies. Because digital information aspires to immortality, is infinitely reproducible, and claims the "aura of information"—the accumulation and management problematics of digital files necessarily emerges as an inevitable outcome of the development of digital technology.

§3.3

All mechanical reproductions are objects in themselves; they carry their own "historical testimony," and are subject to the effects of time and decay as are any other physical objects. This is true for the mechanical reproduction at all levels of its existence; even the photographic negative is subject to decay and loss, just as the metal plate used in printing gradually wears away as it is used to make reproductions. The mechanical reproduction can therefore be regarded as having the same potential to authenticity (via historical testimony) as any other physical work of art.

In contrast to the mechanical reproduction, the digital reproduction is a multivalent object. The physical representation of a digital object, as on a computer screen for example, does not subject that file to the wearing away that physical objects suffer; nor does the copying, sending, or storage of these digital objects necessarily damage them. The digital transfer of files produces perfect, identical copies not subject to the historical testimony of physical objects. In effect, the digital object—the information contained in/as the digital file—is independent of historical testimony. However, the medium that stores the digital file is subject to "historical testimony." This container is distinct from its contents, and should be understood as separate from them.

The types of "historical testimony" that do impact digital files can thus be divided into three types: (1) those that impact the container, whether it is the disk, CD, ROM, or other storage medium, (2) those that effect the digital file in itself as distinct from the storage medium, and (3) the accessibility of the file using contemporary technology (the issue of obsolescent software, hardware, and the files produced with that older technology). A broken CD may render the data it contains inaccessible, but it does not actually destroy the data. A damaged or corrupted computer file is a result of errors made by the system storing and displaying the file, and are not examples of historical testimony, but are more akin to misprints and errors made with the machinery of mechanical reproduction.

The accessibility of a digital object produced with obsolescent technology leaves no trace on the digital object itself; it is the ability to read that file's content that becomes attenuated with time, not the file itself. Its contents remain constant even when we can no longer access those contents. This situation is akin to our ability to read ancient, "dead" human languages written in hieroglyphics or cuneiform: the contents of the text are independent of their storage medium or the format (language) in which they are written.

Technological failures, or glitches, do not constitute a historical testimony for digital objects; instead, they demon-

strate the digital work's nature as second order interpretations presented for viewing. This explains their lack of
physical presence and the uncomfortable relationship between the digital "template" or original digital file and the
physical versions produced from it as print outs, displays on
monitors, etc. The conflict surrounding intellectual property
rights is most concerned with access to the art "object" itself,
since in the digital realm the potential to reproduce and dis-
tribute does not necessarily include the right to read (access)
the work—this is why *every* digital rights management
(DRM) proposal limits and controls access to the (digital) art
work, to the right to read.[6]

§3.4

First order interpretations of historical art works such as the
Sistine Chapel proceed based on the fact that it remains the
Sistine Chapel in all circumstances; however, this assumption
reveals its attenuated character with mechanical reproduction, and announces itself clearly with digital works (if it is
not rendered completely invalid by the myriad variability
between different displays of the same work through the dis-
parate presentations of projectors, monitors, different user
parameters on various computers, etc.) to such an extent that
it becomes less appropriate to think about digital works in
terms of the *specifics* of a particular display than it is to think
about them *independent* of the particular display where they
may appear.

Consider the issue of color, for example. Different computer monitors display color differently, depending on the
age of the monitor, how long it has been in use, the particular
construction of the pixels in its screen, the specific settings it
has at the moment of display, etc. Stores selling monitors will
set up comparisons showing their available models because
these differences impact the appearance of digital works dis-

---

[6] The concept of the "right to read" originates with Richard Stall-
man, of the Free Software Foundation: http://www.fsf.org/.

played on them. The question of color becomes even more variable when consideration of presentation expands beyond desktop monitors to include other kinds of display such as projection, TV broadcast, or even video on cell phones. Each expansion of potential display increases the variation in how a digital file appears, rendering the question of which version is the "authentic version" problematic since the file being displayed can remain constant.

The superficial constancy of a human-readable form does not mean that apparently identical presentations produced by different sources are the same. Three apparently identical images may present the same human readable result, but be generated by incompatible sources. Imagine the following situation: (a) an uncompressed raster file specifying each and every pixel displayed; (b) a compressed version of the same raster data; (c) a version of the same image, but produced and described using vector graphics. The apparent content of the image is irrelevant—it could be a photograph, typography, or simply a collection of linear elements—because any type of image can be stored in these three ways.

The human-readable product of each of these three images are identical, so completely similar that there is no difference between the data on display in a human-readable form in any of these images; thus it is impossible for a human observer to distinguish between them based on their human-readable form.

However, in spite of being apparently identical, each of these images is produced from an individual, separate, digital object. This remains the case with these images no matter how frequently they are rendered human-readable, copied, or otherwise reproduced as digital files. The idea that they are actually the same is an illusion created by the aura of information. It is this aura—that all digital information remains constant/equivalent no matter what types of transformations are applied (in this case both compression and the distinctions between raster and vector storage of image data)—that confuses these distinct files for one another. Each digital file and the rendition of that code as a human-readable object (the apparently identical images) comprise separate, individual digital objects whose human-readable instantiation produces the illusion that they are the same. It is the belief in the equivalency between these distinct data files that contain unique, divergent code that reflects the aura of information in action.

Because the aura of information demands that spectators ignore the presentation (video monitor, projector, print-out, etc.) in considering the "context" of the work—conclusions related to what would be first order interpretations for non-digital works: for example, where the painting is from, how it is lit, how old it is—all these questions generally vanish when confronting a digital projection. Age, materials, etc. do not devolve from the physical materials of a digital work's presentation, but from considerations relating to its symbolic content. To the extent that a digital work has a historical testimony, it is a result of historicizing the style and form of the work (second order interpretations.) That a digital work is shown on a flat-screen in one presentation, a cathode ray-tube in another, and as projection on another occasion does not effect our considerations of that digital work. While the display may change, the digital work is considered to remain the same whatever means are used in its presentation. This dismissal of the variability of digital works suggests that the digital work exists and is understood as being independent of its various presentations. The same dismissal of the physically stored digital file mirrors the dismissals of the specifics of presentations; both are effects of the aura of the digital creating the belief that digital objects are divorced from physicality.

The independence of digital works from their physical presentation is connected to the contingency of both the right to read a digital file and the technological basis of digital (re)production. Where both manual and mechanical reproduction always preserve the physical character of the object, leaving it subject to its particular historical testimony; digital works do not. Any type of printed matter retains its form unless physically assaulted—burying a book in peat moss may result in the book decomposing, with the resultant loss of the book; a digital work cannot be thus assaulted, but neither can it be accessed away from a technological support. Digital files only appear through the variation of display that the above consideration of the issue of color implies.

Recognizing that the lack of historical testimony of digital works creates a framework shifting these objects away from the particular, physical, object-oriented attributes of their presentation towards being a non-object oriented art. The uniqueness of digital works cannot thus be a result of there being "only one," nor can the uniqueness of digital objects be a result of a solitary (individual) character because all "copies" are identical in every way. In effect, for digital works (as with mechanically (re)produced works before them), there is no first order object, in the way there is a *Sistine Chapel.*

The impact of the digital work's particular form of "uniqueness" on intellectual property reveals itself as the issue of access to the work: *the right to read,* rather than to own a copy. Possession and access are separated from one another. With first order objects, such as the *Sistine Chapel,* possession also confers the right of access: having possession guarantees access to the work; with digital works, possession becomes attenuated—it is possible to "own" files on a computer, but not have the ability to access those files' contents. The model that intellectual property thus adopts is much closer to the idea of a bank where only authorized persons may do business and everyone else is turned away unless they, too, invest their money in the bank. In all cases, what the customers have access to, what actions they are allowed, and most significantly how much it costs to perform those acts is determined by the bank. What these "customers" may do is strictly limited by the particulars of their specific investment in the bank.

§3.5

Mechanical reproduction is always limited by the physical materials, both in the form of the (re)productive technology (printing press, photographic negative, etc.) and the materials that form the reproduction itself. This basis imposes duration on the object; until the digital work is (re)produced physically, it lies outside this constraint, even though the digital file is always physically stored, the digital work that file produces remains a separate entity, although nevertheless inherently sourced to this digital file. And because the aura of information leads to the interpretative ignorance of the physical appearance of the work when it is presented to its audience, falling "outside" means that it is not subject to the effects of time degrading it via duration either when reproduced as an object, or in its native, digital form. Thus, the "authenticity" of the digital work lies in it being independent of the effects caused by the passage of time, its use (digital works do not "wear out" the way physical objects will), or via its replication and distribution in a digital form: unlike physical objects, digital works do not exist with physical constraint on the works themselves, only on the ability to store (and transmit) them, as with the limited ability to store files on a hard drive.

The absent physical limit means, in principle, that digital works can be regarded as immortal—making the lengthening of statutory ownership (copyrights, patents, etc.) a necessary and inevitable corollary to the conflict over intellectual property: the maintenance of the property demands that it last as long as the work in question. To do otherwise is to acknowledge the contingency of this *right to read* on the economics of object-based production and consumption that predate the emergence of the digital work. It is a lacuna which follows from the ideology of automation—the perpetual expansion of ownership reifies the fantasy of "self-made" success without recourse to social reproduction; in effect, the continuance of property claims in an immaterial medium is necessary for the valorization of authorship they enable through the dispropriation of agency (this fantasy of autonomy).

The aura of the digital describes the occlusion of the real conditions of physicality from considerations of the apparently immaterial realm of the digital. These constraints and limitations are inherently imposed on all digital technologies, objects and systems. Yet because the specific ways the digital aspires towards the state of information, producing the illusion of completeness, and poses as independent from material reality, the digital, paradoxically, emerges as an immaterial physicality—*spectral,* it is both immanently present and creates the pretext of lacking a substantial, material link to reality.

This supposed rupture—in the form of a penumbral immateriality—is the specific illusion that defines the aura of the digital: the denial of immanent physicality in the face of apparent and structural physical limitations and material basis. The confusion of our ability to identify the falsehood that is the digital immaterialism reflects this aura in action. It is precisely because of the confusion of physical and immaterial that the aura of the digital is pervasive.

The nature of the technology itself—the semiotic, immaterial manipulation and transformation of codes—generates the falsehood that the digital is, in fact, immaterial; contrariwise, it is actually a physicality whose encounters with human actors produce the same divergence between object and form that is familiar in our encounters with language: the symbolic interpretations generated by the digital overwhelm the physical testimony of the digital presentations themselves.

The issue with the aura of the digital is not that there is an inherent connection to the physical, but rather that this very real connection is not only denied, it is stripped from our awareness; this absence is the aura of the digital.

Implicit in the *right to read* is the ideology of the "cutting edge" that renders digital technologies obsolete. With this technological shift from current to antique is a constraint on the particular deployments of the technology—what has variously been called cut-up/mash-up/remix/collage/montage/database-driven work—based around a reassembly of existing materials into "novel" forms. That this aesthetic form has recurred in almost identical approach and form with each

new technology (Dziga Vertov experimented with wax recordings to make "remixes" in the 1920s[7]) suggests these approaches are banal rather than disruptive, (except in the
economic language currently attached to "intellectual property" and copyright). Rather than an "exploration" of the new
technology, these works suggest a Freudian avoidance of the
potential shocks this technology implies through repetition.
The psychological dangers *unheimlich* works may pose are
avoided in advance through the rubric of obsolescence and
the repetitions inherent to remixing existing familiar materials.

§3.6

The nature of digital technology and reproduction creates a
fundamental paradox between the interests of ownership and
the function of technology: where ownership has always already been a feature of possession, with digital reproduction
this connection presents a new problematic. The right to limit access (via DRM) is the key aspect to ownership of digital
works. Control over the right to read digital works finds its
basis in the older laws designed to control printing and publication: copyright laws that codify assumptions about physical objects and the access and ownership of those works.

Because digital works are (primarily) second order non-
object based artifacts, i.e. they are works without particular
physical form (and therefore limited by natural conditions of
scarcity, manufacturing and material), increasing the ability
of the producer to control their digital "property" even when
sold to another person becomes an inevitable consequence of
the steady shift to digital technology for creating and distrib-
uting all aspects of culture.

---

[7] See Vlada Petric, *Constructivism in Films: The Man with a Movie
Camera* (Cambridge: Cambridge University Press, 1987), and Dziga
Vertov, *Kino-Eye: The Writings of Dziga Vertov*, ed. Annette Mich-
selson, trans. Kevin O'Brien (Berkeley: University of California
Press, 1984).

The transformation of everything that can be digitized into a digital form (the universal aspiration to achieve the state of information as instrumentality) follows from the logic of DRM: the conflict over intellectual property is therefore inevitable, as is the elision of agency and the valorization of social action (refracted through the valorization of the author). Object-based works automatically become the consumer's property, and can be given, resold, etc. once possession is attained, but for non-object based works the digital rights management schemas mean that digital works lack this possession-based dimension of property. Even after a work has been purchased, the banking model for ownership obtains: once possession is achieved, the consumer does not own the work—they only have a contingent *right to read*; in its hypothetical form, consumers are unable to resell, give, lend, or share any of the digital works contained by DRM. The mechanisms that control access to digital works also reproduce the conflict they were meant to resolve in a vicious cycle where each new restriction on the right to read intensifies the conflict. In its most basic form, this is a conflict over whether non-object based works are entitled to the same treatment as object-based works.

§3.7

The "aura" of a work of art can be regarded as the tertiary interpretative effect resulting from a third interpretative act that uses past experience to create an awareness of that object exceeding both its physical form and its relationship to tradition. This difference allows the existence of "aura" (contra Benjamin) in mechanically reproduced works, via mechanical reproduction—and thus, also allows "aura" in digital (art) works. Awareness of this kind becomes possible through reproduction even though it exists to lesser degrees in traditional societies where awareness of the art works are "reproduced" as *linguistic* artifacts rather than visual ones. This awareness is imbued with special values (as Benjamin has observed). The earlier works can be understood as being

subjects of verbal (non-visual) reproduction and the awareness this type of reproduction produces generates "aura" that
is consistent with that generated by digital/mechanical reproduction.

Thus reproduction—mechanical or digital—is the source
and vehicle for a work's "aura." A spectator's encounter with
a "famous" work as an object is distinctly different than their
encounter with an unknown work because it is the wide dissemination of that work through reproduction that creates
the particular experience: cultural tourism is based on this
idea of encounters with originals whose "aura" is a function
of their being widely reproduced. The more fully a work is
disseminated, the greater its "aura." Andy Warhol's persona,
and his construction of superstars who are "famous for being
famous"[8] demonstrates the transient, contingent nature of
this conception of "aura," its socially-constructed nature, and
its reliance upon (digital) reproduction for existence.

The semiotic/instrumental immortality enshrined as the
aura of the digital reifies an ideology where the work of "genius" (literally) "lives forever" within the simultaneous frameworks of DRM and digital reproduction. The ownership of
ideas is coupled with the specific material form those ideas
take within digital technology. This semiotic immortality
becomes instrumental immortality in the realm of digital
code executed autonomously by machines: this is the "aura of
the digital." The cultural drive to shift all production to this
immaterial basis—the information economy—reflects how
the ideology of automation enables the expansion of the digital aura.

The aura of the digital signals the digital is the site of a
specific reification dramatizing an underlying conflict between production and consumption: the emergence drama-
tized as digital capitalism—that is, between the accumulation
of capital and its expenditure. By enabling the fantasy of accumulation without consumption, digital technology be-

[8] Patrick Smith, *Andy Warhol's Art and Films* (Ann Arbor: UMI
Research Press, 1986), 195–202.

comes an ideological force reifying the conflict between the limits imposed on the value of capital via expenditure and inflation, and the demand implicit in the capitalist ideology of escalating value. The reciprocity between production and consumption is necessary for the accumulation of wealth (capital) to be anything other than an economic pathology. The lacuna that accumulated wealth presents is one where inflation appears as the necessary corrective—devaluing the accumulated capital in order to maintain the circulation necessary to maintain the dialectic of production and consumption: when capital collects, its value must diminish. The aura of the digital upsets this dialectic by reifying only one side of the construction—the illusion of production of capital without its necessary consumption. The aura of the digital is thus a symptom of the structure of pathological capitalist ideology becoming realized as digital capitalism—a fantasy based upon digital technology without regard for the illusory nature of these transfers, or the reality of the expenditures required in the creation of the digital itself.

Digital technology, its development, deployment, production and access all demand a large expenditure of capital both to create and to maintain. The aura of the digital separates the results from its technological foundation—the illusion of value created without expenditure: a pathological capitalist ideology that demands the valorization of social action it enables through the ideology of automation, coupled with the implementation of controls over digital technology (DRM) as it aspires towards the state of information and assumes the "aura of information" is coincident with the aura of the digital and digital capitalism.

Even though the origins of the "aura of information" reside in the technical parameters of the digital, its role in the capitalist ideology-fantasy of wealth accumulation renders its conception of the digital not only fundamentally flawed, it is also a formulation that supports the disenfranchisement of human agency by the ideology of automation and its transformation into an immaterial commodity separate from concerns with social reproduction. By naturalizing the concentration of capital, the aura of information transforms digital technology into a magical resource that can be used without consumption or diminishment.

The initial effect of this magical resource appeared as the "dot.com bubble" at the end of the 20th century when the internet first emerged as a popular, commercially exploitable medium. This initial bubble was quickly followed by a larger one with an even more explicitly immaterial basis—the 2008 Housing Bubble. These collapses were inevitable since the values they produced depended upon the exploitation of the production without consumption fantasy. The shift in emphasis towards various forms of "DRM" began even before these controls were implemented by technology itself in the form of technology patents, copyright-based registrations and "subscriptions" to software etc., an initial phase seamlessly moving into technological DRM. The (re-)emergence of "walled-gardens" around proprietary hardware-software combinations affirms those connections between the aura of the digital and the aura of information needed to justify capitalist impositions of controls (DRM) over intellectual property and the technical valorization of social activity they accompany. Otherwise, the aura of the digital threatens the status quo because the illusion of profit without expenditure suggests the possibility that the digital could realize a situation where capitalism itself ceases to exist.

Thus, the aura of the digital is Janus-like, suggesting a magical production without consumption, reifying this fundamental ideology as digital capitalism, at the same time as it implies an elision of capitalism itself. However, all these suggestions proceed from an illusion based in a refusal to acknowledge the real expenditures required in the creation, production, maintenance, and access to the digital technologies and the materials made available through those technologies which make these ideological fantasies possible. In this regard, the 'aura of the digital' can be identified with a pathological myopia: it is implicit in the anti-capitalist fantasy of an "end of scarcity" abolishing capitalism, and for the capitalist ideology reified within the illusion of production without consumption. Each belief is therefore an ideological fantasy reified as instrumentality: a product of each denying the actual physicality, and therefore the expenditures and costs, of digital technology.

Chapter Four

The Immaterial Commodity

"Bitcoin" and those 'cryptocurrencies' derived from it are a public system of electronic ledgers recording payments designed to function like legal tender currency. It was proposed in October 2008,[1] and implemented during the bursting of the housing bubble, starting with its registry as a project on the open source software site Source Forge in November 2008, with the first available software for trading Bitcoins released in January 2009.[2] This initial specification for Bitcoin was written by "Satoshi Nakamoto"[3] as a system of exchange employing a decentralized network—peer-to-peer—where individual transactions do not rely on a bank for their authorization, unlike echecks, credit cards, and other types of electronic funds transfer. Cryptographic currencies (crypto-

---

[1] Satoshi Nakamoto, "Bitcoin: A Peer-to-Peer Electronic Cash System," 2008, http://www.bitcoin.org/bitcoin.pdf.

[2] Bitcoin was registered November 9, 2008; the first 'block' was released January 3, 2009, the trading software followed on January 11, and the first use of Bitcoin in a transaction occurred on January 12; see https://en.bitcoin.it/wiki/History.

[3] "Satoshi Nakamoto" may be a pseudonym; see the *Satoshi Nakamoto* page of the Bitcoin wiki: https://en.bitcoin.it/wiki/Satoshi_Nakamoto.

currencies) such as Bitcoin are intended to be electronic ana-
logues of physical cash, protecting their users through a
combination of strong encryption and shared information
about possession—all transactions are recorded publically in
a "block" that contains information about who owns all the
Bitcoins currently in circulation. Unlike national currencies
(legal tender currencies produced by national governments),
Bitcoins are strictly limited in both quantity (the total quantity was constrained by the implementation to 2,100,000)[4] and
the rate of production ("mining") by the linkage of new coin
production to their use in exchange: new coins are a product
of the verification process for the encrypted information that
composes every transaction. A major distinction between
Bitcoins and fiat currencies produced by national mints is
that they exist independently from governmental ability to
"print" money, a constraint inherently imposed by the "mining" process itself, making them a "digital commodity" designed for *scarcity* in the same way that physical commodities
such as gold are scarce; this dimension attracted investment
by securities traders and stock market speculators in 2011
and 2012.[5]

Bitcoin appears to be a "hacker's *currency*" par excellence:
it saves the immaterial labor of computers as the *Bitcoin,* in
the process transforming the mechanical procedure that is
the foundation of the digital into a material exchangeable for
other kinds of production. While the labor involved to produce Bitcoins is immaterial in nature, (it does not involve
physical facture, instead employing the semiotic production
common to digital technology), it still consumes resources—
in the twin forms of the computation performed by the

[4] See https://en.bitcoin.it/wiki/Bitcoin.
[5] There are a number of high profile investors and financial analysts
who have been promoting Bitcoin since 2010; see Max Keiser,
"Some other alternatives to fiat currencies" *Max* Keiser, December
13, 2010 http://www.maxkeiser.com/2010/12/some-other-alternatives-
to-fiat-currencies/, and Chamath Palihapitiya, "Why I Invested in
Bitcoin," *Bloomberg View*, May 30, 2012, http://www.bloomberg
view.com/articles/2013-05-30/bitcoin-the-perfect-schmuck-insurance.

hardware itself and the electricity required to operate it[6]—
and only emerges out of specific types of digital processing.
Bitcoins are not an autonomously arising product of computational activity, but rather the generated outcome of specific
actions. While Bitcoin imitates aspects of the larger internet
structure, it is nevertheless a currency, and so addressable in
terms of socio-economic structure and significance, quite
apart from its technological implication. These ideological
implications of Bitcoin become apparent through a contextual situation of it in relation to the larger political economy:
unlike historical currencies, Bitcoin, as initially proposed by
Nakamoto, enables a perfect form of surveillance over economic transactions, a specific anonymity/privacy issue that
the implementation of Bitcoin has attempted to address as
Simon Barber, Xavier Boyen, Elaine Shi, and Ersin Uzun observed in their discussion of Bitcoin in *Financial Cryptography*;[7] various early implementations of the initial Bitcoin
specification, such as *Bitcoin-Qt* or *BtCoin,* attempt to resolve
this problem.[8] (Other popular alternative implementations
such as *Dogecoin, Maxcoin,* etc. are primarily variants supported by financial speculation in cryptocurrencies, rather
than technologically distinct attempts to restore the privacy
of transactions.) Because all these cryptocurrencies are a developing technology and this issue has *not* been resolved (as

[6] See the summary discussion of how Bitcoin "mines" consume large
amounts of electricity (physical resources) in Katie Davies, "The
Monster Machines Mining Bitcoins in Cyberspace that Could Make
Techies a Small Fortune (but cost $160,000 a day to power)," *Daily
Mail Online,* April 15, 2013, http://www.dailymail.co.uk/news/article-
2309673/Techies-building-powerful-computers-Bitcoins-new-digital-
currency-make-millions.html.
[7] Simon Barber, Xavier Boyen, Elaine Shi, and Ersin Uzun, "Bitter to
Better — How to Make Bitcoin a Better Currency," in *Financial
Cryptography and Data Security,* ed. Angelos D. Keromytis (Berlin:
Springer, 2012), 399–414.
[8] While the problems for anonymous transactions are well documented, the Bitcoin wiki claims there is no such issue. See http://en.
bitcoinwiki.org/Bitcoin_history.

Barber, et al. noted in their 2012 analysis), the present discussion will focus on the initial proposal from which these implementations are derived. The surveillance (pervasive monitoring) embedded in the specifications for the currency itself integrates the authoritarian dimensions of globalized capitalism—a continuous surveillance and valorization of formerly non-commercial behaviors and relationships—*literally* into the system of exchange itself.

This foundation for the "Bitcoin" gives the immaterial labor common to the digital a tangible 'form'—in this case, crystalizing both resources (electricity) and labor expended (computational cycles required to "mine" the coins), in effect, attempting to preserve this immaterial labor in a digitally-derived form that can then be used as a currency, much as commodity-based currencies in the past attempted to preserve labor in an exchangeable form. It is this transformation of immaterial production (semiosis) into Bitcoins that is the essential feature in this case: to extract these Bitcoins requires computational power because the coins are "contained" in mathematical "ore"—*equations*—that require complex processor-intensive labor to solve, as Simon Barber, Xavier Boyen, Elaine Shi, and Ersin Uzun explain in their technical analysis "Bitter to Better—How to Make Bitcoin a Better Currency," published in 2012:

> the generation of new bitcoins happens in a distributed fashion at a predictable rate: "bitcoin *miners*" solve computational puzzles to generate new bitcoins, and this process is closely coupled with the verification of previous transactions. At the same time, miners also get to collect optional transaction fees for their effort of vetting said transactions. This gives users clear economic incentives to invest spare computing cycles in the verification of Bitcoin transactions and the generation of new Bitcoins.
>
> [...]
>
> The bitcoin money supply expands as each block created

may contain a special *generation transaction* (with no explicit input) that pays the block creator a time-dependent amount for the effort (50 coins today, rapidly decreasing). The rate of block, hence money, creation is limited by a *proof of work* of adaptive difficulty, that strives to maintain a creation rate of one block every 10 minutes across the whole network. Bitcoin transaction verification is thus a lucrative race open to all, but a computationally expensive one.[9]

The 'block' is the complete public listing of all confirmed transactions; every coin, and to whom it belongs, is contained in a block. As new coins are mined, they are added to this chain. The resulting coins are thus a product of that labor indicating that it has been expended in their production. This saving of past labor places these digital products in the same category as any other commodity; their designated function as *currency* follows from their linkage to the universal foundation of digital production, the immaterial activity of computers, that is reified in a commodity form as/by the Bitcoin.

However, what this currency brings into sharp focus is not the difference between rentier/fiat currencies and those "backed" by a physical commodity, but contemporary attempts to reify digital or immaterial labor of autonomous systems as an emergent equivalent to physical production, as immaterial physicality. Unlike the physical commodity-basis that is the foundation of traditional currencies composed from a precious material (historically gold or silver)—that is simultaneously also a physical commodity in itself and can be employed for both exchange and has a use value in the production of other commodities—there is no use value contained by Bitcoin. This product of immaterial labor cannot be used in the production of other commodities once it has been created (mined)—unlike other immaterial labor products, the only purpose for Bitcoin is to be currency. The Bitcoin, unlike the physical commodity basis of historical currencies,

[9] Barber et al.,"Bitter to Better," 400.

has only a currency function—as a commodity it is only valuable as a token of exchange either for other currencies, or through social exchange where it is a token dependent on both parties' mutual agreement upon its value: this is the same reification of social relationship apparent in fiat currency itself. There is no other function for Bitcoin other than as currency, and consequently its value depends on social convention.

Social relationships are at the foundation of all tokens of exchange, whether based in a produced commodity or in the reification of that relationship (as with fiat currencies). The "transaction history" that is an inherent part of every individual Bitcoin allows the tracking and quantification (reification) of these social relationships as the currency itself. Thus, Bitcoin occupies an intermediate position between the historical physical commodity that functions as universal equivalent for exchange and the purely social reification of fiat currency. What distinguishes fiat currencies from Bitcoin is that Bitcoin is artificially constrained in an *a priori* fashion. Unlike fiat currencies that can be valued at any amount and so are functionally of unlimited value, and historical currency based in a physical commodity where value is limited by scarcity imposed by production, the Bitcoin simulates scarcity in an attempt to produce value. The scarcity of physical commodities is simulated in two ways: (1) the algorithmic nature of their mining which imposes physical constraints on the generation of Bitcoins, and (2) an absolute limit to the total number of coins potentially available (2,100,000). Other than its (artificial) scarcity Bitcoin resembles fiat currencies in its reliance upon a reified social relationship to ensure its value: it is *not* simultaneously both a token of exchange and a commodity in itself.

This foundation in a social relationship is *not* what Satoshi Nakamoto identifies as the "trust based model" in the initial proposal for Bitcoin. Nakamoto's specification proceeds from a discussion of existing financial payments as being based upon Internet-based commerce using financial institutions, what he termed "trusted third parties," as the intermediary in a system of payments. The underlying "problem" that Nakamoto identified as the *raison d'être* for Bitcoin, specifically that "no mechanism exists to make payments over a communications channel without a trusted party,"[10] is not actually removed from Nakamoto's proposal for Bitcoin:

> What is needed is an electronic payment system based on cryptographic proof instead of trust, allowing any two willing parties to transact directly with each other without the need for a trusted third party. Transactions that are computationally impractical to reverse would protect sellers from fraud, and routine escrow mechanisms could easily be implemented to protect buyers. In this paper, we propose a solution to the double-spending problem using a peer-to-peer distributed timestamp server to generate computational proof of the chronological order of transactions. The system is secure as long as honest nodes collectively control more CPU power than any cooperating group of attacker nodes. [11]

The 'nodes' described in Nakamoto's specification are the computer systems processing transactions, in the process 'mining' new Bitcoins. The "trusted third party" being rejected—the banking system—is subject to various forms of governmental oversight, constrained by laws covering fraud, provides a digital 'paper trail' of the transactions in question, and has an existing system of consumer protections already in place. The proposed replacement, Bitcoin, does not. This transformation is ironic in nature: that the "trusted third party," the global banking system, is *not* trustworthy in itself is the reason for the multitude of legal and procedural oversight mechanisms. In place of these, Nakamoto's design for Bitcoin relies on digital cryptography and limitations on computational power for most users to ensure the validity of

[10] Nakamoto, "Bitcoin," 1.
[11] Nakamoto, "Bitcoin," 1.

a system where the "trusted third party" may be purely technological—the timestamp server—rather than a bank that is already constrained by law:

> The steps to run the network are as follows:
>
> 1) New transactions are broadcast to all nodes.
> 2) Each node collects new transactions into a block.
> 3) Each node works on finding a difficult proof-of-work for its block.
> 4) When a node finds a proof-of-work, it broadcasts the block to all nodes.
> 5) Nodes accept the block only if all transactions in it are valid and not already spent.
> 6) Nodes express their acceptance of the block by working on creating the next block in the chain, using the hash of the accepted block as the previous hash.
>
> Nodes always consider the longest chain to be the correct one and will keep working on extending it. If two nodes broadcast different versions of the next block simultaneously, some nodes may receive one or the other first. In that case, they work on the first one they received, but save the other branch in case it becomes longer. The tie will be broken when the next proof-of-work is found and one branch becomes longer; the nodes that were working on the other branch will then switch to the longer one.[12]

The 'nodes' in this description are the computers engaged in processing the transactions; the 'blocks' are the encrypted transaction keys that identify both parties to the exchange of Bitcoins: it is an automated system constructed to function outside of any human interaction and without requiring human oversight. This system is an example of the law of automation in action, in the process creating a mechanical

---

[12] Nakamoto, "Bitcoin," 5.

procedure to replace existing systems of financial circulation. As such it does not resolve the issue of the "trusted third party" or banking system, substituting a collection of other 'third parties' *not* subject to existing legal restraint or providing protection (the autonomous nodes) for a system based in human oversight and control—that these 'nodes' are, nevertheless, directed by humans is self-evident since they are set up and maintained by humans in exchange for a reward—the newly 'mined' Bitcoins. This substitution of a technological system (timestamp server) for institution where there is an established process to redress and resolve problems—i.e. legal recourse over fraud—is the aura of the digital inflating the *assumption of technological superiority* over established, physical (and historical) solutions. The trustworthiness of this productive system depends on a capitalist incentive—the profit generated by 'mining.'

The Bitcoin proposal does more than eliminate human oversight and legal restrictions from the circulation of exchange values. It is an attempt to replace existing, formally organized, legal systems of protection for all parties in the transaction—the buyer, the seller, and the bank—with one based upon the assumption that the only parties involved in a transaction who need protection are *sellers*: this structural bias further reifies the same capitalist ideology that gives rise to digital rights management (DRM) in the transformation of everything that can be digitized into a digital form (the universal aspiration to the state of information). The only significant parties in such a framework are the *owners* (sellers) whose decisions about how to limit access find literal form in the DRM itself. Bitcoin is the reification of these interests at the level of *exchange* itself; this aspect of Nakamoto's proposal has contributed to its embrace by grey and black markets (such as Silk Road) employing peer-to-peer exchanges[13]

[13] The Silk Road website, accessibly only through the TOR browser, is an anonymous marketplace that only accepts Bitcoin for its transactions, see http://veilednetwork.com/silk-road-url/ and http://en.wikipedia.org/wiki/Silk_Road_(marketplace).

where *getting paid* can be an issue. (The use of Bitcoin escrow at the original Silk Road[14] contradicts Bitcoin's purpose of avoiding the Bank or other middleman.) This embrace is ironic since it is a currency that inherently contains the ability to track all ownership and transactions. Unlike physical currency of all types, and in a fashion distinct from existing systems of exchange, Nakamoto's description of Bitcoin eliminates the privacy afforded to purchases:

> We define an electronic coin as a chain of digital signatures. Each owner transfers the coin to the next by digitally signing a hash of the previous transaction and the public key of the next owner and adding these to the end of the coin. A payee can verify the signatures to verify the chain of ownership.[15]

Every transfer of Bitcoin as Nakamoto designed the system offers the possibility to track the economic activity and associations of anyone using Bitcoin—as Barber, et. al. note, *all Bitcoins are public knowledge.*[16] As a surveillance apparatus, it is difficult to imagine a more perfect way to monitor what and how citizens behave than to link transaction histories to the currency itself. Even peer-to-peer exchanges that would be beyond oversight with a traditional currency become subject to precise scrutiny. In attempting to remove the 'third party' (bank/government) from the exchange process, Bitcoin instead enshrines the authority it attempts to displace. The early embrace of Bitcoin by grey and black markets seeking to avoid the global banking system reflects this irony: the anonymity of "cash" is fundamentally eliminated in favor of a perfect economic surveillance of all transactions. The full

---

[14] Nicholas Christin, "Travelling the Silk Road: A Measurement Analysis of a Large Anonymous Online Marketplace," paper presented at the International World Wide Web Conference, May 13–17, 2013, Rio de Janeiro, Brazil, http://www2013.org/proceedings/p213.pdf.

[15] Nakamoto, "Bitcoin," 2.

[16] Barber et al., "Bitter to Better," 399–414.

visibility of Bitcoin transactions enables the tracking of all informal association networks (all exchanges of value) involving any *particular* Bitcoin, thus providing sellers with demographic information about their customers (and anyone else with the computational power to penetrate the cryptography with metadata about association networks) without offering any possibility to "opt out" from having their privacy violated by the seller (or government). If coupled with an omnipresent government surveillance apparatus, Bitcoin enables a 'Trojan horse' surveillance of those unofficial marketplaces that specifically exist outside standard systems of exchange and which attempt to be anonymous by nature—this surveillance function of Bitcoin contributed to the conviction of Dread Pirate Roberts (Ross Ulbricht) over the original Silk Road.[17]

The valorizing process of capitalist expansion enabled by digital technologies is immediately apparent in the surveillance component inherent to Bitcoin. A further irony emerges from its lack of engagement with the formal banking system: Bitcoin lacks a formal system of recourse when problems of coin ownership, transaction validity, etc. do arise precisely because it is outside established legal frameworks. By creating this "private" currency outside of the legal and historical framework of governmental regulation and management of currency, Bitcoin is an ideological reification of globalized capitalism, and should be recognized as a tool whose alignment with authoritarian values has been masked by how the ideology of automation intersects with the aura of the digital: instead of being a "free" or "independent" form of money that transcends national boundaries, it is a technology of control aligned with globalized concerns over economic surveillance and monitoring the behaviors and associations of consumers' behaviors in the physical world.

[17] See Nicky Woolf, "Silk Road's Dread Pirate Roberts Convicted of Running an Online Drug Marketplace," *The Guardian*, February 4, 2015, http://www.theguardian.com/technology/2015/feb/04/silk-road-ross-ulbricht-convicted-drug-charges.

That in the current implementation and usage, the inherent surveillance is difficult to process due to the use of intermediary "digital wallets" does not eliminate its potential in the future. It is this in-built system of surveillance over transactions happening between individuals, especially since the current system forces the transfer of all the Bitcoins in a digital wallet, with a return transaction (change) being provided, that creates a demonstrable link for (and the value of) each transaction. This process also embeds the public keys for both parties in every transaction, further facilitating the correlation of keys to specific individuals even with randomly generated public key components.

Nakamoto acknowledges the privacy failure inherent in how Bitcoins record their transaction record as part of the currency itself. Nakamoto's solution, however, leaves the ability to "know" the full transaction history in place, just away from the "public" who employ the currency:

> The traditional banking model achieves a level of privacy by limiting access to information to the parties involved and the trusted third party. The necessity to announce all transactions publicly precludes this method, but privacy can still be maintained by breaking the flow of information in another place: by keeping public keys anonymous. The public can see that someone is sending an amount to someone else, but without information linking the transaction to anyone. This is similar to the level of information released by stock exchanges, where the time and size of individual trades, the "tape," is made public, but without telling who the parties were.

> As an additional firewall, a new key pair should be used for each transaction to keep them from being linked to a common owner. Some linking is still unavoidable with multi-input transactions, which necessarily reveal that their inputs were owned by the same owner. The risk is that if the owner of a key is revealed, linking could reveal

other transactions that belonged to the same owner.[18]

The only linkage that concerns Nakamoto's proposal is a "public" one—but it is unclear who composes this "public." However, multi-input transactions—the return of "change" in purchases involving a 'digital wallet' for example—as well as multiple purchases over time with the same vendors both offer the potential to 'unmask' the "privacy" as Nakamoto implements it. As Fergal Reid and Martin Harrigan note in their analysis of anonymity in the *implementation* of Bitcoin:

> With appropriate tools, the activity of known users can be observed in detail. This can be performed using a passive analysis only. Active analyses, where an interested party can potentially deploy 'marked' Bitcoins and collaborate with other users can discover even more information. We also believe that large centralized services such as the exchanges and wallet services are capable of identifying and tracking considerable portions of user activity.[19]

The potential to track users is inherent to the Bitcoin implementation, and it is one where private transactions are, in fact, potentially fully public in spite of the use of cryptography. The availability of this information to sellers is clearly a potential even with the "safe guards" initially proposed. The result is a system where no privacy exists—except from *casual* perusal; the full availability of personal information to the seller is not only potential, it is highly likely given the organization of the system and its embedding of 'a personal ownership history' in the Bitcoin.

The conclusion for Nakamoto's proposed financial exchange system does not solve the problems it identifies—the issue of "trust"—instead adding to those problems the poten-

[18] Nakamoto, "Bitcoin," 6.
[19] Fergal Reid and Martin Harrigan, "An Analysis of Anonymity in the Bitcoin System," in *Security and Privacy in Social Networks*, eds. Yaniv Altshuler et al. (New York: Springer, 2013), 197–223.

tial for a complete dissolution of *any* privacy in economic activity. The statement that "We have proposed a system for electronic transactions without relying on trust." that begins his conclusion is clearly without merit: not only does the system still rely on the reification of a social relationship as the currency, as with the fiat currencies it proposes to replace, it also still requires the currencies' users trust a "third party" who is not involved in the transaction, while at the same time requiring an inherent surrender of privacy—all transactions employing Bitcoins are tracked in the "coins" themselves. The assumption that this information will remain private and secret is prima facie absurd given the history of both DRM restrictions on digital media and software, and the frequent challenges to even the most robust encryption technologies as new, more powerful computers become generally available.

What is apparent in Bitcoin is a dramatic reification of capitalist ideologies and valorization imperatives within/as the Bitcoin technology itself. The dissolution of privacy in Bitcoin is not the "problem"—it is a logical outcome given the valorization demands inherent in digital capitalism's expansion into (formerly) social realms. The transformation of those social exchanges into the currency itself (new Bitcoins are "mined" through the exchange of existing Bitcoins) is a direct expression of this expansion: the valorization of social activities—such as friendship circles, browsing in a bookstore, or shopping without purchasing—becomes valuable data as digital technology valorizes those activities; Bitcoin is the valorization of authorship already present in "social media" taken to its logical conclusion. The creation of a currency from economic activity itself is the application of the same systemic shift focused on the generation of value through semiotic production rather than material facture.

Chapter Five

The Valorization of the Author

The digital translates social activity into commodity forms; the creation of "social networks" challenges traditional conceptions of intellectual property and this change makes clear how the rights assigned to the ownership of information come into question with the development of digital technology. That social networks violate privacy and survive through using their member's information to sell ads is a commonplace observation; the creation of free services enabling anyone with access to them to become an 'author' signals a move away from the productive action of humans and towards the automated surveillance (pervasive monitoring) of data collection, collation, and retrieval. This transformation reflects a fundamental shift in our conception of both identity and authorship—with implications for the idea of intellectual property as well.

Digital capitalism's transformation of non-labor (the various iterations of "social media" and "networking") into a new type of automated, immaterial production, suggests a new form of authorship that is derived from the historically paired varieties of *authorship*—the role and status of the author: there is both an empirical (or naive) interpretation and a critical interpretation of the concepts "author" and "authorship." With digital technology, a third conception of authorship—the digital author—emerges: the valorization of an individual's specific, social behavior, an 'author' made possible by the data management and recording potentials of digital computers. The concept of 'privacy' is therefore utterly foreign to this transformative valorization; the violation of privacy is essential for the transformation of activity into commodity: this is the reason that social networks will and must violate the privacy of their members—for companies such as Facebook or Google to function, they need to collect as much information about their users as possible in order to better tailor sales pitches to the individual interests and tastes of each particular member of their audience—Google's initial demand that the users of "Google+" use their actual names, rather than be anonymous, is a reflection of this desire to more directly and closely associate specific individuals with the database of information collected about them. The resolution arrived at for this transformative use of another's existing, recorded labor has already appeared: the battle between musicians and radio over the use of recorded music (records) on air. With musical performances, the performers are theoretically compensated through various licensing procedures, thus avoiding the unpaid valorization of their labor by radio broadcasters. A resolution to the problems posed by digital technologies is still forthcoming. This issue of "authorship" assumes a new status as (historical) capitalism expands into previous, purely social domains as it becomes digital capitalism; understanding the significance of this new digital author depends on acknowledging the ways it exceeds both the empirical and critical conceptions of "authorship."

The empirical use of "author" is unproblematic: it aspires both to simplicity and to transparency, assuming a direct connection between text and the one responsible for it; it is an ontological connection based on production. For this understanding, the author is the one credited with a "by line": the person responsible for the existence of a specific text. Coupled with an equally simple and transparent conception of "originality," it produces the "plagiarist" as a negative form of author—those authors who falsely claim authorship over works produced by others. DRM formalizes these inter-pretations in technological restraint; for the empirical inter-pretation, the "pirate" no less than the plagiarist (the "false-author") performs actions which establish and support the empirical conception of authorship through the *implicit* em-brace of the claims made. This empirical version of author-ship is the most common, intuitively recognizable even in the critical interpretation's referencing of sources for its argu-ment about a more complex, problematic view of authorship found in writings by Roland Barthes, Michael Foucault, Um-berto Eco, et. al.—each of whom propose some variant of authorship that questions the status and importance of the author in determining the *meaning* of the 'text,' but not its *production.*

The critical understanding is complex, and views "author-ship" as problematic. This critical conception blurs the lines between one author and another based on their sharing of common ideas, etc. that have been suggested as the general (indexical) state of language and meaning; it is a semiot-ic/epistemological approach. By invoking suggestions of a commingling between the empirical version of author and false-author (the plagiarist), the critical view shifts the em-phasis to the "reader" and interpretation of the "text" as Ro-land Barthes makes explicit in his essay *The Death of the Author*:

> The reader is the space on which all the quotations that make up a writing are inscribed without any of them be-ing lost; a text's unity lies not in its origin but in its desti-nation. Yet this destination cannot any longer be per-sonal: the reader is without history, biography, psycholo-gy; he is simply that *someone* who holds together in a sin-gle field all the traces by which the written text is con-stituted.[1]

---

[1] Roland Barthes, "The Death of the Author," in *Image — Music — Text*, trans. Stephen Heath (New York: Hill and Wang, 1977), 148.

His critical view of authorship emphasizes the structural aspects of language and culture that produce the concept of "author" as a specific interpretation generated in relation to a text—what Barthes means by the reader "is simply that *someone* who holds together in a single field all the traces by which the written text is constituted." This concept of authorship, rather than as an *a priori* figure that determines meaning, emerges from the relationship between a specific text and its context. This reversal of relationships is a displacement of the common meaning of 'author' as the determinant of meaning onto the interpreter. The agency of the author in creating the meaning of a text shifts to actions of the interpreter. The designation "Author" becomes an invented (interpreted) role emergent in how the "reader" engages the text; this is the meaning of Foucault's *author-function.*[2]

Yet, this critical view of "author" is not antithetical to the empirical one. Displacing the meanings of a text from the "author" onto the "reader" in Barthes' *The Death of the Author* only appears to reject the empirical author's ontological relationship to the text; it is a fundamentally different understanding of the "author" concept. What Barthes' analysis focuses on is not the physical, material object-nature of a specific text but the ascription of meaning to it; consequently, Barthes' "reader" is epistemological, and so is compatible with the empirical (ontological) concept of "author." His displacement is an issue of *meaning*, not production.

While the critical and empirical interpretations are not mutually exclusive, their conflation leads to interpretative confusion when Roland Barthes declares the author "dead." His claim is at least partially rhetorical since it signals a shift in concerns from the singular, intended meaning imposed by

---

[2] Michel Foucault, "What is an Author?" in *Language, Counter-Memory, Practice*, trans. Donald F. Bouchard and Sherry Simon, ed. Donald F. Bouchard (Ithaca: Cornell University Press, 1977), 124–177.

recourse to an "author," to an open-ended range of potential interpretations and approaches that could be applied with differing results to the same text. This interpretative range suggests an information space such as the "state of information" where multiple interpreted meanings can coexist even when they are mutually exclusive.

§5.1

Roland Barthes' recognition that "all the quotations that make up a writing are inscribed without any of them being lost" could be a literal description of the recombinatory process (collage/montage/appropriation) where the quotations themselves are explicit, physical reproductions of their sources. Instead of problematizing authorship this methodology reifies it and enables the valorization process whereby authors become commodities in themselves: the conversion into material for manipulation objectifies its source, emphasizing not the interpretation but the physicality of the original "text." Barthes' shift in emphasis exceeds Michel Foucault's observation about the emergence of an ontological view of authorship:

> Speeches and books were assigned real authors, other than mythical or important religious figures, only when the author became subject to punishment and to the extent that his discourse was considered transgressive.[3]

Recombinant practices, instead of focusing on transgressions of *discourse,* focus on transgressions of *property.* The legal conflicts over 'sampling' in music support this recognition. The complicity of the critical view in the valorization process derives from the distinction between the epistemological (critical) and ontological (naive) approaches impacts on the interpretation of authorship. If the empirical view acts to limit and restrict authorship, the critical view serves to ex-

---

[3] Foucault, "What is an Author?", 124.

pand it, and this expansion is essential for valorization to occur: valorization of the author as a stand-in for the author's produced works follows from this framework, the digital valorization of social action follows logically as computer technology responds to the expansions imposed by the aura of the digital.

If Barthes' argument that the author's role in writing is to vanish, to become "dead," so that the text may be encountered as a form of "performance," where the one speaking disappears within that which is being said, then Barthes' argument necessarily also expands this largely semiotic and performance-oriented view of interpretations to include context. He argues that authorship is an illusion, and that the structure of all texts is quotational; i.e. that there are no authors in an epistemological sense who (via their unique, original work) can provide a singular final meaning in a text:

> The text is a tissue of quotations drawn from the innumerable centers of culture. Similar to Bouvard and Pecuchet, those eternal copyists, at once sublime and comic and whose profound ridiculousness indicates precisely the truth of writing, the writer can only imitate a gesture that is always anterior, never original. His only power is to mix writings, to counter the ones with the others, in such a way as never to rest on any one of them. ... Once the Author is removed, the claim to decipher a text becomes quite futile. To give a text an Author is to impose a limit on that text, to furnish it with a final signified, to close the writing. Such a conception suits criticism very well, the latter then allotting itself the important task of discovering the Author (or its hypostases: society, history, psyche, liberty) beneath the work: when the Author has been found, the text is explained—victory to the critic.[4]

Within this description it is also possible to recognize the concept of collage, montage, sampling or appropriation—

[4] Barthes, "The Death of the Author," 142–148.

"*his only power is to mix*"—a conception of authorship that corresponds to and implies a "database culture" where the texts any author "creates" simply employ preexisting materials (re)organized, broken down, or (re)arranged into a "novel" form. Fragmentation and subsequent recombination define all semiosis: the production model it provides is serial in nature—a transformation of individual elements through their arrangement into novel patterns governed by past experience and previous examples of type; it is *semiotic production*. The ability to automate productive capabilities depends on this initial dispersion into elements governed by particular 'rules' of structural organization.

In the critical view, the emphasis falls on the interpreter's engagement (via past experience) with any particular text's indexical (appropriational, recombinatory) relationship to all other texts, both previous and future. Within this view, the suggestion that meaning is constrained in any way by the text appears to become nonsensical—it is this specific constraint of meaning that Barthes argues *against*. Understood from within this theoretical framework, the idea that all forms of database culture represent a critique (if not a direct assault) on authorship becomes a logical necessity.

Thus, works that make their quotational nature apparent would be revealing the situation to their audience, making them aware of how authorship is illusory: a simple, easily understood and applied critique; however, this critique relies upon a misconception of the interpreters who encounter a work and the role authors play within this situation, as is revealed by those explicitly quotational works that seek to make the interpreting audience aware of the assembled, "Frankenstein's monster" quality of authorship. Instead of critiquing the "author" as suggested by the critical view of authorship, the critical—in an inversion of what might be expected from Barthes' argument—recombinatory (art) works serve to valorize the author and assert not only its continued survival, but its increased and reinforced importance to the interpretation of recombinant or database (art) works. The fact of quotation in these specifically recombinatory works requires the assertion of priority—*authorship*—implicit as the subsequent use.

As the aura of the digital makes the restriction of access to digital (art) works via DRM inevitable, at the same time it also combines the empirical and critical interpretations of authorship in the valorized form of the "*digital* author." Their combination is essential to the process of transition to immaterial commodity enacted by the digital because it implies an expansion of the empirical understanding of authorship along contextual axes suggested in the critical view and instrumentally enabled by digital surveillance: the conversion of context and interpretation to "authorship." The recombinant modes of production are the most visible, but not the only avenues of this expansion.

§5.2

An interpreter who is unaware of the network of relations that inform the interpretation not only of individual words (terms) in a text, but the various quotations and references implicitly deployed there would not be an interpreter but a direct inventor of meaning: the text would be unknown, *literally* written in a foreign language. Jonathan Culler recognizes this contextual role in his semiotic discussion of Wittgenstein's "Bububu":

> Wittgenstein asks, '*Can I say "Bububu" and mean, if it does not rain, I shall go for a walk?*' And he replies, 'it is only in a language that one can mean something by something'. [...] Once Wittgenstein produced this positing of a limit [to semiosis] it became possible in certain contexts (especially in the presence of those who know Wittgenstein's writings) to say 'Bububu' and at least allude to the possibility that if it does not rain, one might go for a walk. But this lack of limits to semiosis does not mean, as Eco seems to fear, that meaning is the free creation of the reader.[5]

[5] Jonathan Cullen, *The Literary in Theory* (Stanford: Stanford Uni-

The context Culler mentions, "the presence of those who know Wittgenstein's writings," is the crucial component for the meaning Wittgenstein suggested for 'Bububu' to emerge: that if it does not rain, he might go for a walk. Without that context it does not have this meaning; without a context meaning is not possible. It is the reader's recognition of 'Bububu' as possibly referring to Wittgenstein's comment that offers the possibility of it having the meaning Wittgenstein suggested; failing to recognize that about 'Bububu' negates the possibility for this interpretation. In a more general form, this contextuality is also true of all language. Thus, the critical interpretation is inherently contextual: any wholly unique text without specific parallels and contextual identifiers is subject to what can be called "semiotic fantasy": the invention, *tabla rasa*, of meaning.

Past experience is essential to creating fruitful interpretations that are not simply inventions of the interpreter. (This is the *awareness* of "Wittgenstein.") Meaning arises from the relationship between presently examined work and this previous database of knowledge; Barthes' claimed *"death of the author"* does not eliminate past experience, it elevates its importance. The audience's established expertise in recognizing and interpreting *is* what enables the recognition of quotation—of meaning, as Umberto Eco notes in his discussion of serials:

> Any difference between knowledge of the world (understood naively as a knowledge derived from an extratextual experience) and intertextual knowledge has practically vanished ... . What is more interesting is when the quotation is explicit and recognizable, as happens in postmodern literature and art, which blatantly and ironically play on the intertextuality ... aware of the quotation, the spectator is brought to elaborate ironically on the nature of such a device and to acknowledge the fact that one has

versity Press, 2006), 181.

been invited to play upon one's encyclopedic knowledge.[6]

The awareness Eco observes is the same as Barthes' awareness of the "death of the author" since it is the *absence of the
author* that the quotations appear to suggest; however, this is
not entirely the case. The awareness of an *a priori* text that is
sourced/cited by the "sample" presented within a new work
does not necessarily mean the lack of a previous author, nor
does it necessarily mean the non-presence of the author in
the new instance. The ability to recognize the quotation *qua*
quotation requires a double interpretation by the audience/
reader/viewer—the recognition not just of the immanent
placement of the particular quotation, but its status as a *quotation* forces the equally immanent recall of another, absent
'text'—which necessarily invokes the absent presence of both
authors: the one doing the immanent quotation, and the one
who is quoted.

Implicit in Eco's argument is that the significance of the
author is redoubled by this quotation and referencing: aware
of the quotation, the audience feels they are "in on it" with
the new author—i.e., they feel a part of an authorial position
based upon their use of past experience to identify the quotations employed. This factor serves to emphasize the role of
author. The presence of authorial determinations becomes
more significant in those cases where the quotations are explicit and recognized than when they are implicit and unrecognized. By drawing attention to the assembly through
quotation, the actions of the new author gain emphasis and
assert authority over previous texts. In choosing which pieces
to use and which to leave, and what/how to organize them,
the quoting author dominates the earlier text, highlighting
issues around the author's intention.

The use of quotation enables the audiences-who-recog-
nize quotations to assume a superficially critical posture in
opposition to those audiences-who-don't-recognize. Recog-

[6] Umberto Eco, "Interpreting Serials," in *The Limits of Interpretation* (Bloomington: University of Indiana Press, 1994), 87–89.

nition of the quotation may create a false consciousness of a critical position because it can move the engagement away from critical examinations of the text, substituting the "I know that!" of recognized quotation for other possible questions of meaning and use within the new text. Quotation can serve as a nostalgic reverie focusing on past experiences and other texts referenced only in passing.[7] Instead of inviting considerations of authorship, this activity reifies the authorship of both the quoted author and its deployment in the new text, making both authors' presence and position in relation to the texts (current/quoted) more explicit, but their authorship does not disappear in this process—contra Barthes, it is reified *as* the text, as quotation.

§5.3

Digital semiosis (and its implementation as *immaterial production*) originates with the database model for culture implicit in appropriation and sampling, and is suggested by both Umberto Eco's conception of past experience and Roland Barthes' layering of quotations and previous texts (the palimpsest nature of language and interpretation). It is recognizable in almost every avant-garde's approach to new technologies: sampling / appropriation / cut-up / mash-up / remix / collage / montage have adopted new terminologies with each new reproductive technology. It is intimately tied to the common availability of reproductions, but is implicit in the organization of moveable type. The (literally semiotic) recombination of a limited number of physical elements, their storage and organization (upper case/lower case), and arrangement (alphabetical order) differs from digital database culture only in speed of access, variability, and scale.

---

[7] It is the production and modulation of this reverie that forms the implicit "subject" of avant-garde film maker Hollis Frampton's 1971 film *(nostalgia)* where the voice-over narration and the image that narrative describes are disassociated—the narrative precedes the image in the series.

The underlying principles of fragmentation, storage and retrieval remain constant.

Semiotic reassembly of new work from fragments of existing works is characteristic of (artistic) responses—but not limited to them—the emergence of technological reproduction over the course of the twentieth century extends into present uses of digital technologies without any sign of abatement. While digital semiosis has origins with the *katzencavalier* centuries before the twentieth century, art historical discussions of this approach often begin with Pablo Picasso who combined reproductions with his Cubist paintings in the 1910s; the Soviet filmmaker Dziga Vertov who experimented with wax recordings to make "remixes" in the late 1910s and early 1920s.[8] Soviet montage itself owes its existence to experiments with the reassembly of existing film materials. Surrealist Max Ernst cut up engravings to make "novels", and Joseph Cornell re-edited Hollywood films with other movies to create his own film, *Rose Hobart*. The author William Burroughs created "cut ups" with audio tape....As new technologies of reproduction became available, new artists performed some kind of recombination of those materials. The listing of these artists and their works could easily continue. This approach is so common it could be called "typical" when artists confront a new technology: it is essential to the digital technology itself in the form of sampling, logically making semiotic reassembly the primary mode for all digital production.

But what is most striking about the repeating pattern of artistic reuse is the increasingly strident claim that this approach constitutes a "questioning of authorship," especially evident in the later forms that appear at the end of the centu-

---

[8] Vlada Petric, *Constructivism in Films: The Man with a Movie Camera* (Cambridge: Cambridge University Press, 1987); see also Dziga Vertov, *Kino-Eye: The Writings of Dziga Vertov*, ed. Annette Michelson, trans. Kevin O'Brien (Berkeley: University of California Press, 1984).

ry around the idea of "appropriation art."[9] It is against this background that the reappearance of these forms (with new names like "mash-up" and "sampling" and "database") in computer based media art—*new media*—should be considered. This recognition enables an acknowledgement that these procedures are not limited to artistic productions, but are characteristic of all digital, immaterial production.

Their historical continuity with work by the historical avant-garde suggests these approaches (whatever their name) have become banal rather than disruptive since popular entertainment and capitalist finance (in the form of financial 'products') can successfully redeploy these approaches. Acknowledging this fact raises a basic question about how these recombinatory practices challenge traditional author/viewer conventions, as well as why this approach continues to make fundamentally the same claim that these actions constitute a "questioning of authorship." The elimination of the author (and the author-function described by Michel Foucault) disassociates all semiotically produced work from those responsible for it—suggesting the aura of the digital in this action to elide the physical (ontological) author from consciousness.

By examining the belief that recombination "questions authorship," it becomes apparent that these approaches constitute a means to avoid the potential shocks each new technology implies by an assertion of traditional roles for audience and viewer. Thus, their repetition takes on a dual character: at the level of praxis where it appears through the reuse of reproductions (the "raw" material of the work), and at the conceptual level as the specific procedure of adoption and reassembly. Both are subject to the denials characteristic of the digital aura and the aspiration to the state of information. Their implication in agnotological procedures is evident through the process of spreading-out that semiosis enables: the generation of alternative configurations and ar-

[9] There are many sources for this claim, but it figures prominently in Douglas Crimp's "Appropriating Appropriation," in *On the Museum's Ruins* (Cambridge: The MIT Press, 1995), 126–136.

rangements within a given set of potentials makes the agnotologic a natural potential application of semiotic processes concerned with elaboration and expansion. It is the coincidence of agnotological and epistemological constructions that makes the distinction between factual and nonfactual problematic. The recourse described by Foucault's authorship function, where by the appeal to past authority serves as a claim made about the immanent text, exceeds the semiotic process of assembly and organization: it is an emergent valuation not present in the semiosis, but through the recognition and role of quotation *superimposed upon* that semiosis.

Thus, these repetitions, instead of disrupting conceptions of authorship (and originality, etc.), serve as a means to assert these values through the principle of "variation." Umberto Eco has noted that viewers, aware of the rupture in appropriated or quotational works (and sampling cannot be anything but quotational), are aware of their nature as a repetition. What is of interest to the viewer is the way the new work *reconfigures* the old:

> The real problem is that what is of interest is not so much the single variation as "variability" as a formal principle, the fact that one can make variations to infinity. Variability to infinity has all the characteristics of repetition, and very little of innovation. But it is the "infinity" of the process that gives a new sense to the device of variation. What must be enjoyed—suggests the postmodern aesthetics—is the fact that a series of possible variations is potentially infinite. What becomes celebrated here is a sort of victory of life over art, with the paradoxical result that the era of electronics, instead of emphasizing the phenomena of shock, interruption, novelty , and frustration of expectations, would produce a return to the continuum, the Cyclical, the Periodical, the Regular.[10]

With the shift to "variability", the more explicit the quota-

---

[10] Eco, "Interpreting Serials," 83–100.

tion, the more the audience may be expected to recognize it, and thus the more directly it plays the new instance against the original one. Variations imposed through semiosis become the critical focus in relation to the original work. Instead of eliminating the authorship, or even critiquing it, the semiotically reassembled (sampled/remix/appropriated) work emphasizes the role of the author (in the originating source) precisely because it is the differences (if any) that matter: the role of artist-as-author is not minimized here, it is maximized. The artist reestablishes traditional positions for both artist and viewer: the artist dominates, transforming an existing work into something "new." This emphasis on the productive dimensions of semiosis serves to obscure the significance of those sources, even as it valorizes them: it is the "new work"—semiotically generated—that becomes the focus. The earlier work is of great necessity to this process, but it is simultaneously negated by the assertions of novelty made implicitly by the new construct.

This image of artistic domination over materials is familiar—it is the traditional view of "genius" in a different guise. The coupling of such a traditional view of authorship with a consistent artistic practice whose name mutates, (but whose procedures vary only slightly), and which is also a common financial technique in digital capitalism, imposes a specific conclusion about the recombinatory procedure: that instead of challenging traditional notions of authorship, it tends to assert them while inviting the audience to (un)critically engage the work using their encyclopedic past knowledge of the sources for the "new" work. The original sources "disappear" in this sleight-of-hand, following the denials of physicality in the aura of the digital. The audience is active in their engagement with the work, but such "activity" is a potential in any viewing situation and should not be regarded as unique to recombinatory works.

At the same time, this engagement with a "critical" or "active" audience is only superficial. The "activity" is one of comparing the new instance to established forms. This action assumes the prior authority of the existing work. The recombinatory actions exist in parasitical relation (as variations) to their source materials. By drawing together existing materials in new ways, the "variability to infinity" Eco describes comes into the interpretation, creating a false belief in a challenge to authority and the conventional role of the viewer: the repetitions inherent to remixing existing materials escape the psychological dangers *unheimlich* works may pose through a reliance on established expertise and the implicit understanding of the "rules of the game" involved in appropriations.

To claim these semiotic recombinatory practices commonly found in new media—sampling, appropriation, remixes, mash-ups, etc.—challenge traditional author/viewer conventions cannot be accepted as true. As Eco has noted, these practices constitute a shift to a pre-modern convention set where the traditional established work that is the subject of the transformations is elevated in status, and the artist appropriating serves to reify that status, while viewers, aware of the conventionalized variability at the heart of appropriation, recognize in the artist's actions an assertion of authorial dominance over the original work as well as a (paradoxical) subservience to that work.

§5.4

The empirical sense of author appears within and is supported by the practice of quotation and appropriation by digital technology. It emerges in the development of the Internet between 1996 and 2006 first from the practice of *link pages* containing "hyperlinks" on personal web pages, then via "search engines," followed by the later forms of personal sites such as "blogs," and in the concept of "social networking" based on shared links and relationships. The commercial development of "portals," such as the website *Yahoo.com,* that present a variety of links to other sites (in the form of search and as indexed categories of sites), are recognizable as business adaptations of the earlier personal, non-commercial web page.

This kind of authorship is based on interest and citation—social behaviour and human agency—rather than production: the early practice of "surfing" from website to website following their links to each other is the simplest (and most direct) variety of quotational authorship: by linking to another text, the author gains value from the referenced text; blogs retain this linking practice. It is also reified as/in the deployment of social media and social networking—as both "liking" and "following." Authors who have the "best" links within this framework are the "best" authors gaining status (value) within their communities, a position determined by what they appropriate.

Thus, the commercial "portal" presents a great variety of content, and will often incorporate a search feature as a way to gain access (thus authorship) to as much material posted on the Internet as possible; this model is recognizable in both *Yahoo.com* and in sites such as *Technocrati.com* (for blogs) or *del.icio.us* (social networking based on links—"bookmarks") and *Topsy.com* (reifying the authorial nature of links, combined with search). Group-based projects such as open source software, or the various wikipedias where skilled authors collaborate on common projects, are different from the authorship apparent in social networking only in degree. Participation in these activities requires expertise and the same donated labor that builds (is) the databases of social networking.

In every case, value accrues to the business based on its ability to locate and organize 'authorship' and connect that audience to merchants and advertisers; at the same time, authors will actively seek to add their works to these sites, and in the case of *del.icio.us,* open source projects, and social networking generally, such as *Facebook.com* or *Myspace.com,* the business itself is valorized by the work of large numbers of individual authors whose contributions generate the database (are the database) that lies at the center of all these technologies. By shifting all activities into potential varieties of authorship—ranging from personal interests to highly skilled labor requiring training and experience—it becomes possible to recognize the conversion of all activities into potential commodities via authorship enabling the invention of a new digitally-based, immaterial production residing within (over) all social activity.

Valorization proceeds through the appropriation process on both sides of the quotation—as the source who is referenced and as the one who references—as the reversibility apparent in the mirroring of Barthes's death as valorization shows. Thus appropriation becomes a signifier for authorial value: the referencing inherent to semiosis appears literally in this valorization—the more often an author is reused the greater the value assigned to that author. This understanding of authorial significance appears in the rankings (importance) of scientific and medical journals, as determined by the number of citations to articles published by those journals appearing in other articles. In recombinant music, no matter how small the sample, the original artist or artists gain control over the new work that employs that sample by virtue of their being appropriated. Within the structure of websites it is even more explicit: *Technocrati.com* ranks blogs based on how many other blogs link to their contents; *Google.com*'s search results are weighted not just by relevance to the search terms entered but by linkages; advertising rates on websites is based on "click-through"—how many people follow the ad link—not simply on audience delivered as with traditional print and television media. In financialization, this semiotic production leads to multiple levels of tranche, as with mortgage-backed securities that were sold, recombined, and sold again in a cycle of recombining the recombined.

This link procedure reveals the connection between social networking and authorship. Social networking only appears to suggest a transformation of these connections; it is an extension of the author-cult where all actions are reconfigured as quotational, all relationships quantified as affinity groups, and social behaviors are transformed into immaterial commodity (as digitally orchestrated demographics). Barthes' reasons for declaring the author dead become the supports and proof that authors exist. As theorist Nicholas Rombes has noted, the empirical sense of author has proliferated throughout digital technologies:

> Rather than extinguish once and for all the auteur, the rise and hegemony of digital technologies and culture have only reinforced the author concept, and have in fact helped to create new forms of authorship that are being acknowledged in the broader public....And yet, denunciations of authorship have always tended to strengthen the cult and authority of those doing the denouncing. In fact, it was Barthes who called the author into being and whose denunciations helped create the conditions for the dictatorship of the author in the digital era.[11]

These "conditions for the dictatorship of the author" take the form of the assumed critical position assigned to recombinant procedures: recognizing the fabric of quotations, references, and reuses that characterize language and the interpretation of meaning does not mean the "death of the author." It produces, through the recognition of quotations by the interpreting audiences, the simultaneous database nature of culture and the expertise deployed by both author and audience in their encounters via the text. The indexicality Eco observes in the use of direct, obvious sampling from past works serves to valorize both those past works specifically and the role of the author generally. Each new producer, in employing this semiotic reassembly, in becoming an author, also engages in illusory creation—the newly organized work—which has a false independence from its sources.

The mirrorical return of the author marks the expansion and extension of the author concept proposed by Barthes as a critique, not as proof of its disappearance, but as demonstration that anything can be interpreted (thus treated) as authorial. The *authoring* of activities that previously would not have been regarded as authorship is essential to the valoriza-

[11] Nicholas Rombes, "The Rebirth of the Author," *CTheory,* October 6, 2005, www.ctheory.net/articles.aspx?id=480.

tion of these actions: for example, the browsing of products (*Amazon.com*'s "page I made" that lists products viewed while on-site), or the proposition that collecting links to websites of personal interest (*del.icio.us* and social networking generally) can be understood as *productive* actions. By treating these activities as forms of authorship it becomes possible to recognize Barthes' layers of past actions and references being made explicit, and then treated as potential commodities, with *authoring* as the vehicle for the exchange of value. Without the ability of digital computers to record and track actions, this kind of authorship would be infeasible, if not entirely impossible (and improbable), because of the scale of labor required to perform these same tasks without automation.

Expanding concepts of authorship are produced by the digital technologies that enable their existence. Thus expansion is symptomatic of the aura of the digital: the transformation of everything that can be digitized into a digital form (the universal aspiration to the state of information) also transforms every action recorded into a demonstration of individual authorship (the ideology of automation).[12] The universal authoring of lives serves the valorization process that requires both constant surveillance and the imposition of digital rights management (DRM) as a way to extract value from digital works. Expansion of the author concept therefore signals the commodification of all activity and the full emergence of the immaterial production characteristic of digital capitalism.

§5.5

The valorization of authorship demonstrates how the empirical and critical interpretations can interact, reinforcing both the extension of authorship beyond its traditional boundaries (as per the critical emphasis on contextuality and recombination) while at the same time reifying the implicit potential of

---

[12] Betancourt, "The Aura of the Digital."

the empirical interpretation's basis as a productive activity. It is the combination of productive action and contextual extension that creates the digital author. Neither the hypothetical actor of the empirical view, nor the figure vanishing into the ground of its sources proposed in the critical conception, the digital author is an immanent effect of the aura of information operating through the ideology of automation, where all actions, activities, events, objects *(ad infinitum)* become digital, and thus elevated to the state of information.

The digital author is valorized by this transformative fantasy into information, not as consumer or producer (hence a subject with human agency), but as a commodity. Achieving the status of 'author' within a database culture means a transfer of role from actor to commodity—this is the end-result of the valorization process, not simply the maintenance of previously valuable commodities produced by the traditional actors of the empirical interpretation, but an extension of authorship-as-commodification, of author-as-commodity and the dominance of semiosis deployed in immaterial production.

Once all decisions that might previously be considered instances of human agency become instead forms of authorship (the effect of combining the critical and empirical interpretations), the author becomes a commodity: the digital author. It is an inversion of the disappearing-into-context proposed by Barthes, et. al. The digital author emerges as the specific contexts apparent through each individual action: human agency redefined as authorship, as a range of authorial actions that when taken together define a single, specific author. The collection and trading of these authorial entities is simply the logical extension of the business relation implicit in the empirical view's ontology and identified with Foucault's author-function.

Roland Barthes' argument, instead of heralding the death of the author, shows the way to its inevitable extension, expansion and subjugation in immaterial production. It is a side-effect of how the aura of the digital imposes a steadily larger domain for property rights via the concept of "intellectual property" as a necessity for maintaining the circulation of capital. Within a database culture all forms of authorship are potentially valuable, and all information necessarily requires an ontological link to a specific source (the "author"). This then demands the valorization process just as it is the underlying mechanism for the extension and maintenance of authorship. Contextuality thus creates more and new varieties of author and authorship, in the process proposing the eclipse of human agency. The digital author lacks agency precisely because there is no longer any distinction between action and inaction—reflecting the nodal form of the state of information—both are equal. The valorization makes each choice significant and therefore valuable: all decisions produce authorship and so have an equal commodity status.

The valorization of authorship reiterates the fundamental conflict of DRM: the ownership and possession of digital works (such as the digital author). Even as database culture transforms all actions into varieties of authorship, (such as Amazon's "the page I made" that tracked and revealed shopping as authorship), the valorization process implicit in this transformation equally raises the question of ownership: the empirical interpretation's 'author' who acts and so creates the work, or the database collector who is the critical 'author.' In effect the link between the digital aura and capitalist expansion of both markets and commodities inevitably appears as the valorization and extension of authorship along with the simultaneous elision of the ownership role traditionally assigned to authorship by the empirical interpretation. The change in status for digital authors corresponds to the dissolution of human agency inherent in this transition.

However, such tendencies towards elision are not simply linear or unidirectional—instead, by observing one tendency it is possible to recognize a resurgence of human agency at the same time and employing the same means. While recombinant methods *do* valorize the authorship of their sources, they *also* generate novel works whose place and role within this schema are ambiguous. Their ambiguity—as valorizers and violators of the commodities valorized—offers a space for human agency to re-enter. The paradox that ensues from the assertion-elision of human agency suggests the fractious nature of the digital (valorized) author and reflects the Janus face of the digital. The transition to a database culture does not replace previous authorial conceptions. The conflict between these conceptions—naive, critical, digital—is symptomatic of the ideology that defines the aura of the digital. The illusion of production without consumption (in the expansion of authorship via valorization) encounters the physical reality of the particular individuals whose actions are commodified in this process; it collides with the issue of human agency embodied in the authors it valorizes.

The valorization-authorship relationship presents a paradox that depends on human agency, since without human agency, the valorization process cannot proceed (on any level.) What this valorization means for human agency is much closer to the idea of 'disenfranchisement' where agency becomes impotence and actions only proceed so long as the outcome is regulated or predetermined. Since the digital is an imaginary domain (reifying capitalist ideology) where in the guise of 'information' all actions become types of authorship (as informed by the aura the information). From within this framework human agency becomes both the method of valorization and the commodity produced. It is elided in the process of conversion.

§5.6

In returning from the imaginary domain of the digital to the physical domain, the valorization of authorship reveals itself as not as authorship, but as enslavement. By achieving the state of 'author' without compensation for the capital generated through their valorization, these extensions of authorship transform all activity into capital-producing labor (without compensation). Thus the valorized digital author represents a new 'slave' class in database culture, one where the 'slaves' fail to recognize the conditions of their slavery.

The underlying dynamic of the valorization process is not

production—nothing is actually produced that could not exist otherwise—but neither is it a form of consumption. The valorization is semiotic: it proceeds from a shift in meaning, a transferal, accompanied by a process that resembles a form of automated surveillance. It is a form of opportunistic exploitation.

By extending authorship, markets discover an expanded (immaterial) arena for the extraction of wealth, but not one accompanied by an increased production of capital or shift in the production-consumption dynamic. Instead, it is an extension dramatizing the ideology generated by an interaction of the aura of the digital and the aura of information: valorizing authorship serves to more efficiently expedite the transfer and expand the accumulation of existing capital (wealth). As in semiotic production, no new capital is produced by this activity. Each new form of authorship is merely an expansion of an existing market into new areas of (social) activity with the "goal" of converting all (social) activity (uncommodified forms of "labor") into commodities.

Both the recombinant mode and the critical view of authorship serve to increase the aura of (established) digital (art) works. Just as they validate the expansion of authorship, recombinant works are also complicit in the valorization process, serving to increase and extend the value of established works, thus making the imposition of DRM necessary (essential) to maintain and assert the property value inhering in commodity status.

The increase in value that recombination provides is the underlying feature of database culture generally. (It is the economic basis for it, and for its expansion of authorship.) However, no valorization has meaning except within the social relationships that define all exchange values. This connection demonstrates the slavery of the digital author precisely because the expanded, digital author is only possible with the complicity of the individuals being valorized: the transformation of human agency into exchange value is not (generally) reciprocal for the valorized. Hence, valorization serves to produce wealth from the immaterial labor of the valorized: the databasing process that renders all actions equally valuable does not compensate those whose actions are the source of that database.

While the extension of authorship implicitly suggests a differentiation between the semiosis characteristic of immaterial production and the valorization of human agency, the distinction between these is simply one of degree rather than category: both, rendered as information, are commodities within the marketplace. The recombination of existing works increases the value of the appropriated originals as it denies their role in the semiotic process; the transformation of human agency only appears to produce new commodities (authors) for commercial exploitation—in both instances the valorization is not *productive*. It is simply a shifting of functions within an established system (capitalism)—but is neither an enlargement of the 'system,' nor an annexation of additional "spaces" that are not already included within that 'system.' Instead, reifying the ideology of automation, it is exploitation of the ability (already present and in use) of digital technology to record actions and activities. Like the worm that swallows its own tail, these valorizations only appear to produce new sources of capital, labor and wealth. Instead, they are simply a recirculation of existing values: this extension of authorship is therefore a symptom-effect of the fantasy of production-without-consumption that defines the digital. Within such a conception of authorship, the empirical and critical interpretations no longer function as they historical have; each gives way to a hybrid, "digital author" whose identity is apparent in its function as commodity.

This digital author—a commodity—is as foreign to the empirical and critical conceptions of author as the epistemological and ontological authors are to one another. It should be recognized as a third term in the authorship concept, related yet fundamentally independent of ontological and epistemological concerns: where Barthes' "reader" (the critical author) resides in an impersonal construction without history, biography, or psychology—the context of a work's reception, the digital author translates agency apparent in/as history, biography, and psychology into immaterial commodities. They are the parameters defining the differences between one digital author and another. Where both critical and empirical authors are productive—both entail the generation of new texts because both authors entail the extension of agency, the digital author's status-as-commodity presents a closing off of potential production for the digital author, where instead of agency, this author is a token of exchange in a semiotic system of reassembly, surveillance, and constraint.

Chapter Six

The 'Black Box' of Past Experience

Agnotology does not describe the existence of systemic unknowns, but rather the production of systemic uncertainty
through an undermining of the intellectual procedures used
in the creation of knowledge. It employs the same epistemological procedures for creating knowledge and understanding, but with the opposite effect. This systemic uncertainty
develops in the semiotic relationship between current experience and its evaluation *vis-à-vis* past experience—an evaluation described by Umberto Eco's theorization of serial form
in narrative fiction using "past experience"—knowledge created by established competencies and expertise produced
over time.[1] It is these established methodologies that agnotology employs to create uncertainty. Eco's analysis of
popular entertainment as serial in nature uses the paired dialectic of 'innovation' and 'schema,' a construct that implicitly
requires spectators to use an internal model derived from
their past experience with other examples of type in forming
interpretations and anticipating the development of the narrative currently encountered. It develops a conception of
knowledge based in a semiotic process of recognition and

---

[1] Umberto Eco, "Interpreting Serials," in *The Limits of Interpretation* (Bloomington: University of Indiana Press, 1994), 87–89.

relation to past 'successful' interpretations. This construction offers a glimpse of the state of information, suggesting its organization and the variability of discrete samples within an imaginary network of all potential knowledge.

The rise of agnotological procedures within contemporary capitalism is symptomatic of the emergence of a distinctly serial conception of information, its validity, and the 'knowledge' contained within the state of information. The inability to establish the factuality of any claim made, any evidence presented, any empirical proof shown, no matter what the results of an investigation might be, shows the impact of the agnotological effects on knowledge and interpretation. The variability of this serial relationship means there is no longer a space in which we as an audience can agree upon what the epistemic value of any evidence employed in the creation of an interpretation might be: the ability to determine fact has been dissolved by precisely the process employed to produce those facts in themselves—this dissolution of knowledge-generative methodologies reveals the agnotological process in action, and offers a glimpse of the aura of information's aspirations to completeness.

The emergence of the state of information from our internal models that constrain and define the serial requires an acknowledgment of the "black box" in Eco's argument— there is no discussion of how the serial model produced by past experience might arise or how it could work to produce this "past experience" essential to successful interpretation; however, mathematician John Holland's complex adaptive systems (CAS)[2] does offer one model for how serials create these expectations, and provides a logical foundation for describing an imaginary "state of information" that follows from this serial organization of past experience in knowledge. The ways CAS is consistent with Eco's theory of serials has suggestive implications for the relationship between past experience and interpretation in more general terms: a CAS

[2] John Holland, *Hidden Order: How Adaptation Builds Complexity* (Reading: Perseus Books, 1995).

model which accommodates Eco's serial "black box" provides a justification for the variability of interpretation, creating the epistemological foundation necessary to describe the state of information.

The aesthetic model Eco proposes is connected to the way spectators encounter and interpret serial forms. It is a consequence of whether innovation or schema is given priority. Past experiences with the topos of a particular serial define the aesthetic experience the audience has by recognizing specific variations within a predetermined framework. The way serials use viewer expectations is the main source of the pleasure we get from them.[3]

The role of past experience with examples of type in Eco's theory requires a basic explanation of his concept of serial form. In doing so, the "black box" will become readily apparent. The serial aesthetic is a consequence of the serial structures themselves. To be serial means, first and foremost, that the audience for the serial recognizes and acknowledges the ways the audience's knowledge is required to interpret a specific episode in a serial. It is a reciprocal connection between immanence and remembrance.

Eco identifies three serial structures and two temporal relationships used by those forms: the retake, the remake, and the series; the saga and spiral are his temporal structures.[4] The retake is a continuation of an earlier story (Eco suggests *Star Wars* as a good example; *The Matrix* films also qualify); the remake is a new version of an already existing story (the many filmed variations on *Dracula*, or Shakespeare's plays, for example); the series is a continuing story that either develops across time (as with *Dallas*), or it can also repeat episode to episode (*All in the Family* or *Peanuts* are good examples of this variety).[5] Each variation is defined by its relationship to previous models and by how it reworks those schemas to produce a novel example.

[3] Eco, "Interpreting Serials," 95.
[4] Eco, "Interpreting Serials," 84–85.
[5] Eco, "Interpreting Serials," 84–87.

The spectator's interpretations employ frameworks created through previous encounters with similar types in order to anticipate and recognize divergences from established norms.[6] These interpretations are common to all serial forms, not only those employed by the popular media. The difference between art and popular forms is a matter of references and audience, not of form. The relationship between schema and novelty is the focus of a specific kind of spectatorship that defines "seriality" for Eco.

The saga and the spiral use past experience in a different way and present a different conception of fictional time.[7] Each episode of a serial does not necessarily advance temporally. The body of knowledge an audience has about how serials organize their portrayal of time delimits the ways viewers will understand outcome and consequence. Sagas proceed in linear time. They are chronological explorations of characters' actions and history, sometimes reaching epic proportions (as both *Dallas* and Wagner's Ring cycle attest). Spirals do not proceed in linear time; instead, they present variations on a "loop" in which no time elapses, but our understanding of the characters deepens through a continuous variation of set performances. This temporal difference defines sagas and spirals.

A "loop" is the serial form that most requires past experience in order to create complex meanings since, while it is potentially infinite in its variability, each episode is self-contained, making it shallow in its depiction of consequences and history. Our understanding and interpretation of the serial grows through the pattern of repetition and variation in toto. The aesthetic pleasure loops provide is rooted in the variants of form they present:

> In the most typical and apparently "degenerated" cases of seriality, the independent variables are not all together the more visible, but the more microscopic, as in a homeo-

---

[6] Eco, "Interpreting Serials," 91–93.
[7] Eco, "Interpreting Serials," 87.

pathic solution where the potion is all the more potent because by further "successions" the original particles of the medicinal product have almost disappeared. ... We are thus facing a "neo-Baroque aesthetics" that is instantiated not by the "cultivated" products, but even, and above all, by those that are the most degenerated.[8]

Interpreting serial forms requires the audience to recognize that each episode quotes from earlier versions of itself. In *Peanuts,* Charlie Brown has never gotten to kick the football held by Lucy, but the scene of his attempt has been repeated many times. The meaning of Lucy's snatching the ball away at the last moment derives from the audience's recognition of how each sequence is a quotation of all the other sequences generally. This particular scene is a serial structure within the serial that is *Peanuts* itself. Quotation of this type is not specifically recognizable as quotational, since it is fundamental to the serial form itself: seriality is a special kind of intertextuality.

However, Eco notes:

What is more interesting is when the quotation is explicit and recognizable, as happens in postmodern literature and art, which blatantly and ironically play on the intertextuality...aware of the quotation, the spectator is brought to elaborate ironically on the nature of such a device and to acknowledge the fact that one has been invited to play upon one's encyclopedic knowledge.[9]

Explicit quotation makes the serial visible as a synthesis of earlier works, drawing attention to the specific quotation *and* to the ways a serial reflexively quotes itself: the schema is a particular kind of quotation. Audiences draw upon "past experience" to recognize serials in the same way that intertextual quotations do. Each new serial is unique and refer-

[8] Eco, "Interpreting Serials," 97.
[9] Eco, "Interpreting Serials," 88–99.

enced against previous encounters, orchestrating inter-textuality so the expectations spectators have for one episode allow earlier episodes to inflect their immanent interpretations. The audience's familiarity with the cultural context and history for a specific serial mirrors other intertextual devices. Thus serials are always intertextual, and intertextuality is a function of our ability to recognize variation and repetition.

But how these expectations arise, how they evolve, and how they change remains unaddressed, yet omnipresent in Eco's theory of serial form. Each new episode either meets or violates the audience's established expectations, sometimes even at different points in the same episode. Both potentials are valid possibilities within Eco's theory because it is the *expectations* themselves that are the focus of his aesthetic:

> Let us now try to review the phenomena listed above from the point of view of a "modern" conception of aesthetic value, according to which every work aesthetically "well done" is endowed with two characteristics:
>
> It must achieve a dialectic between order and novelty, in other words, between scheme and innovation.
>
> This dialectic must be perceived by the consumer who must grasp not only the contents of the message but also the way in which the message transmits the contents.[10]

Validity derives from the audience being able to recognize both the innovations (differences from expectations) and the schema (the ways that expectations are met). Our role as spectator is crucial. The aesthetic emerges from the audience being able to recognize and appreciate the variations across the serial as a whole. It is the perception of the nuances those variations reveal that is aesthetic. It requires a self-consciously interpreting, anticipating audience. We must use our expertise—past experiences with the schema—to inter-

[10] Eco, "Interpreting Serials," 91.

pret episodes in a serial, acknowledging the ways our experience determines both immediate beliefs about the episode, and our understanding of the relationship between that episode and the schema from which it is derived.

A dialectic between order and novelty requires an internal model for the serial (the schema itself is such a model)— otherwise we cannot recognize any of the characteristics Eco values: variation, repetition, or novelty. By definition, novelty requires a breach of past expectation, while variation and repetition create continuity with it. Eco neither provides an account of how such models arise nor does he provide an explanation for how they change. This absence constitutes a "black box" in his theory of serials. It is crucial to the aesthetic model he proposes.

§6.1

The complex adaptive systems (CAS) John Holland presents in *Hidden Order* as mathematical models of physical phenomena are expectation-generating structures that describe the emergence of order from the individual, disconnected actions of groups of organisms.[11] He is not discussing the kind of interpretive process crucial to Eco's seriality; nevertheless, these two theories have much in common. His model's ability to anticipate outcomes and maintain "ideas" about the world makes CAS a good candidate for Eco's "black box." In describing the spontaneous appearance of order and structure, CAS provide an account of how internal models could work, and the points of contact between CAS and serials suggest seriality may be basic to how we interpret. It also suggests that CAS, understood through the concept of seriality, could provide a general basis for interpretation. Both CAS and seriality are incomplete in themselves as general theories of interpretation.

Holland's complex adaptive systems use the concept of rules to explain how a model is constructed. The creation of

---

[11] Holland, *Hidden Order*, 11.

rules provides a mechanism for both storing previous experience and using that experience to guide future expectations. Holland describes how these rules could act:

> The usual view is that the rules amount to a set of facts about the agent's [interpreter's] environment. Accordingly, all rules must be kept consistent with one another. If a change is made or a new rule is introduced, it must be checked for consistency with all the other rules.[12]

Conceiving the rules in this way produces a rigid framework that does not fluidly change. While viewing the constraints imposed by serial forms in this fashion does have some appeal, it does not "fit" with the description Eco proposes—that variations and exceptions to our expectations are what provide the specific interest generated by a serials' reuse of an already existing schema. Holland disagrees with the "usual view" of rules, and instead suggests a description for how rules could function that is closer to seriality:

> There is another way to consider the rules. They can be viewed as hypotheses that are undergoing testing and confirmation. On this view, the object is to provide contradictions rather than avoid them. That is, the rules amount to alternative, competing hypotheses. When one hypothesis fails, competing rules are waiting in the wings to be tried.[13]

This second description for how rules could work satisfies the sense of immediate accommodation that Eco's description of serial pleasures implies. If we exchange "rules" with "expectations" in the above quote, the problematic "black box" in Eco's theory is replaced with a mechanism for identifying and understanding repetition and variation. Holland's theory does not describe CAS in serial terms, but it is possi-

---

[12] Holland, *Hidden Order*, 53.
[13] Holland, *Hidden Order*, 53.

ble to adapt it to be a general model for interpretation. This adaptation requires the CAS model adopt a serial character itself.

Variation in his serial aesthetic shifts emphasis from originality to variability within the schema. This change of focus signifies a new understanding of serials for Eco:

> The real problem is that what is of interest is not so much the single variations as "variability" as a formal principle, the fact that one can make variations to infinity. Variability to infinity has all the characteristics of repetition, and very little of innovation. But is the "infinity" of the process that gives a new sense to the device of variation.[14]

Appreciating these variants is a consequence of being able to create an internal model where the variations appear as different potentials within that construct. The model describes this situation precisely and, at the same time, explains how viewers can perceive the model within the network of variations.

Established knowledge—in the form of rules that have already been tested—provides a base for extending these models. CAS "scales" like a fractal—each rule combines to make more complex rules and is itself composed of simpler rules. Its structure remains constant at all levels of complexity and combination because the basis of the structure lies in how the CAS model remembers success and failure and adapts to new situations:

> This credit-assignment procedure, which I call a *bucket brigade algorithm,* strengthens rules that belong to chains of action terminating in rewards. This process amounts to a progressive confirmation of hypotheses concerned with stage setting and subgoals.[15]

---

[14] Eco, "Interpreting Serials," 96.
[15] Holland, *Hidden Order*, 53–56.

Holland's "rewards" come in the form of a rule accurately anticipating the outcome: the spectator's expectation is met. This mechanism allows an audience member to recognize a serial, and appreciate the ways that episode both meets and differs from the audience's expectations. What we commonly call "experience" and "expertise" are forms of learned behavior in CAS. What this model makes explicit is the connection between past successes and future successes at all levels of interpretation: Holland's "bucket brigade" demonstrates how abilities and actions can be described as learned skills. It also explains how a schema can arise from the network of distinct, yet similar forms that are episodes in serials. Both variation and repetition act to make the schema appear stronger since both kinds of experience work with established knowledge and understanding.

Repetition strengthens specific rules and weakens others in CAS. Those rules that grow stronger do so because they are proven correct more often than other rules; however, these rules are not unchangeable. They depend upon the viewer recognizing them. The aesthetic aspects of repetition requires the schema since it is the continuance of forms that is aesthetic.

Variation proceeds through a process of substitution and alteration. It is always serial, but the aesthetic model specific to it lies (as with repetition) in the continuance of the schema and its perceptibility in spite of the changes imposed through the process of variation. It is a matter of nuanced changes within an immobile topos. For CAS, these variations prompt specific attention because of the relationship they have to established form—variations serve to strengthen the schema by making it that much more visible as the constants within the variables.

Consider how expectations in *Raiders of the Lost Ark* guide our viewing of Indiana Jones' encounter with the Arab giant. His fight elicits laughter because it breaks the expected convention—followed in that film up to that moment: "the spectator, in order to enjoy the allusion, must know the original topoi. In the case of the giant, it is a situation typical of the genre."[16] It comes at the end of a long sequence of fights with smaller Arabs in a bazaar, each of whom Jones defeats with either fist or bull whip, so when he is confronted by the giant and simply shoots him, the act confounds our expectations. The use of the gun "breaks" the rule established by the earlier fight sequence and, as Eco noted, defies the genre itself. "These imperceptible quotation marks, more than an aesthetic device, are a social artifice; they select the happy few (and the mass media usually hope to produce millions of the happy few)."[17] Recognizing the interplay of quotations is a function of familiarity with the schemas that produce serials; this familiarity is not a formal principle of the work but constitutes extratextual knowledge that lies outside the serial itself. This example suggests that the situation is modeled in different ways, depending upon whether the viewer chooses to interpret based upon the context of the film or the context of the genre.

A later fight with another giant (a NAZI) follows genre up to a point then breaks it in a less humorous way. The second encounter is more dramatic precisely because, as spectator, it is impossible to determine in advance how the sequence will play out. Our past experiences with the serial form *Raiders* employs is applicable, but only to the point where our ability to anticipate is curtailed. The variability takes precedence over the schema in this example. The opposite is true of Charlie Brown and the football: the minute variations are the focus, with the outcome remaining constant. The ways our models and the serial episodes interact is the source of Eco's "neo-Baroque" or serial aesthetic. The CAS model provides a way to explain how this aesthetic arises and how we recognize serial forms.

The ability of different audience members to see the same thing, yet interpret it in radically different ways, demonstrates how our interpretations of serials grow deeper and more complex through repeated encounters with new exam-

---

[16] Eco, "Interpreting Serials," 88.
[17] Eco, "Interpreting Serials," 94.

ples (as the *Peanuts* example shows).[18] The variation that defines the serial form is reflected in our interpretations of that form.

§6.2

There is a high degree of similarity between Holland's CAS and Eco's serials. Complex adaptive systems create models that "remember" and "learn" by using previously successful rules as building blocks for future rules,[19] creating the "depth" necessary for Eco's serial aesthetic. Both Eco's aesthetic and CAS become more complex as a result of greater familiarity. The CAS model, by "scaling" from simple to complex, is very flexible in adapting to new situations. The model dynamically restructures itself to incorporate changes, just as serials contain all their variations and remain constant:

> Evolution "remembers" combinations of building blocks [combinations of rules] that increase fitness. The building blocks that recur generation after generation are those that have survived in the contexts in which they have been tested.[20]

The support for these rules is circular, making novelty the force that causes the model to grow in complexity. Only novel situations test new rules and refine the model further: rules are constrained by the feedback loop producing them. As a general interpretive framework, then, the CAS model presents meaning in serial fashion as a range of immanent probabilities.

Circularity reinforces the tendency towards a consistent interpretation. Charlie Brown and Lucy do not tell us anything new about the schema when Lucy pulls the football away, and yet each time she does, our understanding of their

---

[18] Eco, "Interpreting Serials," 86–87.

[19] Holland, *Hidden Order*, 61–76.

[20] Holland, *Hidden Order*, 79.

relationship grows slightly more complex. This depth of understanding is the "rules" being refined further. Our appreciation of the scene—and its comedy—comes from our understanding of these variations. This corresponds to Eco's dialectic of innovation and schema where innovation is the novel situation, and schema is the established model.[21]

§6.3

The complex adaptive systems model may provide a general explanation of how interpretation proceeds. Its specific strengths when confronting the variability of serials is suggestive when we consider the variety of mutually exclusive theories and interpretations that characterize broader fields of thought.[22] Our ability to accept and evaluate, even employ, multiple, different (even contradictory) interpretations at once has much in common with the problematics connected to interpreting serials.

Being able to describe a process where expectations can arise, shape interpretation, and then evolve places serials in a broader interpretative context. The CAS model may provide a framework for justifying interpretation generally through recourse to a set of potential interpretations—Holland's "rules"—that may apply to any given situation, whether it is a serial or otherwise. Conceptualizing interpretation as a serial form shifts the emphasis in supporting specific interpretations from an external foundation to an internal one where specific interpretations are justified by the existence of alternatives. The momentary superiority of one rule does not invalidate the others. Like serial forms, meaning depends not on specific individual interpretations but on the relationship between specific interpretations and the system that creates them. This shifting of relationships appreciated in itself is Eco's serial aesthetic.

The concept of a probability set whose composition is se-

---

[21] Eco, "Interpreting Serials," 97–98.
[22] Eco, "Interpreting Serials," 95.

rial—a collection of various, competing interpretations—
opens possibilities for justifying interpretation in a flexible
and open ended fashion. A serial CAS could explain and justify these competing interpretations without necessarily forcing us to choose between them in the way that Holland's CAS
does where past experience creates a framework that produces the single most probable interpretation. In contrast, the
serials Eco describe present a set of alternatives defined by
their relationship through variation. When applied to interpretation generally, a serial conception of the CAS model
suggests we consider meaning as a range of potentials rather
than as a singular choice. Even though the model proposed
here is incomplete and tentative, it is suggestive of possible
strategies for justifying interpretations without precluding
their rejection or revision at a later time. Individual interpretations are justified not by comparison to an external truth
but by the existence of other possible interpretations with
shared characteristics that nevertheless contradict each other.

As the state of information develops and becomes dominant, what we observe as a symptom of its activity is the
breakdown of the procedures that create knowledge and establish the reliability of information apparent in the rise of
agnotology specifically, and digital capitalism generally. These validity-producing procedures themselves are what is attacked by the agnotological process. The same epistemological techniques for creating certainty are the foundational
techniques for agnotological generation. What enables their
use within agnotology is the serial relationships posed by the
state of information; however, their action is authorized as
potentially valid not through a recourse to epistemological
reasoning, but via the aura of information that accompanies
the ascent of the digital. In aspiring to the state of information, the aura of the digital authorizes the acceptance of
agnotological results specifically because the contra-results
characteristic of agnotism are always already valid within the
information space described by the state of the information.
Thus, no matter what the result of any investigation subject
to agnotism might be, it is the investigation itself that is in

question: those who already doubt the validity of available studies enmesh themselves more deeply into the agnotological structure by demanding newer, alternative studies, yet in calling for more study they have already begun with the assumption that whatever result they currently have available to them is of no value—the most obvious symptom that their thinking is caught in the trap of agnotism.

The problem posed by a dominant regime of agnotology is that it authorizes doubt about any result—literally any piece of information—that does not match a preconceived frame of reference. It makes challenges to established patterns of thought difficult if not impossible: the affect of agnotology, perversely, is a reinforcement of certainty since it undermines alternatives that could challenge those ideas; thus, it leads to an unwillingness to compromise, and an inflexibility of thought—both essential features of how digital capitalism is an ideological construction capable of governing what would otherwise appear as incompatible, mutually exclusive groups.

Chapter Seven

The State of Information

A concern with paradoxes is one of the hallmarks of the twentieth century. Sometimes confused with a radical relativism in which all possibilities are equally acceptable, this focus on paradox is, in fact, a concern with the limits of knowledge and logic. Only when coupled with an instrumentalist desire to render all potentials immanent does it begin to take on the auspices of relativism based in a misconception of probability: as the concept of serial interpretation suggests, even when there is an array of potential interpretations (for example) there are more and less 'correct' responses within that range; the paradox is a special case, one where a simple resolution is not possible. The transformation from a deterministic, "clockwork" universe in the nineteenth century to the probabilistic one of modern physics marks a radical shift in not only thinking about the physical world, but in how it is modeled, conceptualized, and interpreted. At the same time, similar foundational changes were spreading through other disciplines as well: both mathematics and psychology produced theories of paradox that converge on those employed in quantum physics in describing our interpretation-encounters with the world around us. The interpretative model these fields present is one where contingency and variability are inherent properties of reality and certainty is replaced by uncertainty and the probability set; the traditional, singular "truth" changes into one truth among many. However, it is important to acknowledge that the results of this interpretive structure are *not* relativistic in the typical sense, as employed in the non-specialists' claim "truth is relative"; any confusion about this apparent "relativity" is resolved through a more detailed consideration of this model. Conceptualizing the state of information suggests an epistemology not based on certainty.

The emergent conceptual 'space' these fields have produced has enabled the development not only of modern digital computers, but of the internet, networked communication, and has transformed all aspects of our society. This model suggests that social, political, and cultural meaning proceeds from—in the sense are secondary effects derivative from—this larger conceptual space that can be termed the "state of information." These culturally produced meanings, precisely because they are interpretative effects of how we use information, depend on creating relationships within that information space; however, all these relationships are recursive—once created, the new relations enter into that information space as *further* elaborations of the information space itself; they are easily (and often) confused with the information space.

Nevertheless, the concept of this information space does pose questions about the state of information and its relationship to cultural theory. So, while these secondary meanings and the space they describe are linked in a recursive formulation, totalizing; yet they are also entirely an abstraction that serves a descriptive or intellectual purpose. The space should not be reified: the state of information becomes problematic precisely at the moment it is reified as in the digital aspiration towards that state.

Understanding the state of information's abstract space proceeds from four concepts that occupy a central position in their fields: uncertainty, superposition, schizophrenia, and seriality. The first three describe different aspects of what can be considered a singular phenomenon—the emergence of paradox—while the final term identifies the 'ground' for the 'figure' that is paradox itself: multiple emergent, equally valid, yet exclusive, potentials within a delimited framework. Considering this figure-ground relationship has been an ongoing concern for a variety of distinct fields of empirical study from the twentieth century into the present, this consideration suggests an epistemological framework that requires inconsistency, which is implicit in the interpretative implications of Gödel's Theorem as well as Holland's CAS. Understanding the state of information requires the explanation of how these four concepts interlock since each term describes a specific aspect of how the state of information emerges from empirical observations; nevertheless, it is an abstract construct that is most apparent in the concept of the digital itself.

By attempting to literalize information as instrumentality, the digital aspires to become the physical manifestation of a "state of information" beyond all considerations of validity, empirical reality, or dialectical opposition: an equivalency reified in the idea of information-as-data. It emerges naturally from this idea. The suggestion that the digital transcends physical form through its replacement of physicality with "meaning" embodied in that (denied) physicality is the aura of information in action; the aspiration to achieve the state of information as immanent instrumentality is fundamental to this would-be transcendence; it also becomes apparent in the attempts to create what mathematicians term "completeness" inherent in the various ways the digital is deployed in security.[1] *The digital aspiration towards the state of information is a direct effect of the immateriality assigned to the digital.* The tendency towards reification of the state of information in digital technology (the digital aspiration to the state of information) is a consequence of the immortality of digital information; its perpetual accumulation in databases pro-

---

[1] See Samuel Nunn, "Tell Us What's Going to Happen: Information Feeds to the War on Terror," *CTheory*, September 1, 2006, www.ctheory.net/articles.aspx?id=518.

duces the illusion that it is possible for this information collection to create the type of completeness only possible in the abstract framework of the state of information itself.

The aura of information reveals itself via the digital as a mystification that breaks empirical relationships between information and reality required for validation; it logically develops from the aura of the digital, but where the digital aura strips physicality from consciousness, the aura of information is philosophically relativist, denying the need for observational, empirical, or factual relationships between interpretation and reality. This transformation happens because the state of information suggests that all interpretations are equivalent within its information space—even contradictory, mutually exclusive, or empirically false ones—because there is no distinction between interpretation and information. This understanding relates to Ludwig Wittgenstein's comments about the empirical tests familiar from scientific procedures:

> "An empirical proposition can be tested" (we say). But how? and through what? What counts as its test?—"But is this an adequate test? And, if so, must it not be recognizable as such in logic?"—As if giving grounds did not come to an end sometime. But the end is not an ungrounded presupposition: it is an ungrounded way of acting.[2]

Given the framework of these questions, the *a priori* 'forms of life' that inform both question and test become the grounding for the answer and provide the range of possible, acceptable solutions to those questions; however, to the question that addresses that grounding, *What is it that provides the basis for that ground?* is to open up an infinite regression. It is a question that cannot be resolved without the assertion of an arbitrary factor—the 'forms of life.' Such frameworks for thought emerge precisely because there is an assumption

---

[2] Ludwig Wittgenstein, *On Certainty*, trans. G.E.M. Anscombe (New York: Harper and Row, 1972), sec. 580.

of sequence (as in the logical syllogism), while the state of information specifically does not present sequence, but rather a multiplicity and continuity that denies logical sequence (it is *alinear* rather than *nonlinear*). Jean Baudrillard intuited this critical and interpretative over-extension of the uncertainty posed by quantum physics in his book *Impossible Exchange*:

> The uncertainty of the world lies in the fact that it has no equivalent anywhere; it cannot be exchanged for anything. The uncertainty of thought lies in the fact that it cannot be exchanged either for truth or reality. [...] The uncertainty principle, which states that it is impossible to calculate the speed of a particle and its position simultaneously, is not confined to physics. [...] Uncertainty has seeped into all areas of life. And this is not a product of the complexity of parameters (we can always cope with that); it is a definitive uncertainty linked to the irreconcilable character of the data.[3]

Baudrillard is discussing, without specifically naming or developing, the empirical bases for the concept of superposition. The paradox which lies at the heart of the state of information proceeds from a different situation entirely than the one Wittgenstein investigates, and it is one which is *not* capable of producing answers and certainty—one where the reality that information/interpretation describes is a feature of that information, rather than an independent value. As a description of "all possible interpretations", the state of information is an abstraction; only in its reification does it become problematic and promote relativism. This distinction of information from reality is the reason the digital aspires to the abstract state of information: this state, in reified form, appears as a super-structure beyond the concerns of physicality; this denial of the physical is the defining feature of the

---

[3] Jean Baudrillard, *Impossible Exchange*, trans. Chris Turner (New York: Verso, 2000), 3, 19.

aura of the digital.

§7.1

Central to understanding the state of information (and the triad of uncertainty, superposition, and schizophrenia) is the issue of paradox. When typically encountered, a paradox is a symptom of interpretative failure—it is understood as a point of logical/axiomatic incorrectness—a direct demonstration of inconsistency in a logical system. Mathematician Douglas Hofstadter explains in his book on paradoxes, *Gödel, Escher, Bach:*

> But let us now say exactly what is meant by *consistency* of a formal system...that every theorem, when interpreted, becomes a true statement. And we will say that *inconsistency* occurs when there is at least one false statement among the interpreted theorems.[4]

All parts of a formal (logical) system must be true for that system to be a valid interpretative construction; inconsistency thus means the system is faulty, and a paradox means there is an even deeper flaw in the construction of the system itself. While interpretation as a general concept is not identical to the constructed formal systems of logic (such as mathematics), the formal systems Hofstadter describes are a specialized subset of interpretations: axioms and theorems are rigorously defined versions of past experience and future expectations; their role in a formal system is to render the information needed to construct the system (and any interpretations within that system) explicit. Inconsistent results demonstrate an inherent failure of interpretation; their resolution requires some type of external modification to resolve the incompatibility. Often this change comes from an empirical test against observable reality; however, inherent in re-

---

[4] Douglas R. Hofstadter, *Gödel, Escher, Bach: An Eternal Golden Braid* (1979; repr. New York: Basic Books, 1999), 94.

solving the paradox is a method for locating and improving interpretations—the inconsistency can also be understood as a liminal point of instability where multiple, equally valid interpretations converge: as a nexus where alternatives coexist at the same time and with equal validity. It is this recognition of paradox as a nodal point that creates the state of information. Paradoxes define the indeterminate points of collision and overlap between different interpretations; the state of information is a construct that emerges from how these nodes can be related to one another in a probabilistic space. Quantum physics calls this indeterminate state of overlapping, mutually-exclusive-yet-valid interpretation "superposition."

§7.2

In quantum physics the concept of "superposition" developed because of an inconsistency between the formal, deterministic predictions of physics and the empirical results of experimentally testing those predictions: it is a term describing an apparent, fundamental paradox of physical reality. Physicist David Albert explains it as a paradoxical incompatibility of interpretation and observation. Knowing one observed value precludes being able to identify another:

> We find that we can't ever put ourselves in a position to say, "The color of this electron is such-and-such and its hardness is now such-and-such." It isn't that our color and hardness [tests] are built (somehow) crudely....It's that any electron's even having any definite color apparently entails that it's neither hard nor soft, nor both, nor neither, and that any electron's even having any definite hardness entails that it's neither black nor white nor both nor neither.[5]

---

[5] David Z. Albert, *Quantum Mechanics and Experience* (Cambridge: Harvard University Press, 1992), 15.

Albert's observation that one value, color, is apparently incompatible with the other value—only one of these values can exist at any given moment. It is not that the tests are flawed, nor is it that the phenomena examined act inconsistently—there is something else happening that appears to defy our expectations of a single, consistent result. The solution to this paradox is to describe our predictions as equally valid, yet incompatible sets of probabilities: to abandon singular, absolute results. Viewing interpretation as ranges of potentials is a key feature of the state of information—the expression of any single interpretation as one within a range (or set of distinct ranges) where all interpretations are valid. Nevertheless, only one interpretation is immanent at any given moment. Again, Albert explains:

> The rules for predicting the outcome of a measurement of (say) the hardness of a white electron turn out (in so far as we're now able to determine) to be probabilistic rules rather than deterministic ones.[6]

Quantum Mechanics, in order to accommodate the paradox described by superposition, has been forced into a description of the world based on probability. This kind of interpretation presents opposed potentials as equally possible; instead of there being a contradiction in this description, the extremes become liminal positions of mutual exclusion. This is a 'solution' that does not "solve" the problem; it makes inconsistency into part of the 'rules.' The variability defined by ranges of equally valid, potential interpretations produces an "information space" that collectively 'defines' the interpretant. The state of information derives from the full range of superposed potentials that identify the extremes of this "information space."

Instead of being deterministic and singular, the state of information, following the model suggested by superposition, defines interpretations as multiple, overlapping, mutually exclusive, and explicitly contradictory: it is a network or a spectrum of possibilities, rather than monolithic. It is the existence of the range of potentials that is the guarantee of validity (i.e., all interpretations are valid, their validity being a function of presence within the larger range of equally valid potentials) even though only one particular interpretation will be empirically observable at any given time. The likelihood of empirical observation is simply another dimension of this multidimensional space. The state of information, while an abstraction, thus implies a specific type of (in)-completeness unbounded from human knowledge in the same way that all the members in the set of rational numbers, while immanently describable, cannot be enumerated individually: this interpretative framework generates infinite regression at the same time as it is logically bounded. That the state of information originates within physically immanent observations and empirically describable processes does not negate its inherent nature as construction—it is necessary to acknowledge that the state of information lies outside the frameworks of human conceptualization except indirectly; the process of naming "the state of information" creates the illusion that such a state is comprehensible, that it can be conceptualized; it is problematic precisely because it exceeds our conceptual capacity in the same way that "the infinite" does.

§7.3

The "Necker Cube" is an optical illusion named after the nineteenth-century Swiss crystallographer Louis Albert Necker who discovered it. He noticed that salt crystals appeared to reverse their orientations when viewed with a microscope.[7] Optical illusions provide a direct way to consider the interaction between different, incompatible (superposed) interpre-

---

[7] Louis Albert Necker, *The London & Edinburgh Philosophical Magazine and Journal of Science* 1 (1832): 329–337.

tations[8] and our choices that determine which interpretation we see at any given moment:

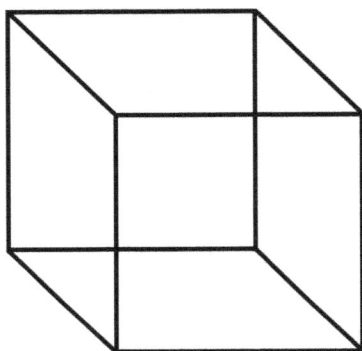

The indeterminate orientation of the salt crystals Necker observed is recreated in this optical illusion (above) by a network of visually ambiguous lines that we interpret as a cube oscillating between an 'up' and 'down' orientation. It presents two possible orientations using the same set of potentials. Which interpretation of the Necker Cube's orientation we see is completely dependent on how we interpret the relationship of the constituent lines. Our understanding of the cube's orientation suggests a feedback loop between our visual perception and our interpretation of the figure's orientation[9]: interpretations and perceptions dynamically interact to resolve the visually ambiguous figure into one orientation or another.

These lines gain their meaning as a cube only from the relationship we choose for them, a decision that happens so

[8] Nancy J. Woolf and Stuart Hameroff, "A Quantum Approach to Visual Consciousness," *Trends in Cognitive Science* 5.11 (2001): 472–478.

[9] Wolfgang Einhäuser, Kevan A.C. Martin, and Peter König, "Are Switches in Perception of the Necker Cube Related to Eye Position?" *European Journal of Neuroscience* 20.10 (2004): 2811–2818.

easily and immediately that we may not be aware of making it. It is determined by our mental arrangement of the elements 'spatially' using our past experiences as a guide. Our visual interpretation of this figure remains constant only so long as the arrangement considered most probable remains constant. However, how we interpret this cube is a dynamic process of examination and engagement; when the interpretation of which orientation is most likely changes, the form correspondingly shifts, demonstrating that this figure's orientation is superposed between two distinct, yet incompatible, orientations. This figure, like all optical illusions, allows us to encounter the variable 'space' of the state of information "directly." Changes in our initial interpretations are what cause these visual shifts. These transformations are evidence for a superposition resolving into a particular outcome.[10] The multiple interpretations of this singular figure reveal the contingent and interactively-determined nature of our selections from the range of potential interpretations.

Interpretive shifts suggest that there are discrete, interactive levels to interpretation. The movement from one interpretation to another in optical illusions is a function of these different levels of interpretation checking against perceptions and failing to match what is being perceived as sensory experience. Depending on how the image is understood to be oriented, all other levels of interpretation are shaped by the expectations it establishes. However, as the Necker Cube shows, our sense perceptions are inconsistent and fully determined by our initial assessments of what we encounter. Our apparent (immanent) experience of the world is only one possibility, a potential understanding that undergoes constant comparison to new perceptions. The "state of information" is a construction for identifying this abstract realm of (un)realized possibilities.

---

[10] Woolf and Hameroff, "A Quantum Approach to Visual Consciousness."

§7.4

Ernest Nagel and James R. Newman explain the foundation and form of Gödel's Inconsistency Theorem in their book, *Gödel's Proof*. Their discussion demonstrates Gödel's claim that all systems of rules (axioms) will produce inconsistencies in the form of paradoxes that cannot be resolved. In epistemological terms, Gödel shows that formalized knowledge derived from logic is, in itself, an inconsistent, tentative proposition:

> Gödel showed (i) how to construct an arithmetical formula G that represents the meta-mathematical statement: 'The formula G is not demonstrable.' This formula G thus ostensibly says of itself that it is not demonstrable....But (ii) Gödel also showed that G is demonstrable if, and only if, its formal negation ~ G is demonstrable.[11]

The appearance of an infinite logical regression—a series of repeating logical contradictions whose "resolution" simply shifts the focus of the contradiction—happens precisely because the formula G is inconsistent. In the formal system of logic, Gödel's Theorem is both correct and invalid at the same moment: it is a true statement of logic that simultaneously cannot be true; its validity exists in superposition; inconsistency is a defining feature in paradoxes of interpretation. Gödel's formula follows the rules for the logical system of symbolic mathematics, but in following the rules, he shows that the system of mathematics is inconsistent:

> Gödel's paper is proof of the impossibility of demonstrating certain postulates....The traditional belief that the axioms of geometry (or, for that matter, the axioms of any discipline) can be established by their apparent self-evidence was thus radically undermined....For it became evi-

[11] Ernest Nagel and James R. Newman, *Gödel's Theorem* (1958; repr. New York: New York University Press, 1986), 58.

dent that mathematics is simply the discipline *par excellence* that draws the conclusions logically implied by any given set of axioms or postulates.[12]

In general terms, what Gödel demonstrates is that the set of assumptions which provide the foundation for logical certainty have an arbitrary basis. This demonstration has consequences for justifying all interpretations since it identifies a fundamental failure of logical procedure: any set of 'rules' can produce paradoxes in the form of unresolvable loops. Regression is the problem posed by questioning Wittgenstein's 'forms of life,' and shows that Gödel's demonstration extends beyond mathematics and formal logic, a point raised by Nagel and Newman in their introduction. Inconsistency is a fundamental component of our interpretations generally, although it only becomes apparent through a process of interpretative engagement or in atypical situations where ambiguity dominates and singular interpretations reveal themselves as contingent.

§7.5

The clinical description of schizophrenia is a cognitive disease that develops from a mental state of superposition that psychologists call "ambivalence."[13] In his original description of schizophrenia, Eugen Bleuler concluded that its basis was a *pathological ambivalence*[14] that exaggerates typical situations into a conflict resembling superposition, a type of mental paradox:

(1) *Ambitendency,* which sets free with every tendency a counter-tendency.

---

[12] Nagel and Newman, *Gödel's Theorem*, 10–11.
[13] Eugen Bleuler, *The Theory of Schizophrenic Negativism*, trans. William A. White (New York: Journal of Nervous and Mental Disease, 1912), 266.
[14] Bleuler, *The Theory of Schizophrenic Negativism*, 266.

(2) *Ambivalency,* which gives to the same idea two contrary feeling tones and invests the same thought simultaneously with a positive and a negative character.[15]

These definitions repeat the inconsistency identified by Gödel; while the human mind is not a formal system such as mathematics, it is the source of such systems. The demand that the world be ordered within a specific, *a priori* interpretative framework is schizophrenic; all interpretations have a schizoid component. The pathological varieties of schizophrenia emerge precisely because of a dysfunctional response to these superposed potentials.

Psychologist Mark Garrison views the indeterminate character of the ambiguous as the cause of schizophrenia: the difference between a pathological and 'normal' thought process arises from how the ambiguity of superposition is "handled" by the interpreting mind; the kinds of variability his model requires are coincident with those proposed in quantum physics by the concept of superposition. In schizophrenia, ambiguity polarizes into ambivalence (superposition), blocking 'normal' solutions. Garrison's retheorization of schizophrenia proposes a model for understanding how the mind "solves" the problems posed by superposition through "opposition"—the autonomous generation of negated interpretations:

Opposition solves not only ambivalence but also indecision, forcing an either/or decision or no decision at all. Ambivalence occludes multiple alternatives, ambiguity, and multiple meanings (polyvalence), forcing a dominating tension of opposites. Ambivalence—pathologized—both shrinks the world into oppositions and prevents (blocks) movement through it.[16]

[15] Mark Garrison, "The Poetics of Ambivalence," *Spring: An Annual of Archetypal Psychiatry and Jungian Thought* (1982): 224 [213–232].

[16] Garrison, "The Poetics of Ambivalence," 223.

Faced with an array of equal potentials, the tendency to collapse variability into ambivalence is a method to force an interpretative selection. What makes schizophrenia different from 'normal' thinking is not that the opposition is unresolved—it is that schizophrenia presents a pathological inability to cope with multiple (superposed) potentials or alternatives. A 'normal' resolution is one that remains within the established parameters of Wittgenstein's 'forms of life.' Garrison notes:

> The psyche must cope with the configuration of ambiguous fragmented experience into contrary tendencies and oppositions, and it must find its way through the maze of resemblances it makes from these ambiguities. Overlay this myth-making process with the various demands from the environment for singular, rational actions—the myth of continuity and the fantasy of singularity—and the potential for ambivalence is great indeed.[17]

This theory of consciousness has an element of essentialism to it, mediated by its limitations. It is not an account that proposes a complete explanation; instead, what Garrison advances is the thesis that the conditions of a superposed, uncertain reality—both in the physical and interpretative senses (i.e. the state of information)—has produced a set of coping mechanisms for the inconsistency of our interpretations; this transformation from a range of potentials into a dualistic pairing, an either/or opposition, is exploited by agnotology, not through a pathological blocking of resolution, but through the substitution of an alternative set of potentials—a different either/or dialectic—that creates the uncertainty about selecting an appropriate resolution to the inter-pretive problem. This ambivalence about how to proceed with the fundamental analysis enables the creation of an interpreta-

---

[17] Eugen Bleuler, *Dementia Praecox, or the Group of Schizophrenias* (New York: International Universities Press, 1950), 271–286.

tion, *not* a pathology of interpretation (agnotological interpretations proceed normally, as with any other normal interpretive process), which characterizes the agnotological procedure.

This model of schizophrenia reveals two kinds of ambivalence acting on interpretation; both are operative in normal and agnotological constructions. The first is a natural feature of the physical world that all interpretations must address on multiple levels: not simply that of physical sense-data, but on subsequent elaborations of that sense-data into the lived experience we have in encountering reality. This ambivalence is inherent to the universe and exists independent of the observer. The second kind of ambivalence develops in the mind of the observer as a means to check the interpretations of the ambivalent environment; both function in interpretation as a means to resolve superposed potentials through recourse to empirical observation and via past experience and expertise. It is the application (and validity) of this past experience that agnotology brings into question. Mathematician John Holland's CAS models these past experiences as a "bucket brigade" that assumes successful interpretations will make future interpretations based on them more likely to be successful. It builds on past success as a way to help insure future success, i.e. the past acts as reference for the future. This procedure enables us to make sense of the world around us by using our past experience to shape future interpretations. The interpretative process that is pathological in schizophrenics begins with the same basic set of perceptual cues and processes that constrain and direct all other interpretations, even those more complex than simple perception.

All interpretations are necessarily subject to schizophrenia since they function as divisions and limitations of interpretative possibility *a priori:* Wittgenstein's 'forms of life' describe these successful past experiences. They provide an apparent commonality for our ability to communicate about the world around us. *Pathological ambivalence* suggests the development of an unresolvable inconsistency that forces the mind to adopt other solutions than what 'normal' minds employ. This possibility is consistent with Bleuler's observations of schizophrenia as a disease defined by symptoms with no apparent psychological cause; the description of the schizophrenic pathology, which is a failure of adaptive interpretation, is distinct from that state's physiological basis in the mind. The schizophrenic mind chooses a potential response that is not as likely as those chosen by 'normal' minds; this is a direct result of blocking created by unresolved ambivalence. The choices made are part of the same "information space" as normal decisions, but follow from idiosyncratic foundations. The development of agnotology inverts this relationship that enables the separation of functional and pathological, substituting unresolvable contradictions for the established, successful resolutions, resulting in not only a diversion of established resolutions, but also the inability to generate further resolutions specifically because the foundations of those resolutions are in doubt and remain unresolved—it offers instead the suggestion that *all* solutions are idiosyncratic.

§7.6.a

The approach to interpretation suggested by the concept of superposition, and elaborated through the consideration of the Necker Cube and Gödel's Theorem, creates a framework for understanding interpretation that is indeterminate; single interpretations resemble nodes in a network of intersecting probability scales—positions within a series of possibilities. This relational nature of interpretation is what allows the agnotological to emerge as anti-knowledge while still proceeding through the normal process of ambivalence resolution. The state of information emerges as a necessary abstraction produced by this approach; attempts to render it immanent using digital technology are simultaneously an aspiration to the state of information and a symptom of the aura of information acting upon the application of digital technology.

By employing Holland's CAS model as a means to resolve the logical 'black box' of past experience in Umberto Eco's theory of serial form, the nodal model for interpretation emerges from the relationship between past experience and the immanent decision to choose one potential interpretation instead of another; the state of information is a logical consequence of this model.

§7.6.b

Umberto Eco's conception of "serial" means, first and foremost, that the audience for the serial recognizes and acknowledges the ways the audience's knowledge is required to interpret a specific episode in a serial. It is a reciprocal connection between immanence and remembrance; it implies a model for interpretation that is centrally focused on the interpreter actively working to resolve indeterminate potentials—precisely those situations identified by the concept of *superposition*. The spectator's interpretations employ frameworks created through previous encounters with similar types to anticipate and recognize divergences from established norms.[18] In selecting one interpretation from within a set of potential interpretations—a choice that is subject to later interpretative reversals—produces contradictions and oscillations between equally likely interpretations (as in the Necker Cube). It is the provisional nature of this interpretative choice that is significant, and it produces an expanded field of potential interpretations when the possibility of interpretative inconsistency is admitted into the framework as a limiting factor which describes those positions of greatest incompatibility. This interpretative construct generates a greatly expanded field of potential, valid interpretations, and at the same time creates a logical justification for those alternative interpretations, thus enabling the potential for agnotological procedures to challenge any established interpretation. It is this indistinguishability of agnotology-as-interpretative-procedure that produces the affect common to all

---

[18] John Holland, *Hidden Order: How Adaptation Builds Complexity* (Reading: Perseus Books, 1995), 53.

agnotologies—the creation of an unresolvable uncertainty: agnotology seeks to generate a superposed set of potential interpretations.

§7.6.c

The inconsistency "superposition" represents, and which enables the emergence of agnotology, provides the mechanism for adaptation in Holland's CAS model. His description uses natural selection to choose the best-working example from a group of potential solutions.[19] "Best-working" interpretations meet the needs of the interpreter in encountering the environment examined. The interpretative demands are constrained by the feedback loop which produces them, generating new interpretations based on earlier successes.[20] Inconsistency is essential to this process; the ability to allow inconsistencies to exist simultaneously and to evaluate those inconsistencies for relative degrees of success is a logical necessity in this structure. It requires a ranking of interpretations based on their "fit" to the specific situation being encountered. When modified by Eco's serial framework, these interpretations become ordered as with nodes in a network.

The concept of "superposition" suggests understanding interpretation as a "probability set" presenting a range of tentative possibilities rather than a singular, deterministic result. While Holland's CAS does provide a method for addressing superposed potentials, it can also potentially 'lock' interpretation into a singular position, making the kinds of interpretative shifts that are readily apparent in viewing the Necker Cube a problematic situation. The instant flipping between one orientation and another implies the coexistence of (at least two) mutually exclusive interpretations that are essentially (and easily) interchangeable. The serial version of CAS justifies these competing interpretations without neces-

---

[19] Holland, *Hidden Order,* 79.
[20] Holland, *Hidden Order,* 61–76.

sarily forcing us to choose between them.[21] Both are equally valid interpretations defined and mutually supported as valid potentials by their relationship through variation. The probability set as a whole—the existence of a series of mutually exclusive (and intermediate) interpretations—is the site of "validity" rather than any singular interpretation. These alternatives do not undermine interpretation; the probability set as a whole authorizes alternative potentials at the same moment as any singular interpretation achieves apparent 'validity.' The mutually assured validity of interpretations in the state of information emerges from the extension of superposition and optical illusions to other types of interpretation that are less obviously (apparently) in superposition.

Interpretation proceeds by employing inconsistency as a technique, thus seeking to create superposed potentials rather than avoiding them, since it is through encountering and addressing these undecidables that interpretative success emerges. Holland's CAS model requires that even when there is no obvious contradiction, that one is created—ambivalence in psychology is the generation of these oppositions; what emerges from this ambivalence as pathological schizophrenia is the quantity, strength, and unresolvable nature of these conflicts. Its specific strengths when confronting the variability of superposition is suggestive when we consider the variety of mutually exclusive theories and interpretations that characterize broader fields of thought; at the same time, Gödel's Theorem suggests that the appearance of inconsistencies within any interpretative schema is inevitable. Our ability to accept and evaluate, even employ, multiple, different (even contradictory) interpretations at once suggests an empirical basis for the nodal approach to interpretation.

The role of past experience in interpretation serves to mask the inconsistent aspects of everyday experience; that the world appears neither uncanny nor inconsistent is a necessary result of how Holland's building blocks function: in-

---

[21] Umberto Eco, *The Limits of Interpretation* (Bloomington: University of Indiana Press, 1994), 97–98.

terpretation adopts the most likely potential that is consistent with what has already proven successful. Only in specific situations where alternate and equally potential interpretations emerge does the underlying superposition visibly "appear" as in the Necker Cube, or with paradoxes generally.

§7.6.d

The "nodal" view of interpretation identifies any singular, immanent interpretation as a choice from a probability set whose composition is serial—a collection of various, competing interpretations. This view opens possibilities for justifying interpretation in a flexible and open ended fashion; the nodal model is one where interpretations are 'nodes' in a multidimensional space of potentials; collectively, these nodes describe the state of information—"information space." Because the nodal model appears superficially quantifiable, it implies the potential to become instrumentalized through the application of technology—i.e., specifically via the digital. It is precisely the analogy of a nodal (or network) conception of interpretation that suggests the possibility of transition to instrumentality; however, this application is reification.

Being able to describe a process where expectations can arise, shape interpretation, and then evolve provides a framework for justifying interpretation generally through recourse to a set of potential interpretations. Conceptualizing interpretation as nodal shifts the emphasis in supporting specific interpretations from an external foundation (immanent empirical correctness) to an internal one: specific interpretations are justified by/through the existence of alternatives with common features: 'truth' conceptualized as a spectrum of potentials. This process creates a state where all potentials coexist as information. The momentary superiority of one interpretation does not invalidate the others; a shift to another possibility is always potentially immanent. Like Eco's serial forms, the nodal approach to meaning depends not on specific individual interpretations but on the relationship between specific interpretations and the system that creates them and which they collectively define. The digital's ability to manipulate data directly leads to the general aspiration to manipulate and contain the "information space" itself; this is the aspiration of the digital to the state of information; this aspiration requires a limitation and reification of that space, collapsing its variability into a limited, a priori series of potentials—the illusion that this space, however large, is infinite is the aura of the digital in action.

Nodal interpretations are justified by the concept of mutually assured validity: the validity of one interpretation is established through its relationship to other potential interpretations. In this schema "past experience" is a method for choosing highly probable interpretations from the range of potentials, but does not eliminate the potential to shift from one interpretation to another: it is not a source of validity for any single interpretation against another. The abolition of a dialectical/dualistic basis for interpretation produces the apparent (superficial) egalitarianism of the state of information where all interpretations are valid potentials. This is not a philosophically relativistic construction because this entire "information space" exists in "superposition"; only one potential can be valid at any given moment. The "nodes" are abstractions that do not actually exist within that space, but rather are features of our interpretations falling within the parameters of the space itself, useful in conceptualizing their relationships to each other.

Even though the nodal interpretative model proposed here is extremely schematic, it suggests possible strategies for justifying interpretations without precluding their rejection or revision at a later time; it is a means for selecting individual potentials from within the state of information. Yet, it is important to recognize there is a distinction between the nodal approach to interpretation and the interpretative "space" that approach inherently suggests—the state of information is an abstraction implied by, but independent of, the nodal approach itself.

§7.7.a

The instability of the Necker Cube becomes the instability between different levels of scale within a given construction. What we commonly call "experience" and "expertise" are forms of learned behavior. Faced with an array of equal potentials, the ambivalent nature of perception forces an interpretative decision; without making an initial choice about relationships and organization, there can be no evolution towards successful interpretations. Barthes' observations about initial interpretative choices are true for all meaning-bearing constructions:

> Distance and proximity are promoters of meaning. Is this not the great secret of every vital semantics? Everything proceeds from a *spacing out* or *staggering of articulations.* Meaning is born from a combination of non-signifying elements (phonemes, lines); but it does not suffice to combine these elements to a first degree in order to exhaust the creation of meaning: what has been combined forms aggregates which can combine again among themselves a second, a third time.[22]

Barthes is discussing the organization of Mannerist painter Giuseppe Arcimboldo's composite heads, but he could just as easily be discussing the *paranoiac-critical* paintings of Salvador Dalí, or the *Graphysics* of contemporary painter Rostarr. These observations are also true of how we transform the marks on a page, wall, or screen into letters that become words, which in turn become sentences, paragraphs and so on. It is the scaling-up of organization that generates constructions that when related, via successful past experiences, are able to become meaning-bearing.

---

[22] Roland Barthes, *The Responsibility of Forms: Critical Essays on Music, Art, and Representation*, trans. Richard Howard (Berkeley: The University of California Press, 1985), 141.

Consider *Negative Space Traveler 7* (2008), a painting by New York-based painter Rostarr. In interpreting this painting, we create order in the network of lines by deciding on a series of relationships that generates figures; these decisions structure what we see, and are part of the work's significance. The appearance of the figures in these paintings requires an interpretation of abstract lines as representation; it mirrors the choices made in interpreting the Necker Cube.

Rostarr, *Negative Space Traveler 7* (2008). Copyright Rostarr; used with permission.

These figures are a potential, but equally possible is the apprehension of the image as a network of abstract ribbons, overlapping. Each image remains in superposition until one or another potential becomes a dominant interpretation for the viewer. It is this shifting of interpretations that Rostarr calls "Graphysics" in an explicit acknowledgement of the superposition present in these paintings.[23]

The transformation effected here is a shift between a variety of pure abstraction familiar from Minimalist paintings by Frank Stella that becomes a network of faces and anthropomorphic forms. The emergence of form is a specific choice by the viewer, and gives these works a dramatic anthropomorphic character: they invoke an internal, subjective reality whose instability reflects the shifting character of the state of information.

§7.7.b

The crucial factor in these interpretations is "successful past experiences"—these correspond to the 'forms of life' that Wittgenstein suggests are *a priori* to any encounter; however, the success of these past experiences is dependent not on the interpreter, or a particular interpretation, but the ability of other interpreters to also produce a similar interpretation when confronted by the same initial material. Abbott and Costello's *Who's on First?* demonstrates this problem:

> Costello: Well then who's on first?
> Abbott: Yes.
> Costello: I mean the fellow's name.
> Abbott: Who.
> Costello: The guy on first.
> Abbott: Who.
> Costello: The first baseman.
> Abbott: Who.
> Costello: The guy playing...
> Abbott: Who is on first!
> Costello: I'm asking you who's on first.
> Abbott: That's the man's name.
> Costello: That's whose name?
> Abbott: Yes.

---

[23] Rey Parlá, "Organic Harmonies," in Rostarr, *Wreckless Abandon* (Miami: O.H.W.O.W., 2008).

Costello: Well go ahead and tell me.
Abbott: That's it.
Costello: That's who?
Abbott: Yes.

This comedy routine depends upon a recognition that *"who's"* and *"whose"* sound the same. We laugh at their predicament because we understand how easily it happens, and how frustrating it is when it does. Abbott does not explain the 'rules' of substitution to Costello, and the simple explanation, *that the first baseman is named Who*, depends on our ability to recognize a shift in function for the word *who*. The comedy in this routine is thus sadistic: it emerges from the semiotic torture of Costello and his inability and rising frustration with Abbott's refusal to answer his question. In reality, they are speaking entirely different languages.

What each of these instances involve is a differential between the author and the reader; the staggering of articulations proceeds based on a set of rules which the reader either implicitly deploys in interpreting, or must discover through trial and error in order to render the alternative, declarative meaning in "who's on first." This is a dynamic process of engagement, not a passive one where the interpreter simply receives the instruction from the author. It requires the selection of appropriate interpretative engagements in order to arrive at a semblance of meaning.

In tracing the parameters of an interpretation, what emerges is a shifting set of relationships not only between the elements that are being interpreted, but between the author (Abbott) and the reader (Costello). The shifting relationships between elements are a signpost for the shifting nature of nodal interpretations. It reveals the authorial differential between Abbott, Costello, and the audience who recognizes the dynamic and is complicit in the comedy being performed.

Our interpretative ability to "back-up" and change our initial assumptions based upon their applicability to a given situation allows us to resolve paradoxes. It is this feedback process that is crucial to Holland's CAS model for adaptation (and interpretation). Language and communication are nei-ther automatically functional, nor are they necessarily unam-biguous in meaning. The transition from the state of infor-mation to the reality of interpretation depends on how we apply our knowledge of the 'rules': thus, appearance of mean-ing is determined by other interpreter's ability to recognize that interpretation as well—this is the distinction between the abstract state of information and its emergence within any specific interpretation. It is this initial decision that shapes the entire interpretative process that follows. As the inability to communicate in *Who's on First?* results from the inconsistency between 'normal' and specific uses, the associa-tive procedures of the rhetorical "jumps" evident in this dia-logue demonstrate that superposition is a methodology for 'rule' discovery, providing a means to test and a technique for expanding interpretative results.

§7.7.c

Meanings become pathological specifically when they are unique to a singular interpreter. According to psychologist Mark Garrison, the experience of superposition we encoun-ter in Abbott and Costello's routine is an essential compo-nent of communication; without it there could not be the kind of creative thinking called "poetry" or "rhetoric." As Garrison observes, it enables communication of ideas not immediately apparent:

> Jung characterized Bleuler's understanding of ambiva-lence [superposition] as the "fusion of one function with another."...Rhetoric demonstrates that ambivalence is fundamental to language for it is in rhetoric that all as-pects of ambivalence converge....In a metaphor taken lit-erally, communication is blocked and meaning cannot move....Mediated by recognition and acceptance, it is therapeutic, imaginative, originating and joining. It is a

phenomenon crucial to psychological experience.[24]

Rhetorical devices perform the transformation of 'normal' speech into a poetic construction that encourages associative understanding. Persuasion in rhetoric works through the transposition of values without the use of logical structures; this is the effect of superposition collapsing. This transfer occurs because both the speaker and listener agree—implicitly—to accept the superposition of associative speech.

Without the agreement between speakers that meaning will proceed according to specific 'rules,' where the words used have clear roles, we cannot communicate; for the interplay that creates the comedy in *Who's on first* elides these roles and is both the confusion and the joke, (as does the confusion of reality and metaphor Barthes describes in the example below). There is an overlap between Garrison's ambivalence and Barthes' semiotic theory: both suggest a central role for inconsistency in a model of communication and *mis*communication. Crucial to Barthes' explanation of his semiotic procedure is the metaphor taken literally:

> One of the techniques of the poet Cyrano de Bergerac consists in taking a perfectly banal metaphor in the language and exploiting its literal meaning. If the language says "die of grief," Cyrano conceives the story of a condemned man whose executions sing him tunes so lugubrious that he finally dies of grief over his own death.[25]

This narrative is absurd, comic in its implication. It proposes a relationship that recognizably distorts the role of language and the power of metaphor—songs do not kill people, no matter how depressing and sad they may be. Our interpretations perform this jump "without" thought; it is a tacit agreement based in our past experiences with the 'rules.' This type of agreement is often called *transparent* because we do

---

[24] Garrison, "The Poetics of Ambivalence," 226–229.
[25] Barthes, *The Responsibility of Forms,* 141.

not become aware of our complicity in accepting its terms or our role in maintaining and deploying these conventions whose purpose is the containment of ambiguity so we can communicate. We are familiar with the 'rules' for this kind of statement and the rhetorical connection it makes; it is the types of shift that the state of information describes.

§7.7.d

The concept of "semiotic disobedience," as developed by law professor Sonia K. Katyal,[26] describes the on-going conflict over intellectual property as a function of political speech; however, she includes in her framework the

> [a]ppropriation and occupation of intellectual, tangible, or even bodily property. I call these recent artistic practices examples of 'semiotic disobedience' because they often involve the conscious and deliberate re-creation of property through appropriative and expressive acts that consciously risk violating the law that governs intellectual or tangible property.

Katyal further elaborates:

> This article defines semiotic disobedience to include a number of approaches to visual, actual and verbal representation, including vandalizing, subverting and "recoding" certain kinds of intellectual, real government, and private property for public use and expression.)[27]

The emphasis on physical properly in a discussion of intellectual property is only to be expected; however, this emphasis obscures the disruptive functions of recoding; these proceed by enabling superposition to emerge. What these transfor-

[26] Sonia K. Katyal, "Semiotic Disobedience," in *Washington University Law Review* 84.2 (2006): 489–570.
[27] Katyal, "Semiotic Disobedience", 493, 493fn18.

mations perform is a change of meaning through a systematic shift of 'rules' that result in a changed resolution to the paradox of interpretation. This change reflects a differential between the potentials employed at any given moment and the possibilities contained by the information space itself.

The systematic reappearance throughout the twentieth century (under new nomenclature) of remix/appropriation/ mash-up/montage/collage—the reassembly and alteration of manufactured materials into new art objects, whatever the name used—and of Duchampian found objects, commodity sculpture, even the transformation of commonplace objects in Pop, are all variations on this disruption of conventional engagements. Initially all these actions share a common shift in category from everyday object to artwork; in performing this shift they violate an established semiotic system of organization in favor of other, implicit and valid yet unexpressed, values. It is through a shifting of potentials described within the state of information that these changes appear both natural and logical to us in retrospect, yet they all are examples of the superposition implicit in the state of information itself.

Katyal's conception of semiotic disobedience addresses graffiti and other kinds of "culture jamming" that are deployed directly as political speech, but which impose a shift in engagement between audience and object; however, all these depend on the transformation of established meaning and order and its replacement with an alternative. The validity of this transformation is established by the state of information's suspension of validity: interpretation is an ambivalent phenomenon that reveals the authority of official statements are one political position among others. The superposition emergent in the state of information is deeply threatening to established orders—both of political domination and political resistance—because it subverts the messaging codes of each.

Jose Parlá's painting, *Temporary Autonomous Zone* (2008), is a typical wall-sized painting: covered with swirls of his stylized calligraphy, it includes a single piece of poster stating

"US TROOPS OUT NOW," torn and ragged, an official statement that dominates the painting. The decay of the poster implies the instability of the political message it conveys; as much as the collage employed is itself always already an example of semiotic disobedience, this political statement both covering earlier and covered by later layers invokes a superposition of meaning. While explicitly a political statement, at the same time it lacks the urgency appropriate to the message conveyed—NOW appears to be long past—thus, attenuated. Its specific political message becomes something historical; life moves inexorably on, incorporating both the dominant powers and objections of the dominated into its matrix: visualizing the equivalence of positions identified by the state of information.

Jose Parlá, *Temporary Autonomous Zone* (2008). Copyright Jose Parlá; used with permission.

Parlá's painting superposes the anti-Iraq war protests with pro-war sentiments through the handling of the poster: ripped, dirty, worn, it becomes a sentiment that is simultaneously demanding and passive. It becomes possible to think of the demand in multiple ways simultaneously: as having failed, succeeded, or even having been superceded by other, more pressing concerns. The transformation from immanent to past leaves the status of its proclamation in doubt; the multiplicity of potentials that results destabilizes all the possible positions that can be held in relation to the poster's statement—support, denial, apathy—become merged as equal potentials. Each is justified as a valid potential, but also countered by the immanent presence of the alternative: they are an assertion of possibilities, of alternative political situations. This paradox is reflected in the ambivalence of the title, *Temporary Autonomous Zone*,[28] itself a reference to Hakim Bey's book, the issues evoked by the ambiguity in the painting reflect upon its intertextual namesake.

§7.8

"Superposition" describes both the paradox and our inability to interpret a solution to the problem it presents by discussing how an observer interprets an experiment. Albert notes that superposition requires that we believe both possibilities simultaneously:

> The standard way of thinking about what it means to be in a superposition somehow flatly contradicts what we unmistakably know to be true of our own mental lives.[29]

The concept of superposition prepares for a new model of conceptualization. It appears as a means to "resolve" the contradiction by not resolving it. Instead of finding a way to reject the resulting inconsistency which our interpretations produce, superposition suggests these inconsistencies are the point of the theory; it produces a set of alternatives which suggest any interpretation will eventually fall victim to its own immanent inconsistencies: Gödel's Theorem shows that all formal systems must be incomplete. The implication of

---

[28] Hakim Bey, Temporary Autonomous Zone (Brooklyn: Autonomedia, 1985), http://hermetic.com/bey/taz_cont.html.
[29] Albert, *Quantum Mechanics and Experience,* 15.

these developments is that reality is *in flux,* continuously subject to investigation, transformation, and argument.

Instability of relationships, and the consequent uncertainty—the ambiguity of the state of information as a description of reality—provides the epistemological authorization for the emergent production of agnotology common to digital capitalism. This agnotology exploits the suspension of validity presented by the state of information to achieve its particular effect on interpretation and knowledge: the superficial slide into relativism that the aura of information proposes is the enabling factor for agnotology's counter-production. By proposing alternative interpretations based on similar (or even the same data), but proceeding with different, implicit assumptions, agnotology is symptomatic of the aura of information. The socio-political exploitation of the information space's resolution of interpretative conflicts through superposition is the agnotological process: the use of agnotology to create uncertainty for economic or political benefit; a reification of the state of information without recognizing the dimension of validity (constrained by logic and empiricism) in that space. The demand that all interpretations be accepted and evaluated equally—the positive aspect of the nodal relationships—presents as a negative corollary the agnotological dissolution of certainty as a means to prevent political engagement or action: consider the various demands occasionally heard both before and after the crises of 2008 about "audit the Fed" or "audit Fort Knox" or "audit _____." All these political calls-to-action have a basic problem: it is *not* what the results from the audit might be, but the *credibility* of any result produced for those making the demand. It is not a post-modern plurality or relativity of values, but representative of something else, a different process, whose action superficially resembles relativism, but is not.

As with other sites of agnotologic action, such as demands that American President Barack Obama produce his "real" birth certificate (which continued even after he produced the actual document), the issue with these calls for an "audit" is fundamentally an issue of how agnotology has undermined the knowledge-creation and validation process: there is systemic uncertainty about the factuality of any claim made, any evidence presented, any empirical proof shown. This is the relativism posed by the aura of information in action—it does not matter what the results of any audit might be because there is no longer a space in which we as an audience can agree upon what those results might signify, what the epistemic value of that evidence might be: the ability to determine fact has been dissolved by the process employed to produce those facts in themselves.

It is the breakdown of the procedures that create knowledge and establish the reliability of information that are attacked when agnotology comes to dominate. Thus, no matter what the result of such an audit might be, it is the audit itself that is in question. The ones calling for these audits begin with the assumption that whatever audit they currently have available to them is of no value—the most obvious symptom that their thinking is caught in the trap of agnotism.

The problem posed by a dominant regime of agnotology is that it authorizes doubt about any result—literally any piece of information—that does not match a preconceived frame of reference. It makes challenges to established patterns of thought difficult if not impossible: the affect of agnotology, perversely, is a reinforcement of certainty since it undermines alternatives that could challenge those ideas; thus, it leads to an unwillingness to compromise, and an inflexibility of thought—both of which are 'solutions' to the problem of ambivalence described by Bleuler and Garrison. The pathological dimensions of this response are apparent in the ways this 'certainty' blocks the ability to revise, reconsider and accept alternative potentials as (even potentially) valid.

The variability and limits of interpretation that developed during the twentieth century in quantum physics and mathematics lead to the emergence of the state of information; they are also preconditions for the invention of contemporary digital computer technology. The apparent "naturalness" of the interpretative framework that produces the state of information is closely related to the invention of these technologies, their widespread dissemination, and the current cultural aspirations towards the state of information exhibited by the digital generally. The consequences of this approach remain uncertain precisely because it presents an expanded field of interpretation. Although bounded by pairs of mutually exclusive potentials (as most obvious in the Necker Cube's orientations), the epistemology the state of information implicitly creates is not a system built from dialectics or dualities, but from a range of potentials that include intermediate and hybrid interpretations. The traditional problematics of a knowledge system based on certainty and particular value dissolves into a nodal conception where these values persist, but as dimensions of the system itself.[30]

If dialectic thinking is essentially alchemical—a collision of opposing forces that creates a new, superior result—the expanded field of nodal interpretation is essentially superposed: the result is held in suspension awaiting a collapse into the specifics of a singular result (that remains fundamentally transient). At the same time, the expanded field of interpretation is one where *all* interpretations—even those later disproved empirically—have 'validity' within the range of potential interpretations *as* interpretations; this situation describes the state of information clearly: a description of "all possible interpretations." There is no distinction made between the empirical validity and non-validity of an interpretation because both exist within the range of potentials and their empirical validity is just one of the dimensions that define them as nodes inside the interpretative range generally; this distinction enables the recognition of valid and invalid interpretations (thus avoids falling into a reductive relativism) while at the same time acknowledging the validity of an 'invalid interpretation' within the range of potentials. This recognition is epistemological in nature.

---

[30] The implications of such a construction exceed the parameters of this preliminary description of the state itself.

Chapter Eight

The Demands of Agnotology::Surveillance

Security is a network of social modes autonomously enacting authority (the security apparatus[1]). Central to this framework is the aspiration to the 'state of information' where vast amounts of information are collected and stored precisely so that they can be deployed instrumentally in predicting future behaviors as well as policing past actions. This framework is the interrelationships of surveillance, labor, and capital, which are immediately apparent in Edward Snowden's revelations, starting in 2013, about the scope of the United States' National Security Agency (NSA) pervasive monitoring programs. The authorization for expanding the scope and increasing the breadth of the information collected by the NSA originates with this aspiration to the state of information; however, it is simply one dimension of the political economy of digital capitalism, and so cannot be considered in isolation. Addressing the challenges posed by pervasive monitoring requires a recognition that it is not an isolated phenomenon—it is reflective of a broader collection of mutually

---

[1] Giorgio Agamben, *What is an Apparatus?* trans. David Kishik and Stefan Pedatella (Stanford: Stanford University Press, 2009), 7.

reinforcing tendencies in digital capitalism itself. Surveillance, however broad and omnipresent, nevertheless is simply an epiphenomenon resulting from other, more fundamental demands posed by digital capitalism.

Contemporary surveillance has its origins with earlier forms of surveillance: this issue was an on-going concern in the twentieth century, immediately apparent not only in fictional works (George Orwell's novel *1984*), but in the political realm as well (the scandal over wiretapping in the 1970s known as "Watergate"). Yet there were only occasional moments when the extent of the surveillance being undertaken ever became apparent; its clandestine nature has limited analysis and consideration of its role in digital capitalism. By nature, surveillance is surreptitious, secretive, suspected—but only rarely demonstrated—at the same time, it also demands deception about its existence, a fact that Orwell noted in his novel. The uncertainty prior to Snowden's revelations is reflective of these ambiguities: those memoranda and other documentation leaked to the press by Snowden, unlike similar leaks and claims made in the decade prior to his highly visible release of NSA documents, provided direct evidence of not only the (formerly) conspiracy-theorists' claim that surveillance was omnipresent, but the extent of its technical capacities to record, integrate, and process the vast amount of data generated by automating this surveillance so it no longer required human oversight. To assert the materiality of the digital against disavowals of the physical dimensions of these technologies, in opposition to the "aura of the digital," is essential to this analysis. Digital automation increasingly performs tasks that were formerly the exclusive domain of human intelligence, in the process enabling a broader and more complete surveillance than ever before. The ability to automate the recognition of faces, the ability to listen and transcribe speech—both tasks that require a different kind of intelligence than that found in a clockwork mechanism—has enabled a pervasive monitoring of everyone's every activity rather than a small portion of those performed by selected individuals—this expansive surveillance system is what

Snowden revealed.

The broader significance of this confirmation is neither technical, nor even an issue of privacy: surveillance has become a tool not only of governments, but of business, and of crime. The databases produced through this pervasive monitoring have become productive domains in themselves, creating value through the autonomous digital rearrangement of the information they contain. This new variety of unintelligent production impacts the organization and structure of society as a whole, creating a systemic crisis for capitalist value production that is unlike the periodic financial crises precipitated by a decline in the rate of value production over the past two hundred years: the deployment of surveillance, independent of any particular purpose, is linked to the inherent instability of digital capitalism; the forms of digital automation that enable pervasive monitoring are the root cause of this instability.

However, surveillance is only one half of a complementary pair. The systematic production of uncertainty ("ignorance") termed 'agnotology' provides what surveillance itself cannot: the control and limitation of interpretations (the *use value* of information). Intimate connections between surveillance and agnotology emerged following Snowden's announcement to the press—it was not the document's contents released by Snowden that provided the confirmation of the surveillance program's factuality; it was the response to their release by the United States government that demonstrated not only that the documents were true, but that their contents were of great importance. The tendency to dismiss this information with a "we know this already" response misapprehends their meaning: the confirmation of Snowden's claims is a momentary breach in the agnotology that has historically surrounded information about these broad programs of observation-recording-analysis. Confirmation brought this agnotological dimension into focus, allowing a consideration of how one reinforces the other. These linkages are not apparent when considered in isolation; resistance only becomes possible after their mutually reinforcing relationship becomes visible. This examination of the political economy of the security apparatus through the agnotology::surveillance dynamic is diagnostic in nature. It seeks to make understanding *what* responses, if any, are possible.

§8.1

Linkages between agnotology, hyperreality, and surveillance converge in the security assemblage: a paradigm of observation and control whose function is both immaterially productive (it enables the autonomous semiotic generation of value) and restrictive (it enables the mobilization of physical/immaterial force to defend this immaterial production). These productive-restrictive activities are distinct, yet mutually reinforcing—they form a dynamic cycle masked by the aura of the digital's stripping of physicality from conscious consideration. Without this distanciation of the physical, the productive-restrictive cycles would become apparent through their necessarily disenfranchising actions as human agency is usurped by automated processes and autonomous oversight. The security assemblage appears as an impartial, disinterested alternative to the variable contingency of human agency: its uniformly applied mechanical responses create an illusion of objectivity. This autonomous response is a crystalized ideology, an inflexible restriction iterated by the all-or-nothing logic of digital protocols that are incapable of ambiguity, plurality, or contingency apparent in the "right to read" implemented as Digital Rights Management (DRM)—either you have authorization or you do not. Authorization implicitly demands a continuous monitoring and maintenance where its authoritarian dimensions—what has been termed "pervasive monitoring" by the Internet Engineering Task Force (IETF) in "BCP 188: Pervasive Monitoring Is an Attack"—become readily apparent not only in the immaterial "space" of digital technology, but in the physical world as well. However, the IETF'S description of "pervasive monitoring" should not be limited to immaterial forms of surveillance:

Pervasive Monitoring (PM) is widespread (and often covert) surveillance through intrusive gathering of protocol artifacts, including application content, or protocol metadata such as headers. Active or passive wiretaps and traffic analysis, (e.g., correlation, timing or measuring packet sizes), or subverting the cryptographic keys used to secure protocols can also be used as part of pervasive monitoring. PM is distinguished by being indiscriminate and very large scale, rather than by introducing new types of technical compromise.[2]

The indiscriminate nature of this surveillance—that it captures *all* communications, not only those being specifically targeted for examination, is its necessary and sufficient criterion; the analysis this surveillance offers depends on a vast data collection and collation. Yet this surveillance is not limited to those actions online; it is applied to everyone, both in the physical world and the immaterial realm of the Internet: pervasive monitoring also includes how these digital technologies have been applied to surveillance in the physical world, for example, with facial recognition on streets and in stores, passive traffic cameras that capture and log vehicle movements, and the monitoring of geo-location through cellphone tracking. All the contemporary machineries of surveillance depend on digital technology—whether employed as immaterial production or socio-political control—serving to reify the security assemblage in this implementation of pervasive monitoring itself. These technologies function both for commercial interests and for governments in much the same way: DRM is the most visible prominence of this implicit, ubiquitous system that directly impacts the human readable form of digital objects, but this most apparent example is precisely an isolated surfacing of larger, dominant systems for control and observation that lie within the "data-

[2] See Stephen Farrell, "BCP 188: Pervasive Monitoring Is an Attack," Internet Engineering Task Force document, May 2014, http://www.rfc-editor.org/rfc/rfc7258.txt.

base" that enables immaterial production.

These multivalent dimensions of "security" in digital capitalism reify the convergent aspects of agnotology and surveillance—each is a reciprocal justification for the other: agnotology renders established knowledge uncertain, requiring greater detail and contextual understanding; surveillance provides this understanding, but at the same time produces so much data that its interpretation becomes uncertain because of the destabilizing effects of the equivalences posed by agnotology. Their linkage is a "virtuous circle" in which each begets the other, making their expansion inevitable: the logic providing these justifications is inherently circular, but this circularity is not a flaw of the system, but its precise focus—a circularity necessary for digital capitalism to become dominant.

The prophylactic disenfranchisement of human agency enables the generation of new domains for commercial expansion by transforming *non-productive use values* into new forms of value via immaterial production through the surveillance capacities of digital technology: the transference of this implicitly policing action is apparent in the shift to digital capitalism itself. Once a physically productive economy becomes one based on semiotic manipulation, the foundation of production undergoes a fundamental transformation from facture to reconfiguration—the database as a model. This transformation simultaneously enlists pervasive monitoring via surveillance (data collection) as the technical means for both the expansion of productive capacities and their defense against any socio-political challenges that might emerge. This change invokes surveillance at its most basic level: the immaterial securities that are so central to the circulation of values within digital capitalism depend on the database for their recombinative processes. It is precisely this protocol of recombination and permutation that characterizes digital semiosis as distinct from the meaning-construction of a *human-oriented* semiotic process. The resulting values are unintelligent; their meaning for the database is dependent on the full set, rather than as individual configurations. It is through this unintelligibility that digital production aspires to completeness, revealing its link to the 'goal' of all securitizing processes. This semiosis is the digital aspiration to the state of information coupled with the innate need of digital capitalism for a continuous growth of values. The semiotic expansion of immaterially generated values is apparent in how capitalist productive 'domains' expand within society; all these activities are a reflection of attempts to reify the aura of information in immanent form. This instrumentality demonstrates how aspirations to the state of information become a literal tool of control and prediction (the security assemblage). Thus, agnotology is not a *cause,* but a *symptom* of the expansive nature of the semiotic processes embedded within and enabled by digital capitalism.

Disjunctions between physical assets and their role as immaterial tokens in semiotic production (via the database) reflect the structural demand in capitalism for continuous expansion (growth). Semiotic production is unintelligent, generating values through logical operations rather than directed, coherent action; it is autonomous, but unconscious. Agnotology is uniquely suited to the demands of digital capitalist surveillance by interrupting the evaluative process assumed to lie at the base of all market decisions (the "rationality of markets")—agnotological uncertainty makes any choice appear equally "good" (valid)—conventionally closed only by the utility (use value) of those interpretations: it emerges when the contingent relationships between production and representation are recognized as being arbitrary, whose meaning is unstable, with dependencies relative to their particular application at any given moment, a process inherent to the unintelligence of semiotic facture. This continuous expansion of immaterial production is a simultaneous expansion of value accumulation without restraint. Eliding differences allows the semiotic manipulation of values; the "openness" of interpretation expands without constraint. This shift is performed by the complex relationship of physical and immaterial commodities in the valorization process mediated by agnotology and surveillance.

Connections between agnotology and hyperreality provide the foundation for the 'security assemblage.' Their similarities are readily apparent: *agnotology* is a particular failure of knowledge and interpretation (focused epistemologically on the methods and procedures by which we arrive at conclusions, think), while the *hyperreal* is a specific effect on perception/conception of the physical world itself (focused ontologically, transforming the underlying interpretation of the physical). Both have a semiotic character, but with divergent foci. Their impacts on interpretation originate with the same semiotic function in digital capitalism: the substitution of the semiotically produced for immanent physicality, enabling/contributing to the capitalist demand for the expansion of markets into new, previously unvalorized domains. These processes act together as enablers for semiotic recombination, each reinforcing the other in the denial of physicality inherent to digital capitalism.

§8.1.a

The semiotic dissolution of 'reality' into interpretations contingent on a collection of *a priori* assumptions—the hyperreal—is a precondition for the dominance of agnotology. The processes inaugurated by the rupture between the hyperreal and the conception of the (historical) reality it supplanted are logically circular, self-reinforcing methodologies: where 'the real' was considered uniform and inviolate, the hyperreal is contingent and fabricated. This shift is not a "crisis of meaning," but a transformation of meaning *qua* meaning, from a singular construction (linear) to a multiplicity of contingent potentials (network). The aura of information and the aspiration towards the state of information dominate this process of semiotic production: they are eminent in the network of different (competing) contingencies as any 'the real' enables the reification of information as/within a database upon which various 'operations' produce momentary, unintelligent interpretations—semiotic (re)configurations—that can and will be challenged by later emergent alternatives.

Hyperreality is a shift to a "contingent epistemology" that reveals/depends on a fundamental uncertainty about ontology: in replacing 'the real' with its (semiotic) double, those empirical foundations commonly employed as a check on interpretations become subject to flux, variability, and instability. The ability to distinguish causes from effects, epistemological from ontological concerns, and knowledge from uncertainty depend on a stable system of signification that is no longer available with the emergence of hyperreality. Elision of *a priori* distinctions, their conflagration, is the operative demonstration that the hyperreal is dominant: the particular breach in epistemological understanding undermines knowledge in other domains in a mutually disruptive fashion. The meta-stable (contingent) nature of the hyperreal was noted by Jean Baudrillard in his prominent theorization, "The Precession of Simulacra," that developed the semiotic dimensions of the hyperreal explicitly as an ontological instability that creates epistemic doubt:

> All the hypotheses of manipulation are reversible in an endless whirligig. For manipulation is a floating causality where positivity and negativity engender and overlap with one another, where there is no longer any active or passive....Is any given bombing in Italy the work of leftist extremists, or of extreme right-wing provocation, or staged by centrists to bring every terrorist extreme into disrepute and to shore up its own failing power, or again, is it a police-inspired scenario in order to appeal to public security?[3]

The nature of "any given bombing" (its ontology) becomes a demonstration of the hyperreal: because all 'terrorist' actions are done to evoke a specific *political* result, and so are not neutral, naturally occurring events, their underlying, intentional purpose is also always a specific political goal that de-

---

[3] Jean Baudrillard, *Simulations*, trans. Phil Beitchman, Paul Foss, and Paul Patton (New York: Semiotext(e), 1983), 30–32.

pends on the ontological origins of the event itself, quite apart from the 'terrorist' action. In assessing these events, what renders them comprehensible as *political actions* is the creation of an interpretation revealing, demonstrating, and/or inferring this innate purpose (identifying the ontological nature of the particular event). The "'ignorance'" that hyperreality describes is of a different character than traditional 'ignorance': it is an "'ignorance'" that is superposed between true/false, certain/uncertain, known/unknown. In place of opposition, these positions lose their distinctness and become *equivalent*. Baudrillard's argument suggests those developments now recognized as agnotology: any interpretation is more accurately understood as a direct product of the particular model—*simulation*—employed to gene-rate a specific interpretation (understood as the organization of 'facts' and their meaning). The range of mutually exclusive interpretations he poses for any such "terrorist" act are superposed: all these potentials cannot be true at the same time, yet distinguishing one from another is problematic, if not impossible. Digital semiosis reiterates the protocols of hyperreality: the resulting values are unintelligent, their meaning dependent on the full set, rather than as individual significations. Which particular interpretation is selected as "true" reflects the innate biases of the human interpreter, rather than a logic of 'facts.' (The hyperreal is mute to binary oppositions such as true/false, factual/counterfactual, real/unreal that rationalize superposition into singularity.) Interpretation depends on *a priori* models; the hyperreal/agno-tological disrupt human agency not through a *dis*avowal of meaning, but through a surplussage of superposed potentials.

Employing models to create interpretations demonstrates 'the real' is specifically semiotic precisely because 'the real' is contained by its model (simulation) in a web of interdependent interpretations where any given 'fact' is at one and the same time another model and series of relationships whose stability ('factness') is contingent on their arrangement within the particular interpretation. The semiotic nature of interpretation is not limited to significance (meaning), but includes other forms of interpretation that are also subject to the same contingency under hyperreality: affect, causation, sensory experience...the instability (or contingent nature) of all interpretations in hyperreality is agnotology. Each particular interpretation depends on a network of potentials focused around *how* the event-being-interpreted is conceived in advance of its interpretation by the model used to produce that particular understanding: its nature as a *political* action in service of a particular *political* end is therefore dependent on the *specific model* employed to evaluate it, shaping conclusions in advance of their creation: agnotology is the particular "ignorance" of hyperreality that is the inability to select a 'fact,' any 'fact.'

§8.1.b

The meta-stability Baudrillard identifies as symptomatic of the hyperreal is the affective result of agnotology—that no interpretation can be definitively chosen is precisely his point. This model itself is symptomatic of how contingencies collapse 'certainty' into its opposite: an infinite regression of signifiers around a 'fact,' any 'fact'—thus, agnotological. Our inability to separate one potential interpretation from others reflects the shift from a realm of facts (reality) to one based in a logic of semiosis (hyperreality)—this transformation of knowledge and its foundations in argument is the effect of agnotological processes in action. The network of these potential interpretations and relationships (even those that are mutually exclusive) define the event-being-interpreted through a web of potential relationships and exclusions (the state of information). The editorial selection and fabrication of a singular interpretation reflects one set of 'facts' that may be countered by an alternative set that is equally potential, plausible, yet mutually exclusive and contradictory: this shifting of connections is the aura of information in action. The uncertainty of this situation reflects how the initial rupture (the hyperreal) challenges *established* knowledge; it describes an epistemological failure of empirical and logical relationships that disrupts not only epistemological but ontological knowledge as well.

Agnotology engages in semiosis precisely by ungrounding the conventional limitations imposed via utilitarian concerns (the demand that *use value* be homologous with a particular *use*). The apparent opposition of these two features of digital capitalism is ironic since both function in the same fundamental way to expand/generate new domains for capitalist valorization. Semiotic production creates value limited only by the scarcity of capital. What appears in this new unbounded mode is a surfeit production of *use values* without function (*use*); it separates agency from efficacy, resulting in all evaluations of significance coming to depend on irrational (affective) procedures quite independent of any potential result or application.

Hyperreality and agnotology are mutual reflections enabling the expansion of digital capitalism through the surveillance demanded by this aspiration to the state of information: the final potential Baudrillard suggests—"a police-inspired scenario in order to appeal to public security"—is not an accident or coincidence; 'terrorism' always serves as opportunity for capitalist expansion into unvalorized domains. The distinction between the intrusion of the police and the intrusion of commercial interests in digital capitalism disappears with the decomposition into translation/ recording of all activities as data, and the concurrent emergence of pervasive monitoring as autonomous productive action. In an interview with *The Atlantic* in 2010,[4] Google CEO Eric Schmidt makes this innate linkage between surveillance and production both threatening and obvious:

> We know where you are. We know where you've been. We can more or less know what you're thinking about.

[4] See Derek Thompson, "Google's CEO: 'The Laws are Written by Lobbyists'," *The Atlantic*, October 10, 2010, http:// www.theatlantic.com/technology/archive/2010/10/googles-ceo-the-laws-are-written-by-lobbyists/63908/#video.

[...] Your digital identity will live forever...because there's no delete button.[5]

The potential immortality of digital files means that, unless destroyed, their information remains available and accessible in perpetuity—the collection and reconfiguration of data necessitates the maintenance and expansion of the database. Without this ever expanding archive, the valorization produced by semiotic production cannot proceed: it depends on the ability to generate novel relationships. Demands for increasingly intrusive data collection is an integral part of how semiosis interfaces with surveillance—it becomes the primary activity of this production: *surveillance is its own end product.* This assertion of dominance enabling and enabled by continuous, omnipresent surveillance makes authoritarianism the logical form of this political economy: whatever the organization of society, it will inevitably tend towards concentrations of power and authority as these are reflections of the structural demands imposed by the dynamics of the security assemblage.

§8.1.c

The annexation of new domains for digital capitalism requires the replacement of 'the real' with the hyperreal, since this shift *is* the fundamental condition for semiotic production's dominance; the 'security' network (most apparent as surveillance itself) is a fundamental dimension of semiotic production. The commercial and authoritarian dimensions of surveillance merge and overlap in this process: the NSA surveillance programs disclosed by Snowden are simultaneously both a government collection protocol that employs commercial digital technology and resources (Snowden himself was *not* a government employee, but rather an "outside

---

[5] See Yasha Levine, "The Psychological Dark Side of Gmail," *Alternet,* December 31, 2013, http://www.alternet.org/media/google-using-gmail-build-psychological-profiles-hundreds-millions-people.

contractor" working for a commercial enterprise[6]) and data-bases of valuable commercial data. Semiosis removes 'intent' from the crystalized form that *purpose* assumes in the data-base, expanding into previously non-semiotic realms, mirror-ing the expansion of capitalism into unvalorized domains, in the process demonstrating how digital capitalism has broken *value* generation free from any constraint imposed by *use value.*

Surveillance is the logical antithesis of agnotology: it acts to produce certainty rather than uncertainty. 'Security' pro-vides a far-reaching, nebulous justification for a range of ac-tions, from expansions of surveillance (immaterial pro-duction), to war and imperialism (primitive accumulation). Baudrillard's "police-inspired scenario in order to appeal to public security" serves as an underlying excuse for violations and suspensions of human rights, due process, and habeas corpus. All the various interpretations enabled by the in-strumental database are united by an implicit threat—whether physical (violence) or immaterial (default)—that justifies imposed/intrusive authority ('police action') as a protective measure. 'Reality' has become an effect of what data has been collected and stored, as David Cole noted in his discussion of how the NSA uses their surveillance-generated database to make assessments of threat:

> NSA General Counsel Stewart Baker has said, "metadata absolutely tells you everything about somebody's life. If you have enough metadata, you don't really need con-tent." When I quoted Baker at a recent debate at Johns Hopkins University [*The Price of Privacy: Re-Evaluating the NSA, A Debate,* April 7, 2014], my opponent, General Michael Hayden, former director of the NSA and the CIA, called Baker's comment "absolutely correct," and

---

[6] See Luke Harding, "How Edward Snowden Went from Loyal NSA Contractor to Whistleblower," *The Guardian,* February 1, 2014, http://www.theguardian.com/world/2014/feb/01/edward-snowden-intelligence-leak-nsa-contractor-extract.

raised him one, asserting, "We kill people based on meta-data."[7]

The expansion/assimilation of data becomes the totalizing nature of the database via the recording/recoding: semiosis reifies this continuous surveillance as instrumentality; the database is 'reality.' Everyone is potentially a 'terror' threat. It identifies those allowed to live and those who are killed, shift-ing responsibility from the human agents who give the orders to kill, to the digital system's encoding and arrangement of data. The question the database requires is (as with any 'ter-rorist action') one of purpose: *what is it for?* The NSA pro-gram known in the mid-2000s as "Total Information Aware-ness"[8] makes the answer literally apparent, and its digital aspirations explicit: to convert the state of information into immanent instrumentality. Security researcher Wolfgang Sutzl identified this fundamental purpose with the ability to contain and anticipate outcomes, linking it to the *instrumen-tal* function of a productive apparatus:

...[T]he actions through which security is "performed" concern the construction of physical and informational architectures of seriousness and essential "sameness." Here, everything happens the way it happens because other possibilities have been rendered impossible.[9]

The "uniformity" Sutzl describes is a consequence of the digi-tal recording itself—the transformation of all actions and

[7] David Cole, "We Kill People Based on Metadata," *New York Re-view of Books*, May 10, 2014, http://www.nybooks.com/blogs/nyr blog/2014/may/10/we-kill-people-based-metadata/.
[8] The 'Total Information Awareness' Program has been extensively discussed and covered in the press. For a summary, *The Center for Media and Democracy* provides background on such programs through their "Source Watch" website: http:// www.sourcewatch.org /index.php?title=Total_Information_Awareness.
[9] Wolfgang Sutzl, "Tragic Extremes," *CTheory*, September 9, 2007, http://www.ctheory.net/articles.aspx?id=582.

events into data (following the aura of information). Ideology is reified as technology, its demands become the only potentials possible in an attempt to contain and limit those alternative potentials always already present in the state of information. Producing value (economic or political) by reconfiguring and rearranging data has as its goal this total containment of future outcomes; its predictive capacity is an aspiration to the state of information—a system attempting to create an instrumentality of "completeness"—and is the reason that the agnotology arising from this state simultaneously requires/enables its antithesis, surveillance.

§8.1.d

All selections and choices become contingent, an effect of attempts to render the state of information as instrumentality: incompatible interpretations are equivalent within this database, ironically reflecting the demands posed by agnotology. The irrationality and arbitrariness of this agnotological marketplace reflects the priorities of the database (the aura of information): *all* positions are equivalent as data points; the conception as information (data) disregards its meaning (*use value*)—collapsing historical dualities of true/false, real/unreal, life/death. Agnotology produces a 'capitalist market' where no rational decision is possible in a dynamic where the demands of the security assemblage create the conditions for agnotology through surveillance, reinforcing the demand for greater certainty posed by pervasive monitoring itself. In the absence of epistemological checks against 'reality,' any decision becomes inherently a reflection of irrational factors extrinsic to evaluation. The disenfranchisement of human agency the database produces is the reiteration of this shift, a disavowal of responsibility for actions onto the matrix of surveillance data, separating effect from choice—a result uniting both the political and commercial dimensions of the agnotology::surveillance dynamic.

Meaning is independent of the database itself; the collection of data and its relations follow semiotic rules of combination, but without the lexical concern for their significance. Data reflects only the uniformity of the digital protocol—reifying and aspiring to the state of information—all positions, even when contradictory and mutually exclusive, coexist as discrete datapoints awaiting semiosis. This process is not capable of concern with the meaning (*value*) of what has been collected, indexed, referenced, and compiled. The nature of these values depends on how the database is employed—whether for commercial or political reasons, the results are irrelevant to the form and collection of data; values only become apparent through semiotic (re)configuration. Their significance (the *use value* of a particular semiotic configuration) is beyond the scope of what has been catalogued; it is the nature of the semiotic processes within the database that any significance generated remain unrecognized. This valorization of (previously private) non-productive action enables the transformation of all formerly non-productive activities into varieties of labor from which *value* can be extracted through the creation of a broad new arena for economic development without corresponding compensation: the 'digital author'—the subject of the surveillance created and reified in/through the database itself. The ambivalent nature of this production reflects a semiotic reassembly with both political and commercial functions, where any values created are shifts in categorization and internal relationship specific to the database (the valorized liquidation of *use value* via surveillance). Such a process is not dependent on human agency—it is instead automated through algorithmic analysis, a semiotic production without human intervention or direct oversight.

§8.2.a

The 'security assemblage' originates with the everyday understanding of "security": a cluster of ideas focused on protection, freedom, and vigilance—as well as a specific meaning in *financial* terms: the linkage of legal obligations to specific debts. This assemblage's formulation is coincident with capitalist investment practices generally; this fact emerges when we remember that investments are called "securities." The underlying displacement or postponement of the 'desired' result (the definitional 'goal')—actually producing "security"—is required for the security assemblage to function, a symptom-effect of the underlying capitalist dynamic embodied in it: the investment in an expected but nevertheless *hypothetical* (i.e. the "risk" of investing in a stock) future "payoff." This offset of results from means creates a linkage of expanding surveillance following the logic of surveillance itself: the limitations discovered by surveillance necessitate further examination, inaugurating a fractal-like infinite recursion, recalling Michel Foucault's observation in *Birth of the Clinic* that "knowledge invents the secret."[10] It is precisely the observational demands of empiricism that those domains *not* subject to observation become apparent. Once set in motion, the demands of "security" require perpetually intensifying effort, apparent in surveillance itself. This continuous, expansive demand is not a failure of surveillance, but a demonstration of its efficacy.

Because the security assemblage's main purpose is the impossible task of eliminating all "risk," it provides the ideal capitalist product: one that all citizens must purchase, but which can never actually be delivered—all profit, no risk; it is the imaginary "free lunch" reified in the aura of the digital. Continuously expanding investments in security coupled with the increasing expenditures on surveillance they necessitate are fundamental features of the security state, as is the continuous expansion of pervasive monitoring into all aspects of life. These technologies and protocols of observation-recording-analysis were recognized by the IETF as being *uniformly* deployed by criminals, corporations, and governments in their assessment of the impact that pervasive monitoring has on privacy. The transformative effects they note demonstrate the agnotology::surveillance dialectic at work:

---

[10] Michel Foucault, *The Birth of the Clinic: An Archaeology of Medical Perception* (London: Routledge, 2003), 200–201.

[Pervasive monitoring is an attack that] may change the content of the communication, record the content or external characteristics of the communication, or through correlation with other communication events, reveal information the parties did not intend to be revealed. It may also have other effects that similarly subvert the intent of a communicator. [...] The motivation for PM can range from non-targeted nation-state surveillance, to legal but privacy-unfriendly purposes by commercial enterprises, to illegal actions by criminals. The same tech-niques to achieve PM can be used regardless of motivation. Thus, we cannot defend against the most nefarious actors while allowing monitoring by other actors no matter how benevolent some might consider them to be, since the actions required of the attacker are indistinguishable from other attacks.[11]

As the introduction to this report notes, there is no *a priori* means to distinguish between actors (criminal/corporate/government) in terms of how they use the tools of surveillance. The methods and technology employed in pervasive monitoring is *neutral* to the human intent of its deployment, reflecting the underlying nature of the database and its reification of the state of information. This is the reason the IETF terms this surveillance an "attack." It is the technique itself that produces the problem it seeks to resolve: it is continuously countered by the agnotology that provides its proximate justification[12]—thus there is a continual expansion (the "pervasive" in '*pervasive* monitoring') because achieving the "completeness" that is the goal of this security-through-surveillance is impossible.

However, this duality—agnotology::surveillance—is an adaptive network that impedes resistance and ensnares all activities attempting to escape or evade its logic (to the extent

---

[11] Farrell, "BCP 188: Pervasive Monitoring Is an Attack."
[12] James Tully, "Communication and Imperialism," *CTheory*, February 22, 2006, http://www.ctheory.net/articles.aspx?id=508.

that 'terrorism' can be seen as a variety of 'anti-globalization protest,' it is a failure because it generates and substantiates the security assemblage.) This amorphous, absorptive complex reflects the requirements created by security's structural aspiration (shared by the digital) to achieving the state of information as immanent instrumentality of prediction and control: based in semiotic networks of relationships, this process is infinite, uncompleteable, thus continuously demanding more data gathered through ever greater surveillance. Schmidt's comment, "We can more or less know what you're thinking about,"[13] documents this instrumental goal through the presumption that what the surveilled "think about" and what those thoughts *are* coincide with the materials interceptable via surveillance. His presumption that what is collected in the database is capable of completely describing those individuals being examined demonstrates the authoritarian dimensions of this instrumentality: those who are so fully described that their thoughts are predictable cannot be considered "free" in any sense of the term.

Attempts to unmask this construct inaugurates the infinite regression of hyperreality where what one finds 'beneath' one semiotic mask is simply a second, a third, each identifiable by the progressive ease of its rupture: the underlying nature of the hyperreal is its construction as constellated signs, themselves moveable into new arrangements. The infinity of interpretations develops the arbitrariness of semiotic disassembly into a regression of successive layers, producing a vertigo of interpretation recognizable in the aura of information itself—an unbounded process that is a reification of the state of information. The agnotology::surveillance dynamic cannot be challenged along traditional lines of rational interrogation, logic, or evidence: these are always already captured by this process since they posit a retrograde return to *use value* (immanent 'reality'); concern for a metaphysical value created through ethical (moral) considerations of social reproduction is cast aside by a technological determinism

[13] Levine, "The Psychological Dark Side of Gmail."

that replaces the human with the autonomous digital—social functions supplanted by digital efficacy. That this shift is also simultaneously a function of digital capitalism presents a direct demonstration of how it deploys information collection (pervasive monitoring) in its aspiration to achieve the state of information as an immanent instrumentality without regard for social or legal constraint.

§8.2.b

The periodic crashes of capitalism are a symptom of the over-extension inherent in capitalism itself, apparent in cycles of excessive production Karl Marx described in the nineteenth century:

> The stupendous productivity developing under the capitalist mode of production relative to population, and the increase, if not in the same proportion, of capital-values (not just of their material substance), which grow much more rapidly than the population, contradict the basis, which constantly narrows in relation to the expanding wealth, and for which all this immense productiveness works. They also contradict the conditions under which this swelling capital augments its value. Hence the crises.[14]

The "crises" Marx identifies are specifically financial, and instead of offering expansions and potentials for capitalist growth, they are destructive of value: it is the contradictions between "expanding wealth," the conditions of production, and the purpose of capitalist production generally that creates the crisis. The difference between physical facture and semiotic facture become apparent in the role that crisis has in Marx's account, and its role in semiotic production. The cri-

---

[14] Karl Marx, *Capital*, Vol. 3, ed. Friedrich Engels (New York: International Publishers, 1999), 181; online version, eds. Tim Delaney and M. Griffin, https://www.marxists.org/archive/marx/works/ down load/pdf/Capital-Volume-III.pdf.

sis of the nineteenth century is one of over production out-
stripping demand and the capacity to generate profit. In digital capitalism "crisis" arises from inabilities to meet the
demands posed by the scarcity of capital's constraints on
semiotic facture: it is only through the addition of an external
source of value that the system can continue. The shift from
capital as repository of value to capital as title to future production forces an expansion into previously unvalorized domains; surveillance mirrors the capitalist colonization of
these same domains: they are different aspects of the same
process of expansion where any crisis, natural or manmade,
can provide an opportunity for exploitation as a revenue
source for capitalist expansion. The perversity of this system
arises because there are a finite number of external sources,
and when those are depleted, the system necessarily enters a
crisis.

However, moments of 'systemic failure' are not indicators
that capitalism will implode; instead what occurs is a re-
trenching that results in an expansion of capitalist processes
into new domains in what journalist Naomi Klein called
"disaster capitalism." Her book of the same title explained
the exploitation of disruptive social events as a method of
economic expansion:

> On August 5, 2004, the White House created the *Office of
> the Coordinator for Reconstruction and Stabilization*. [...]
> The office's mandate is not to rebuild any old states, you
> see, but to create "democratic and market-oriented ones.
> [...] The work is far too slow, if it is happening at all. For-
> eign consultants live high on costs-plus expense accounts
> and thousand-dollar-a-day salaries, while locals are shut
> out of much-needed jobs, training and decision-making.
> Expert "democracy builders" lecture governments on the
> importance of transparency and "good governance," yet
> most contractors and NGOs refuse to open their books to
> those same governments, let alone give them control over
> how their aid money is spent. [...] But if the reconstruc-
> tion industry is stunningly inept at rebuilding, that may

be because rebuilding is not its primary purpose. According to [Shalmali Guttal, a Bangalore-based researcher with Focus on the Global South], "It's not reconstruction at all—it's about reshaping everything." If anything, the stories of corruption and incompetence serve to mask this deeper scandal: the rise of a predatory form of disaster capitalism that uses the desperation and fear created by catastrophe to engage in radical social and economic engineering. And on this front, the reconstruction industry works so quickly and efficiently that the privatizations and land grabs are usually locked in before the local population knows what hit them.[15]

'Systemic failure' offers digital capitalism an opportunity to expand through the liquidation/elimination of competition—both economic and political (consider the repressive effects that spread through the United States of America as a result of 'terrorist' actions in 2001). These 'systemic failures' make the security assemblage explicit—what is *secured* is the ability of capitalist expansion to continue: reconstruction after a natural disaster, rebuilding after war, or "recovery" is primarily an opportunity for the profit-generating *process of stabilization*: expanding demands for *new* production. The ideal situation for this unconstrained capitalist expansion is an open-ended conflict without apparent criteria for victory or readily attainable grounds for an end to the conflict itself: the "Cold War" between the United States and the Soviet Union during the twentieth century provided a similar framework for expansion and revenue generation to the "War on Terror." Actions that lead to a reduction or resolution of the conditions creating 'terror' are less significant than the exploitation of the those actions as a means to further establish and expand these processes; it is precisely how surveillance seeks to justify its violations of both legal and

[15] Naomi Klein, "The Rise of Disaster Capitalism," in *The Nation*, April 14, 2005, http://www.thenation.com/article/rise-disaster-capitalism/.

historical limits on its expansion throughout the social.

Security necessarily employs ever increasing monitoring: surveillance, data mining, and "coercive interrogation" (torture) are all part of the same cycle of observation-recording-analysis that defines the 'security assemblage.' It does not matter what the proximate cause (source) is—or whether it is successful in the attack—any particular challenge to the authority of this system is thus irrelevant *a priori,* since each event only serves to strengthen the systemic demand for pervasive monitoring: in the security assemblage, a failure in the instrumentality of information demonstrates the need for greater surveillance, not its futility.

§8.3.a

Where law acts to ameliorate, security seeks to dominate through a totalitarian control not just of actions but of all *potential* actions. Security becomes an impossible goal because it postulates and requires the complete ability to monitor and predict all future behaviors; the conjunction of an ascendant 'security assemblage' and the emergence of the digital is not coincidental—the attempt to actualize the assemblage depends on the digital processing and immediate recall encased within the database itself. Semiotic production (via the database), the hyperreal, and agnotology reflect the same structural demand in capitalism for continuous expansion (growth). Their development is mutually reinforcing as they are complementary dimensions of the same implicit processes in action: the shift to a semiotic model of production that itself has a modular, recombinative character.

Automation is ideally suited to the inherently permutational character of semiotic production: the logical rearrangement of a limited quantity of variables into all possible configurations. This is the logic of the database deployed as productive methodology—one that can proceed without human agency since it is mechanical, rather than one which requires the intervention of human judgment. This kind of production is most immediately apparent in the use of High

Frequency Trading (HFT) systems: computers and software employ algorithms that automate decisions about stock purchase orders including price, timing, and size without human intervention; HFT generates financialized profits from the exchange of stocks, commodities, and other derivatives in the financial markets. For these computer programs, speed and proximity to the financial markets (via high speed data connections) are essential to their ability to generate multiple, sequential trades in microseconds. It is this factor that necessitates their being automated systems using digital technology.

HFT reveals one of the clearest examples of the semiotic procedures of digital capitalism in action. The Nanex analysis of the first "flash crash" in 2010 demonstrates how agnotology can be translated into forms that impact automated systems as well, simply by using the sequential nature of data processing (i.e., the linearity of computers) to create immanent uncertainty.

The first HFT "flash crash" in the financial markets happened on May 6, 2010. This event presents a model for how agnotology can emerge within autonomous digital systems; machines lack the comprehension of meaning characteristic of agnotology in human interpretations—agnotology can only be created through exploiting the structure of the machinic instrumentality itself: it arises through an asymmetry of information in an otherwise "open system" where all participants have equal access—a reflection of the 'transparency' digital systems need for pervasive monitoring to be fully efficacious. It seems reasonable to assume that this exploit will become the norm unless rules are implemented to prevent it. Their analysis noted the agnotological effect and considered its implications within the financial markets:

Approximately 400ms before the eMini sale, the quote traffic rate for all NYSE, NYSE Arca, and Nasdaq stocks surged to saturation levels within 75ms. This is a new and surprising discovery. Previouisly, when we looked at time frames below 1 second, we thought the increase in quote traffic coincided with the heavy sales, but we now know that the surge in quotes preceded the trades by about 400ms. The discovery is surprising, because nearly all the trades in the eMini and ETFs occurred at prevailing bid prices (a liquidity removing event).

While searching previous days for similarities to the time period at the start of the May 6th drop, we found a very close match starting at 11:27:46.100 on April 28, 2010 -- just a week and a day before May 6th. We observed it had the same pattern -- high, saturating quote traffic, then approximately 500ms later a sudden burst of trades on the eMini and the top ETF's at the prevailing bid prices, leading to a delay in the NYSE quote and a sudden collapse in prices. The drop only lasted a minute, but the parallels between the start of the drop and the one on May 6th are many....

The quote traffic surged again during the ETF sell event and remained at saturation levels for nearly 500ms. Additional selling waves began seconds later sending quote traffic rates back to saturation levels. This tidal wave of data caused delays in many feed processing systems and networks. We discovered two notable delays: the NYSE network that feeds into CQS (the "NYSE-CQS Delay"), and the calculation and dissemination of the Dow Jones Indexes (DOW Delay).[16]

The italicized text identifies the agnotological function in operation here: the "congestion" caused by the large number of quotes forces other HFT systems (those not already aware of the quotes because they didn't generate them) to process these requests—creating an information gap between one system and all the others. The discrepancy in information possessed by one system generating quotes vs. all others who must process those same quotes, enables the system which generated the quotes to gain a competitive edge because it

[16] *Nanex Flash Crash Summary Report,* September 27, 2010, http://www.nanex.net/FlashCrashFinal/FlashCrashSummary.html.

does not need to process the sequence as a whole to assess its impact. For information processing systems, what we can see with this action is the automation of an agnotism and its application to the HFT computers. The time required to process the series of quotes has an impact on what the other HFT systems will do, but first they must address the entire sequence; the system generating those quotes already has this information.

Because successful interpretation depends specifically on both access to relevant information, and the more specific ability to apply and employ it, the organization as a whole has an in-built bias towards the accumulation and concentration of information maximally. The baseline condition for success within such structures historically has been one determined by an information differential: those lying at the greater end of the gradient tend towards success and dominance, with those falling at the lesser end tend to fail, excluding such mediating factors as already established positions and authorities that tend to replicate themselves. Information differentials scale between aggregate actions by individuals within this construct. It is the means by which we evaluate claims and establish basic facts that agnotology challenges: *dissent* over foundational information and basic questions of what the 'facts' *are* produces agnotology, with the concomitant, necessary result that agnotology blocks our ability to create ordered, logical interpretations. In this regard agnotology behaves in a schizoid fashion, splitting and conflating the relationship of cause and effect, their identity as logical sequence.

§8.3.b

Since the automation in HFT is typical of all forms of digital facture—the digital procedures all having the same foundation as instrumental code—the question to ask is *whose desires does it serve?* Automated facture has a different character than the autonomy of the (human) agency it replaces: the particular form of a digital work when rendered for human viewing/encounter makes the *purpose* of both the code and the particular data stream it engages apparent, whether it "is" a movie, a piece of music, a text or anything else: the data itself is encoded *for* human purposes. The illusion that our devices function without our input, without responding to our desires and demands, is a reflection of their (human-originating) design, and the functions these machines are constructed to achieve—the superficially mysterious, perfect nature of the digitally manufactured, its magical aura—works to obscure the underlying physical reality of the digital and its subservience to human choices and agency—these foundations are all hidden by the aura of the digital. The creation of agnotological effects depends on individual human agency whose cumulative impacts emerge with variable coherence at different levels of social organization; the dependent relationship between the functioning of the digital technology and the demands made by the desires of human society (providing its formal basis in capitalism).

Without a social function—given and directed by the human agency that puts these devices into action—the digital, however active the device itself may be, is unintelligent. It is confronted by immaterial production's generation of *value* without function (*use value*): that digital technology is designed for and functions in service to particular human demands is lost when the aura of the digital dominates. Technology is a crystallization of human agency externalized in/as the machine; not only do we forget their physical basis as devices, we also forget their dependence on human desires and demands, enabling the transfer of agency to the autonomous system. Like all machines, digital software and hardware are constructed to meet specific human-originating goals, and these goals are the 'reality' of function (the *use value* of the machine), not the instrumentality it creates (its *use*).

The social realm of human desires and needs are of an entirely different order than their instrumentalities. The connections are implicit, rather than explicit, and so require a jump of interpretation to move from one level of this construction to another: the structure as a whole is necessarily interrelated to the political economy and social organization of the human society that produced it. And it is here that the duality of the digital becomes apparent from its earliest moments as a (military) technology being developed in American universities during the 1950s and 1960s.

§8.4.a

Digital technology intersects with the political economy and the *problema* posed by human agency (labor) in this convergence of agnotology, hyperreality, and surveillance. Agnotology hijacks the traditional need to accumulate information (literalized in/by digital technology's storage and databasing of data without reference to its nature, factuality, meaning, or interconnectedness) through its relationship to the state of information: it necessarily introduces equally valid, yet contradictory, information and interpretations. The issue becomes not simply a matter of economic or class structure, but of relations of greater and lesser control produced, maintained, and reified by *how* digital technology and the ideology of the digital reinforce each other in this accumulation of alternatives that generates ambiguity around issues of basic factuality and fundamental knowledge; the database and its semiotic processes proceed without the possibility of recognition or comprehension of any meaning thus produced.

The underlying implication of capitalist valuations (the concept of *exchange value*) is that *value* resides in productive action where currency represents a promissory note secured by future production; in digital capitalism, *use value* becomes a productive (immaterial) source of 'new' *value* via the semiotic process itself—this is the immaterial facture specific to digital systems. Automation entails a shift entirely unlike human labor, as Marx noted about the inherent connections necessitated by labor, society, and capital:

> The capitalist process of production is simultaneously a process of accumulation....But with the development of

social productivity of labor the mass of produced use-values, of which the means of production form a part, grows still more. And the additional labor, through whose appropriation this additional wealth can be reconverted into capital, does not depend on the value, but on the mass of these means of production (including means of subsistence), because in the production process the laborers have nothing to do with the value, but with the use-value, of the means of production. Accumulation itself, however, and the concentration of capital that goes with it, is a material means of increasing productivity. Now, this growth of the means of production includes the growth of the working population, the creation of a working population, which corresponds to the surplus-capital, or even exceeds its general requirements, thus leading to an over-population of workers....by applying methods which yield relative surplus-value (introduction and improvement of machinery) it would produce a far more rapid, artificial, relative over-population, which in its turn, would be a breeding-ground for a really swift propagation of the population, since under capitalist production misery produces population.[17]

While Marx is describing literal population growth, such an interpretation would be incomplete: while the quantity of human labor does increase, its growth is a given, no matter what happens. The replacement of human labor by machines, however, has an immediate and dramatic impact: a 'working population' that exceeds the productive requirements of capital for labor. Price inflation—the increased price of commodities and the consequent devaluation of currency—is recognizable as a superficial increase in value counterposed by the equalizing force of currency devaluation: there are no "profits" being produced, only a reshuffling of promissory notes against future production, foreshadowing digital capitalism. These costs of this labor, what Marx called "variable

[17] Marx, *Capital,* Vol. 3, 150–151.

capital," are resolved as automation supplants human agency into "constant capital": the costs of machinery and raw materials without the variable expenditures posed by human labor. The result is an apparent production of value without an expenditure of any *values* produced by human labor: the generation of commodities through autonomous labor suggests a fundamental rupture in the production of values within capitalism, implying the irrelevance of human labor and social foundations for value in digital capitalism; this implication is the aura of the digital splitting physical from immaterial concerns, even as it elides the physical entirely.

§8.4.b

Marx's conception of uniform labor power (untrained productive ability) inherently requires a basic 'lack of skill.' Its negation of social reproduction (dissolution of human agency) is inherent in this paradigm shift as it transforms compartmentalized human labor to automation and then to immaterial labor—from human activity to autonomous, semiotically generated commodity. Automated production and the earlier fragmentation of the assembly line are a challenge to human agency through their displacement of the skilled craftsman's expertise and productive capacity. This fact finds ironic implementation through the rejection of 'decoration' (the most apparent marker of highly skilled hand labor) common to the art and design movements at the end of the nineteenth century focused on the critique of industrial production. The linkages of commercial and moral concerns in Adolph Loos' discussion of production, "Ornament and Crime" (1910), is typical of the paternalistic view of labor intrinsic to capitalism—what in the United States was called the "Protestant Work Ethic"—a linkage that enables and validates what are primarily commercial determinants and excuses for the social stratification of society and the forms of value generated through automation. Loos' rejection of human agency ensures the displacement of skilled labor by unskilled labor, a factor in the industrialization of the 'arts and crafts movement' in the United States, a shift enabled by the assembly line and later reaffirmed in the automation of human productive capacity:

> The advancement of culture is synonymous with the removal of ornament from objects of daily use. [...] It represents a crime against the national economy, and as a result of it, human labor, money, and material are ruined. Time cannot compensate for this kind of damage.[18]

Loos' claim that the rejection of ornamentation is necessary for cultural development masks the underlying difficulty posed by the production of ornamentation: it required skill and was associated with careful craftsmanship. The 'de-skilling' this rejection of decoration entails is implicit in Loos' argument: 'wasted capital' is the primary focus of his theory-manifesto; it is concerned with justifying and validating what would appear to be unfinished commodities (lacking the surface finish provided by decoration). The highly skilled work needed to create these decorations also required more manufacturing time than the production of simple, unornamented objects that simultaneously required less skill and so could be more easily automated:

> Ornament is wasted manpower and therefore wasted health. It has always been like this. But today it means wasted material, and both mean wasted capital.[19]

His actual justification for the rejection of decoration (human, skilled agency applied to production) is financial—eliminating the additional capital expended in producing decoration—has been disguised as a moral crusade against degeneracy. The argument against ornament is commercial, a

---

[18] Adolph Loos, *Crime and Ornament: The Arts and Popular Culture in the Shadow of Adolph Loos*, eds. Bernie Miller and Melony Ward (New York: XYZ Books, 2002), 30–31.

[19] Loos, *Crime and Ornament*, 33.

supposition that hides an underlying concern with productivity: it takes longer to produce an ornamented object than one without it—these "savings" result in higher productivity, i.e. more objects produced. This concern with rate of production necessarily implies a process of surveillance over those engaged in the labor, a monitoring of their work process and rate of facture—a dimension that becomes literally a new form of production through pervasive monitoring.

The transformations produced by urbanization, industrialization, universal literacy, and the democratic access to information fundamentally shifted this earlier condition, but without altering the baseline assumption that more information is equivalent to success—it is this ideology that is reified in the 'security assemblage' as attempts to create an instrumentality of information. Yet, there is a crucial difference between the values generated by an information-rich environment via databases linked to digital technology, and those created by the information-poor one: pre-industrial societies' social structures self-replicate, not because information is less available, or necessarily less easily stored, but because it is less transmissible—accessible—to those who might otherwise use it; agnotology reproduces this condition within highly automated, *inforich* digital capitalism through the hyperreal by undermining the interpretative process and creating decoherence about social, political, and environmental conditions.

The problem posed by the *inforich* society is not one of access to information—accessing information becomes a commonplace through the always-on computer network—but rather the issue of coherence. Agnotology acts to generate decoherence: it undermines the ability to determine what information is factual and valid for constructing interpretations. At the same time, the concept of "factuality" becomes something that has been termed "truthiness"—information that appears to be valid. Yet agnotology is more than simply 'ignorance,' or a result of an information gradient or differential. The agnotism that is so apparent in digital capitalism generally is one where unusual and seemingly unlikely claims are presented without any acknowledgement that there is conflicting or contradictory evidence. The decoherence generated by agnotism serves established hierarchies within the political economy by rendering 'human resources' impotent to effect changes or challenge established social organization; inability to resolve 'controversy' within the socio-political domain is one of the most visible symptoms of this decoherence in action.

§8.5

Human agency requires a reciprocal relationship with the immanent physical world; it is this capacity to alter and effect the physical environment that is apparent in the emergence of Modernism and industrial capitalism following the Enlightenment's invention of humanism in the eighteenth century. Capitalism's definition as a worker's externalization of their productive capacity—human agency—is an adaptation of this emphasis on individual activity as productive model grounded in the social reproduction of human society. The emergence of agnotology is demonstrative of the shift from the historical capitalist production to one without reference or concern for the social: the recording and observation immediately recognizable as pervasive monitoring is one dimension of a general emergence of digital automation and facture that only becomes possible when the social itself is subject to dissolution.

Immaterial production reveals the law of automation in action as intellectual labor first becomes a commodity, then is simplified into autonomous processes—following the historical trajectory in the nineteenth century's deskilling of labor inherent to assembly line production. This apparent alienation of human agency is innate to capitalism—the externalization of productive capacity was its first, definitional moment. Digital capitalism remains basically linked to a humanist conception of production through externalized agency; it is equivalent to the Modern period in its elevation of humanist values (agency) above all else, as demonstrated by contemporary wage disparities in the United States between the CEO's salary and the salaries of those who perform labor: the decider—the CEO—has a high salary because of the high degree of agency, while those who perform the actual labor are deserving of only a tiny salary because they do not have agency: those without agency are without value. The reassertion of human agency is not a critical response to the alienation posed by digital capitalism, but a dimension of the system producing the alienation itself. It is the situation of value *in* agency that enables capitalism itself.

Until the advent of digital technology, intellectual labor fundamentally required human agency (it could not be automated); only the CEO still retains this inviolability, hence the salary disparity. The issue of human agency, rather than a 'barbarous relic,' remains a fundamental constraint on all production and value generation precisely because *value* is a crystallization of specific social demands that are coincident with, and ultimately dependent on, human agency. It is worth remembering that all currency (money) is a reification of a social relationship—without this human dimension, value ceases to exist. *Value* is what the security apparatus acts to protect, replacing the social (the reified combination of human agency and the intelligent relationships accompanying that agency) with its own instrumental connections and procedures, autonomous and unintelligent so that the (historical) foundation in human agency shifts to the autonomous digital system.

The transition to automation necessarily violates the basic foundation of capitalism itself: that workers exchange their labor (externalized productive capacity rendered as a 'commodity') for payment that is then recycled as the funds that labor spends to purchase the products of their own labor. The integrity of this foundation is violated as automated production replaces workers without enabling their shift into other forms of production—in the permanent replacement of human labor by automated processes: what emerges is no longer the classically defined 'capitalism' of Marx.

Agnotology produces an alienated human agency quite

apart from the historical (traditional) definition of capitalism itself: a reversion to earlier modes of human agency does not escape this problematic; it is these modes that have produced it. Challenges to human agency are at one and the same time the challenges digital capitalism poses for the social, demonstrated by the contradiction of value where agnotology acts to preserve value in the same way that the aura of the digital strips physicality from consciousness. The dehumanization of production that is the ultimate effect of the law of automation does nothing to address issues of *value*; quite the contrary, it makes questions of value production become central to any critical analysis, inherently leading back to the construction of the social realm. The elimination of human agency from production is reproduced by pervasive monitoring; surveillance itself is an alienation from *value* emergent in the hyperreal's rupture with the conditions of physicality. It is a fundamental transformation of *how* the social is constructed, indicating a fundamental shift in the nature of capitalism itself. Value becomes not a social relationship but a technical assertion backed by authoritarian domination. The security assemblage acts to maintain the established order, preventing the emergence of alternatives; the heterotopias offered by agnotology act to dissipate what cannot otherwise be contained. The aspiration to the state of information coupled with semiotic production renders agency moot.

The dynamic of agnotology::surveillance functions simultaneously as affirmation of this hierarchy and as the means for its perpetuation even as the system it serves grows more precarious. The problem is neither a question of agency, nor automation, nor even value production: instead, it is the paradox that lies at the foundations of capitalism in its development within Modernism. The Modernist concern with self-determination, individuality, and autonomy (agency) finds form in capitalism with workers' externalization (alienation) of their own, internal "productive capacity." It is no longer a matter of choosing to act or not act, to do or not do, *agency is contained*: it is rendered powerless by the instrumentality of agnotology::surveillance—methods of resistance and opposition developed in the nineteenth and twentieth centuries are neutralized in advance of their action. This is the problem that the Critical Art Ensemble directly addressed in their 1996 analysis *Digital Resistances* where the concept of 'tactical media'—a specifically undefined concept in their proposition—demonstrated the security response to theoretical challenges.[20] It is the undefined that becomes problematic in this system of authoritarian domination, that which retains the ambiguous character of the absent object, invisible except for the displacement it induces around itself, a factor that is an innate feature of how pervasive monitoring is a *neutral* system, serving all masters equally whatever their purposes, as the Critical Art Ensemble noted in 1994:

> The primary concern among the military/corporate cyber police (Computer Emergency Response Team, the Secret Service, and the FBI's National Computer Crime Squad) is that nomadic strategy and tactics are being employed at this very moment by contestational groups and individuals (in the words of authority, "criminal" groups). The cyberpolice and their elite masters are living under the sign of virtual catastrophe (that is, anticipating the electronic disaster that could happen) in much the same way that the oppressed have lived under the signs of virtual war (the war that we are forever preparing for but never comes) and virtual surveillance (the knowledge that we may be watched by the eye of authority).
>
> The current wave of paranoia began in early 1994 with the discovery of "sniffer" programs. Apparently some adept crackers are collecting passwords for unknown purposes.[21]

The 'terror' that the Critical Art Ensemble identifies at the

---

[20] Critical Art Ensemble, *Digital Resistance: Explorations in Tactical Media* (Brooklyn: Autonomedia, 2001).
[21] Critical Art Ensemble, *Electronic Civil Disobedience* (Brooklyn: Autonomedia, 1996), 28–29.

dawn of the Internet in the 1990s as mass medium is identical to those elements that pervasive monitoring is ineffective at identifying: the dimensions of meaning that transform semiosis into value. The *unknown use value* the information collected might have is precisely what makes it dangerous, makes countering and containing its potential a necessity. The challenge is not one of agency, but inherent to the observation-recording-analysis cycle itself: the transformation of unintelligent semiosis to meaning.

The rise of agnotology as an affect distinct from 'ignorance,' disinformation, misinformation, lies, or other propaganda can be traced to its basis in undeceidabilty: unlike its (apparent, historical) parallels whose foundations are essentially nonfactual and can be recognized as such, the foundations of agnotology merge with and undermine the discursive process itself; the "'ignorance'" it produces does not reflect a lack of information, but rather is the mirror-like doppelganger of knowledge, dissipating action and challenge through a meta-stable hyperreality—actions without discernable reasons (*use value*) will have limited to no impact on the conditions of reality, and lead inexorably to what psychology terms "learned helplessness"—a situation that innately supports the established hierarchy and order, while at the same time justifying the restriction, elimination, and criminalization of dissent/opposition through the 'security assemblage.' Disenfranchisement is the purpose of the security apparatus, shifting the maintenance of value from the social realm to the reified digital. What has been secured in this process is the future.

Chapter Nine

The Scarcity of Capital

The collapse of the United States' "Housing Bubble" in 2008 is the logical and inevitable result of the illusion of production without consumption. However, in spite of the financial collapse, the bailouts of insolvent financial institutions, and the on-going disinflation, credit, and value collapse, the institutions receiving bailouts became stronger as a result of the bailout[1] indicating a fundamental change to the relationship between the physical commodity-form and immaterial values identified with currency and financialization. Financial "bubbles" are an inevitable result of a systemic shift focused on the generation of value through the semiotic exchange and transfer of immaterial assets. In the case of the "Housing Bubble," those assets being traded were based on mortgages—debts generated without regard for the reality of underly-

---

[1] Simon Johnson, former chief economist at the International Monetary Fund, quoted on *Bill Moyers Journal*, April 16, 2010, http://www.pbs.org/moyers/journal/04162010/profile.html: "The big banks became stronger as a result of the bailout. That may seem extraordinary, but it's really true. They're turning that increased economic clout into more political power. And they're using that political power to go out and take the same sort of risks that got us into disaster in September 2008."

ing, physical assets and the labor needed to meet those debts. The failure to address the immanent source of the problem precipitating the crisis—the default on underlying mortgages—and instead focusing on the financial institutions (whether it is through "bailouts," regulation, or investigation of "fraud") is a demonstration of the shift that has occurred from a physically productive economy to one based on semiotic manipulation; this situation has not been addressed by conventional media or analysis, and requires a consideration of how other, systemic factors of immaterialization are determining the kinds of choices available in order to engage these crises when they arrive.

How the collapse of the "Housing Bubble" has been addressed internationally reveals and validates the transformation from productive labor to semiotic manipulation, and consequently, in the various government "bailouts" focusing on reifying the immateriality of markets against physical limits by suspending mark-to-market valuations of assets,[2] an

[2] Alan Greenspan, "Letter to SEC Chairman Richard C. Breeden," November 1, 1990, states: "The Board believes that market value accounting raises a substantial number of significant issues that need to be resolved before considering the implementation of such an approach in whole or in part for banking organizations. Accounting methodology should be developed to measure the results of a particular business purpose or strategy; it is not an end in itself. For an institution whose business purpose is to trade marketable financial assets on an intra-day basis, for example, closing daily market values would measure the success or failure of that particular business purpose. An end of the day balance sheet, marked to market, is clearly the appropriate accounting procedure in the example. Generally, the business strategy of commercial banks, on the other hand, is to employ their credit insights on specific borrowers to acquire a diversified portfolio of essentially illiquid assets held to term. The success or failure of such a strategy is not measured by evaluation such loans on the basis of a price that indicates value in the context of immediate delivery. Clearly, one aspect of value in an exchange is the period of delivery. But the appropriate price for most bank loans and off-balance sheet commitments-is the original acquisition price adjusted for the expectation of performance at

action thus enabling the generation/maintenance of the immaterial values created in the asset bubble. The continuing disjunction between physical assets and their role as immaterial tokens within a system of exchange are suggestive of larger, more systemic crises to come: the underlying problematic of debt generated as a side-effect of immaterial production (the transaction costs posed by the semiosis, subsequently doubled by bailouts that serve to regenerate or "reinflate" the initial asset bubbles through additional sequences of sale and resale sponsored by government agencies for the protection of the markets and those who profit from them) hypertrophies the underlying pathology by creating additional debts and, paradoxically, by increasing the value of assets whose uncertain values are the cause of the initial panic, evident in the collapse of the asset bubble itself.

Debit-versus-production was a systemic dynamic in the early twenty-first century "Housing Bubble," revealing a semiotic process (a procedure of sampling/remixing), and the denial of the importance of the actual, physical commodity form: property owners' ability to pay their debt whose fragmentation, combination, and reduplication resulted in the (digital) investment security. It was both the exchange of these derivative securities and the extension of credit to almost anyone who would request it (in the form of "0% down," "Alt-A," or interest-only mortgages) that generated the immaterial securities sold in the capital markets, producing an expanding network of assets and the steadily escalating values necessary for wealth extraction. At the same time, the significance of the physical asset was denied in a literal demonstration of the aura of the digital's break with physicality, where new values were primarily created by the repackaging/semiotic manipulation of securities generated from mortgages (CDOs and other mortgage-backed securities), and secondarily from the accompanying sales of actual real estate. The physical commodities (houses) were only signifi-

maturity. It is only when that price differs from the book value of the asset that an adjustment is appropriate."

cant to the extent that they could provide debts; the transfer of these debts (mortgages) into securities (Collateralized Debt Obligations) for semiotic manipulation and resale in derivative markets (accompanied by "insurance" in the form of Credit Default Swaps). Once translated into a virtualized form, their physical basis and link to productive labor was denied. The collapse of the "Housing Bubble" in 2008 precipitated from increases in the payments mortgage holders needed to provide each month on their housing debt due to their adjustable rate mortgages increasing their monthly payments above a value they were able to pay.[3] This denial of the physical basis is apparent in the Troubled Asset Relief Program's (TARP) focus on the virtual, semiotically-manipulated investment securities derived from mortgages,[4] rather than on preventing further defaults on the underlying mortgages themselves; it is the default of the mortgage holders due to the scarcity of capital to meet their mortgage obligations that created the collapse of the "Housing Bubble" itself, and caused the "Credit Crisis" in 2009.

Ruptures between physical asset and virtual commodity become apparent in TARP's acquisitions of the devalued mortgage-backed securities: the value of securities whose redeemability had fallen into question was conserved by removing them from circulation *at full value* (hence it was a bailout). The underlying physical limit imposed by the scarcity of capital created the "freeze" of credit in 2009. Scarcity of capital appears via the problematic function of fiat currency, a lacuna formed in the dynamic of immaterial values expanding up to the limit of the physical ability to meet those demands. Agents within this system have their roles prede-

[3] See Benjamin Bernanke, "Four Questions about the Financial Crisis," speech given at Morehouse College, Atlanta, Georgia, April 14, 2009, www.federalreserve.gov/newsevents/speech/bernanke20090414a.html.

[4] The TARP program was launched by the Federal Reserve Bank on October 14, 2008. For more information on that first and subsequent programs, see http://www.treasury.gov/initiatives/financial-stability/TARP-Programs/Pages/default.aspx.

termined by the nature of the system itself; it is not a matter of an elitist conspiracy that digital capitalism acts as it does, so much as it is the requirements of systemic equilibrium that force specific actions.

Real estate formed the evident basis for the 2008 bubble and precipitated its collapse: those mortgages that were re-combined and portioned into multiple, derivative assets—their superficial value based in payments made by mortgage holders each month—had in fact become secondary to the exchange and sale of the derivatives, credit default swaps (in-surance), and other secondary, superstructural assets gener-ated from them. It was the widespread creation of these derivatives based on housing debt that was the wealth-producing force in the expansion of the "Housing Bubble" in a self-reinforcing cycle where the production of additional derivatives acted systematically to spur mortgage (debt) crea-tion; when the mortgages with adjustable interest rates in-creased the monthly payments beyond a value the actual mortgage holders were able to pay, the bubble burst in the panic over which derivative assets were no longer valuable, endangering *all* mortgage-backed securities (and the insur-ance issued as "protection"). The problematic nature of these defaulting mortgages was, and remains, an issue of wages vs. debt.[5] Nevertheless, TARP's focus in dealing with the prob-lems posed by this economic collapse was not on physical assets (the mortgages in default or in danger of default or the issue of wages used to make payments on this debt), but on the virtual, semiotically-manipulated investment securities derived from them. This apparent discrepancy has received little attention or consideration.

Scarcity of capital within this construction becomes ap-parent via the inherent imbalance emergent in the breach between existing values and the number of potential future claims posed by a derivatives market whose value is signifi-cantly larger than the quantity of immanent labor (physical, automated and immaterial) available to produce new physi-

[5] Bernanke, "Four Questions about the Financial Crisis."

cal values to match those claims; however, it is not a question of commodity values vs. speculative values, but between rentier claims (titles to production values) and production capacity. It is this mismatch between capital and rentier claims that was exposed by the collapse of the 2008 "Housing Bubble" and that became apparent as the "Credit Crisis" of 2009. Bank insolvency, for example, emerges precisely because investors held more claims on value-to-be-produced than there are available values to be claimed. This type of failure is a feature of how semiotic transactions develop values independently of physical assets.

The illusion of production without consumption that produced these crises is central to my conception of the digital proposed in chapter three, "Aura of the Digital." The digital is a symptom of a larger shift from considerations and valuations based in physical processes towards immaterial processes; hence, "digital capitalism" refers to the transfer of this immateriality to the larger capitalist superstructure. Because the digital is a semiotic realm where the meaning present in a work is separated from the physical representation of that work, the "aura of the digital" describes an ideology that claims a transformation of objects into that semiotically-based immateriality. At the same time, the digital appears as a naturalization of the concentration of capital, since the digital itself poses as a magical resource that can be used without consumption or diminishment, leading to a belief in accumulation without production. This shift from a basis in limiting factors and scarcity is inherent to the immaterial form posed by the digital; at the same time, it denies how scarcity of capital is imposed by the dual forms of interest and profit on capital expenditures.

The force that is evident as the immaterial form of digital capitalism is a transformation of the underlying relationship between the universal equivalent, based in the physical commodity-form, in its role as *currency* in Marx's formulation, and its valuation, independent from its role as marker-of-exchange, as physical commodity. Gold and silver are no longer *intrinsically* valuable, but rather exhibit a fluctuating value relative to the socially produced fiat currency. The change in the US Dollar from its historical basis as a currency "backed" by a precious commodity (such as gold or silver) to one without such a basis marks the change from exchange via the physical commodity-form to an immaterial exchange whose basis is purely social rather than physical (the fiat currency); this shift demonstrates an extension of immateriality into the political economy as a whole. (It is less a radical change than an incremental transition that emerged in the abandonment of the Bretton Woods agreements, and consequently in the role adopted by the US Dollar as the global reserve currency in the 1970s.)

While the underlying structural logic that precipitated the economic crisis of 2008 has its foundations in the same ideology of immateriality that is apparent in the aura of the digital's denial of physical reality, the factors that produced this immateriality are evident in the internal structure of how this semiotic system drives its participants towards immaterial values. At the same time, those semiotic structures of financialization, exchange of titles to future production, and ideology of rupture between physical and immaterial values leads recursively to a debt cycle emergent in the large-scale bubbles of the "Housing Bubble" (2000s), the "Dot.Com Boom" (1990s), and the "Savings & Loan Collapse" (1980s) in the United States; similar bubbles have emerged internationally in Japan and Europe over the same period, revealing how the escalation of values apparent in the semiotic, immaterial production of digital capitalism is both internationally systemic, unsustainable, and unavoidable.

This new immaterial basis contributes to other shifts in production and labor. Semiotic manipulation replaces physical asset-basis reality (in the physical commodity form), and immaterial labor replaces physical production, revealing the process of reification that legitimates immateriality as a vehicle for wealth production: the reason the Federal Reserve and Troubled Asset Relief Program bailouts in the "Housing Bubble" of 2008 focused on the liquidity of the banks, and were concerned with the flow of credit,[6] lies with this market-based semiosis generating wealth without expenditure via a spontaneous creation of exchange value *sans* labor or consumption of resources (it is transactional rather than productive). This fantasy is a fundamental condition of digital capitalism. It is a system attempting to expand without limit, inevitably encountering physical constraints imposed by the scarcity of capital, which precipitates the recognition of a collapsing "bubble," thus, crisis.

An accelerating shift towards immaterialism—values created without productive action—is apparent in the historical rise of the digital in the United States: the issuing of a rentier currency based on debt (on December 23, 1913 with the Federal Reserve Act, which created the Federal Reserve Note); the shift from currency based in the universal equivalent commodity, the "gold standard," to a fiat currency (on August 15, 1971); the transition to a financial economy focused on immaterial labor (the trend of manufacturing to shift to Asia during the 1980s, and the rise of globalization in the 1990s); and finally with the emergence of the aura of the digital (with the widespread adoption of digital communication technology at the heart of the semiotic financialization that enables these asset bubbles, a trend starting in the 1970s, accelerating in the 1980s, and fully emergent in the 1990s with the initial Dot.Com boom). In all cases, these transformations describe a fundamental social shift from concerns with physical, tangible equivalency to an immateriality described by the aura of the digital—the illusion of an infinite domain capable of producing value without expenditure, coupled with a denial of physical costs and limited resources—as it merges with the systems of value production and exchange.

[6] While this move followed the suggestion of Hyman Minsky for the Federal Reserve to be the "lender of last resort," it also did nothing to address the underlying problem with the "Housing Bubble" of 2008; see Stephen Mihm, "Why Capitalism Fails," in *The Boston Globe*, September 13, 2009, http://www.boston.com/bostonglobe/ideas/articles/2009/09/13/why_capitalism_fails/.

The "Housing Bubble" of 2008, no less than the "Dot.Com Bubble" of 2001, and the collapse each triggered, demonstrate the pervasiveness of this ideology and the shift to semiosis in immaterial (financial) transactions in place of physical production. Digital capitalism can be identified with the simultaneous appearance of these interlocking social-economic conditions, each of which reinforces the ideology of immateriality apparent in the aura of the digital.

Immaterial currency and physical labor generate a disparity between the demands made by titles to future wealth reified in the fiat currency, and the ability of labor and production to meet those demands. Its fundamental basis favors imbalances and collapses following/producing financial bubbles; this rupture between physical labor and immaterial 'production' reveals a system that inherently cannot maintain equilibrium. Understanding this new condition requires a reconsideration of Karl Marx's foundational definitions of commodities, the physical commodity-form, and the universal equivalent in relation to value and labor. The dynamic tension of this relationship manifests itself through the semiotic process of currency generation via the extension of credit: the creation of liens against future productivity encapsulated in the iteration and exchange of immaterial 'commodities' within the marketplace—what is termed "financialization."

§9.1

In conventional Marxist theory the distinction between the physical commodity-form and the role of the universal equivalent commodity is not significant precisely because the universally equivalent commodity, *currency*, maintains a dual identity: as both agent of exchange in transactions, and as physical commodity-form in itself. The foundations for this conception are in Marx's *Capital, Volume 1,* and his subsequent considerations of the commodity-form depend on the maintenance of this duality. The transition to immaterial production emerges from a breach of the duality between currency and commodity-form: when the universal equivalent is no longer also a physical commodity-form, which is the case with *fiat currency,* the consideration of the dynamic of currency as independent from the commodity-form is essential. The two cannot be assumed to continue to move in tandem as different aspects of the same entity.

Nevertheless, the relationship between *currency* (money) and *labor* remains central to the dynamic of immaterial production and the escalating values of commodities. The development of rentier and fiat currencies are basic components of this process of wealth extraction via immaterial labor. The paradox of immaterial value and futurity in fiat currency can be recognized in the essential nature of fiat currency itself: first, that the currency is a reification of the pure social relation that is Marx's definition of "currency," in place of the dual social-commodity nature he identifies; and second, as a rentier form, it functions as a title to future labor, not as a representation of past labor. These differences make significant alterations to the definitions posed in *Capital, Volume 1.* Marx begins his analysis with the discussion of foundational concepts of labor, value, and commodity, speaking only briefly about a universal equivalent (currency) based in the exchange of physical commodities being simplified through the use of a single commodity-form to stand for exchange value:

> The simple or isolated relative form of value of one commodity converts some other commodity into an isolated equivalent. The expanded form of relative value, that expression of the value of one commodity in terms of all other commodities, imprints those other commodities with the form of particular equivalents of different kinds. Finally, a particular kind of commodity acquires the form of universal equivalent, because all other commodities make it the material embodiment of their uniform and

universal form of value.[7]

The general form of relative value, inherent in all commodities, is Marx's foundation for the symbolic value identified with money: it is the foundational principle of exchange that produces "money" through the universal equivalence between the value of the underlying physical commodity (gold) that is "money" and value of other commodities. The current situation where there is no physical asset providing a basis for exchange value is beyond the scope of his description; it is a key distinction between the paradigm he constructs and the contemporary political economy: an individual commodity, when employed as a general equivalent for other commodities, becomes the "universal equivalent." Thus, a capitalism dependent upon fiat currency divorced from any connection to a physical universal asset (such as gold or silver) is beyond the scope of the historical foundations of Marx's theorization; a reassessment of his foundational definitions is thus required to understand the parameters of this changed scenario. The separation of currency from physical asset is an essential enabler for contemporary immaterialism.

The concept of "fiat currency" plays an important role in the contemporary dynamic of digital capitalism. Unlike the formulation of currency in Marx, digital capitalism lacks direct physical connections to tangible commodity values. Whereas Marx's concept of "exchange value" acts as a repository for value produced by past labor (i.e. the physical commodity-form is literally "in" the material basis of currency), in digital capitalism there is no "saving" of past labor value: separated from the physical basis of the universal commodity, exchange value does not have a foundation in productive labor since it is no longer simultaneously a signifier for relative value and a physical commodity in itself. The separation of currency from its historical basis in a tangible commodity necessarily generates a virtualized (digital) value separated

[7] Karl Marx, *Capital,* Vol. 1, trans. Ben Fowkes (New York: Penguin Classics, 1992), 160.

from any tangible basis in material reality. Separating the commodity aspect (gold/silver/etc.) from the exchange value of currency alters the basis of exchange itself.[8] The exchange value fiat currency demonstrates is not derived from the commodity nature of the money itself; in digital capitalism these relations between commodities—relative value—become a purely social relation that denies any basis in past labor: what it enables is a shift into rentier claims on future labor—as agent for putting production in motion. This shift is apparent in the systemic paralysis caused by the credit crisis in 2009.

The contrast between the virtualized currency of digital capitalism and traditional currency is stark: traditional currency was a physical commodity whose value within the economic system was clearly defined, whose symbolic value was directly connected to its commodity nature, and whose relative value to other commodities was limited by the physical production embodied in the physical, universal commodity-form itself. These traditional units of exchange were either directly formed from a universal commodity (i.e., gold coins), or stood in for it (i.e., were theoretically redeemable as this universal equivalent). Within digital capitalism such a transaction is no longer possible. The exchange value of traditional universal commodity-forms is now unstable, shifting precisely because the material commodities no longer function as universally exchangeable currency. That role is occupied by the immaterial value of fiat currency.

Freed from the limitations posed by a physical basis in commodities, the quantity of currency in circulation can increase exponentially, yet appear to retain its value since there is no physical commodity-form whose physical limit will constrain value. The potential collapse posed by the "Housing Bubble" in 2008 appears precisely when the relationship between the quantity of currency and its value in relation to other commodities (in this case, mortgage-backed debt, itself an immaterial claim on future production) comes into ques-

[8] Marx, *Capital*, Vol. 1, 141–154.

tion: thus the systemic danger posed by such collapses emerges as an inherent property of the currency itself.

§9.2.a

Marx described physical values two ways: (1) as objects of utility, what Marx terms *use value,* which is the material commodity itself,[9] and (2) as depositories of past labor, or *value,* in which the *exchange value* is represented as money and retains its value because of the commodity basis:

> Gold confronts the other commodities as money only because it previously confronted them as a commodity. Like all other commodities it also functioned as an equivalent, either as a single equivalent in isolated exchanges, or as a particular equivalent alongside other commodity-equivalents. Gradually it began to serve as a universal equivalent in narrower or wider fields. As soon as it had won a monopoly of this position in the expression of value for the world of commodities, it became the money commodity.[10]

This dualism collapses when we consider the reified social values of digital capitalism. There is no commodity equivalent to the fiat currency, thus fiat currency undoes this preservation of values generated by past labor through/as currency. Fiat currency is neither an embodiment of productive action, nor a repository of already-generated-value precisely because it is not a commodity, and cannot be translated into a commodity. The underlying social basis for currency— the *acceptance* of a universal equivalent—becomes the *only* value reified in currency (money) as the exchange value of currency; this virtualization is symptomatic of a transformation of the system of exchange from one based on physical labor and productive economy to a virtual economy. This

[9] Marx, *Capital,* Vol. 1, 126.
[10] Marx, *Capital,* Vol. 1, 162–163.

development is the precondition for finance to emerge as the immaterial production that characterizes digital capitalism.

Unlike physical commodities (such as corn and iron), which can always be exchanged in a direct, physical transaction (a quantity of corn exchanged for a quantity of iron), in fiat currency the value of commodities is no longer expressed through an exchange of value, but rather in a transactional debt: it becomes an exchange of titles to future production; to purchase gold or silver, for example, is to translate the value of fiat currency into a speculative asset whose value over time is unstable precisely because it is not "fixed" as representative of past production, but in relation to production to be performed. These claims against future labor substitute for the historical duality of social relation and tangible commodity. This transaction is rentier in nature: it suggests that the elementary form of commodity value is not expressed through relationships between commodities of any type, but rather through the ability to exchange the currency for labor to be performed, (also known as debt). Marx's concept of "equivalent value between commodities" no longer applies since there is no commodity already produced by labor mediating this exchange of values.

Fiat currency functions to set labor in motion (i.e. as capital), not as a reserve where value is conserved; in the process of this shift, it renders commodities valueless precisely because they are no longer equivalent, except in terms of their expression via claims on future productivity—in an immaterial value not in immanent physicality. In this construct, *futurity* (future-labor-production) comes to replace the historical universally equivalent commodity (gold); *futurity* is transformed into the universal commodity, and the economy it produces depends upon the ability to receive and manipulate credits (i.e., financialization), rather than through the management and distribution of commodity production.

However, it is not a quantitative relation between physical commodity-forms (a quantity of commodity X exchanged for a quantity of commodity Y), that is directly visible in the proportion of exchange values between objects of one sort and those of another sort—in digital capitalism the nature of exchange value becomes a variable social relation distinct from (and unrelated to) quantitative relations. The dynamic of exchange value *qua* fiat currency reifies a social foundation that Marx identifies as characteristic of all currency, changing the symbolic relationship that originated in the relative value of commodities into/as the fiat currency itself. This dematerialization of commodity values reflects a fundamental shift from material production to immaterial labor, and by extension, the automated labor of computer systems, and the rise of semiosis apparent in the transactional wealth generation of financialization.

§9.2.b

Because of the dual costs of physical production—once through the expenses of raw material, and then a second time through the transaction costs imposed by the rentier nature of fiat currency—digital capitalism privileges the generation of value via immaterial exchange where there is only the transaction cost of the fiat currency itself. Precisely because physical production is exchanged for claims on future production in the asymmetrical valuation of immaterial exchange demonstrates how labor has already been expended before it has been performed (i.e. is a debt to be paid). Given this transformation, the shift from a capitalism based on physical labor and production to digital capitalism based on semiosis (the exchange of titles to future production via financialization) is inevitable. It is forced onto actors within the system of digital capitalism by the demand to maximize wealth extraction—profit; it is the logic of the system itself that produces this change. The production of value within digital capitalism is thus necessarily and inherently extractive—a symbolic-order manipulation where physicality (to the extent that it still applies) is a mere pretext for the transactional exchanges that create increased value; "production" within this virtual realm is a matter of semiosis (the symbolic manipulation of financialization), rather than physical production. Unlike Marx's construct, where the value of a commodity remains constant so long as the labor time required for its production remains constant,[11] in digital capitalism, commodity values necessarily escalate because of their indebtedness against future production via their valuation within the virtualized exchange reified in fiat currency. To repay the debts they pose, values must increase.

Being severed from the limitations of the physical commodity-form—where currency can only expand in proportion to the physical material it is exchangeable for—allows dramatic increases in currency-in-circulation. The result is a cycle where claims against future production expand until they encounter the limiting factor: the ability of labor to meet the titles levied against its future production; this constraint is the scarcity of capital. The scarcity of capital limits expansion precisely because the emergent imbalances between claims on future labor and the ability to meet those claims are traditionally resolved through price inflation/currency devaluation—the instability of exchange values inherent in fiat currency's translation into commodity objects. However, digital capitalism poses a special situation for this traditional resolution to the asymmetry of value and labor, since digital capitalism develops from fiat currency replacing universal equivalent, *and* from the transition to the virtualized values of semiotic transactions characterized by financialization.

Fiat currency in digital capitalism does not enable the storage of past labor value. The system of exchange and circulation of currency (credit) that is the basis of these semiotic transactions cannot allow the fiat currency to be devalued without threatening the acceptance of the social relationship that enables the currency itself: digital capitalism is threatened with immanent collapse when the circulation of credit ceases. Thus, the focus on the financial institutions becomes inevitable in the bailouts and actions taken to contain the collapsing bubble: the physical basis (real estate in 2008) that precipitated the crisis is an epiphenomenon when considered

[11] Marx, *Capital*, Vol. 1, 137.

in relation to the semiotic transactions those physical assets enable.

§9.3

While digital capitalism may appear to be an affective form of capitalism, and to a certain extent it does deploy affective measures to achieve its ends, a more correct designation is *agnotologic* capitalism: a capitalism systemically based on the production and maintenance of ignorance.[12] The accusations of fraud against banks such as Goldman Sachs for creating derivatives "designed to fail" and then claiming that these commodities are of the highest value demonstrates how this process of misinformation designed to obfuscate, confuse, and confound functions to create ignorance. This situation is partly a function of ideological blindness, and partly a reflection of the all-too-human desire to believe in positive scenarios such as the well-known, but hypothetical, "free lunch." Coupled with an affective performance, the agnotological dimension can only produce a social dynamic of misinformation.

This agnotism affects all participants within digital capitalism, precisely because it is the enabling factor for the perpetuation of the cycle of bubbles and the escalation of values they create. The limited horizons produced within this social network of agents and immaterial assets constrains the range of potential solutions to those that reinforce the established dynamic; this is the Ponzi formulation in action—as with the caucus-race in *Alice in Wonderland*, there is no alternative but to run faster simply to remain in place. It is this perverse dynamic that generates the need for affective remedial services. Juan Martin Prada's affective capitalism is thus a symptom of the disassociation between the reality of capitalist

---

[12] This term follows the suggestion by Robert N. Proctor, who proposed *agnotology* to describe the systematic, false production of "science" designed by the tobacco industry to create confusion about the health risks of smoking tobacco.

economy and the alienation it produces:

> Therefore, it seems to be almost evitable that the increas-
> ing computer automation of the productive and man-
> agement processes in companies should only be able to
> generate the mere effects of closeness, affective simula-
> tions of service for the user, who will not cease to com-
> plain about the lack of contact with actual "flesh and
> blood" people when hiring services, solving doubts or
> presenting complaints.[13]

The affective labor created to address this alienation is part of
the mechanisms where the agnotological order maintains its
grip on the social: managing the emotional states of the consumers who also serve as the labor reserve is a necessary precondition to the management of the quality and range of
information. The creation of systemic unknowns where any
potential "fact" is always already countered by an alternative
of apparently equal weight and value renders engagement
with the conditions of reality—the very situations affective
labor seeks to assuage—contentious and a source of confusion, reflected by the inability of participants in bubbles to be
aware of the immanent collapse until after it has happened.
The biopolitical paradigm of distraction, what Prada calls
"life to enjoy," can only be maintained if the underlying stric-
tures remain hidden from view. If affective labor works to
reduce alienation, agnotology works to eliminate the potential for dissent. This elision is essential.

Creating *values* through the production of immaterial
values that are constructed around a fictitious basis in tangible assets (there are more derivative assets than can be
matched to physical commodities) requires that the valorizing process apparent in the semiosis remain unacknowl-
edged. The biopolitical paradigm of distraction serves this

---

[13] Juan Martin Prada, "Economies of Affectivity," *Caring Labor: An
Archive,* July 29, 2010, https://caringlabor.wordpress.com/2010/07/
29/juan-martin-prada-economies-of-affectivity/.

semiosis by keeping the social agents occupied in affective pursuits and fantasies of economic advancement (home ownership as "the American Dream" being the lure for the "Housing Bubble"). Without these tangential considerations distracting the human resource, the valorization process would be impeded as the concept of production is extended to all parts of the social domain, and subsequently deployed in the escalation of values inherent in the financialization process.

§9.4.a

The US Dollar (the "Federal Reserve Note," issued by the Federal Reserve Bank, an *independent* federal agency guaranteed by the United States Treasury) occupies an unusual place in the realm of currency: simultaneously both a rentier currency and a fiat currency, it is also employed not only within the national political economy of the United States, but internationally between nation-states as the global reserve currency. The US Dollar performs the role not only of universal equivalent between commodities, but between alternative currencies as well; it embodies the relative value of *all* exchanges within the global political economy.

Where fiat currency is inherently based on liens against future productivity, when *all* currency is issued by an independent organization, (i.e., the Federal Reserve Bank in the United States), the debt-basis is hypertrophied: rentier currency comes into existence by being lent (i.e., having a rent imposed at the moment of its creation even when *not* a fiat currency), and like other types of fiat currency, it is a debt that fundamentally cannot be repaid because it requires an amount of repayment greater than the quantity of currency in circulation.[14]

[14] Bob Chapman, "Liquidity Injection Won't Cure Wall Street Disease," *The International Forecaster,* October 15, 2008, http://the internationalforecaster.com/International_Forecaster_Weekly/Liquid Liquidity_Injection_Wont_Cure_Wall_Street_Disease.

§9.4.b

That the Federal Reserve System in the United States resembles a Ponzi scheme has been noted by a variety of observers, including former Assistant Secretary of the U.S. Treasury Paul Craig Roberts, and former New York Governor Elliot Spitzer.[15] Considering parallels between the Federal Reserve and the Ponzi scheme is therefore instructive: as these observers have suggested, the larger Federal Reserve system can be understood through the Ponzi scheme.

At their simplest level, Ponzi schemes are a microcosm of capitalist accumulation that remain in equilibrium only so long as (1) the number of investable claims against future profits remain constant, and (2) there are sources of income that do not require repayment (thus falling "outside" the system of exchange and circulation). Yet, collapse is potentially immanent even with these constraints—profits generated by "investments" are only sustainable so long as they are being drawn from sources outside the network of titles to future wealth (the investment system itself).

In the larger Federal Reserve System, increases in value for fiat currency apparent in price escalation are counterposed by the equalizing force of currency devaluation: there are no "profits" being produced, only a semiotic manipulation in the form currency circulation (promissory notes against future production). However, the ideology reified in the aura of the digital suggests the problem posed by inherent instability and potentially immanent collapse can be resolved via the shift from physical production to semiotic (immaterial) production, or financialization. It is an ideological position that takes capitalism's requirement to extract infinite wealth from finite resources and reifies it as a productive teleology through/as the Ponzi nature of this formulation. The generation of asset "bubbles" is not only required by this

[15] Daniel Tencer, "Spitzer: Federal Reserve is 'a Ponzi scheme, an inside job'," *Global Research*, July 28, 2009, http://www.global research.ca/index.php?context=va&aid=14559.

system, it is the demonstration of the system in action that these "bubbles" appear. Rather than an unusual circumstance, such developments are required by the nature of the currency system itself. When coupled with the immaterialist ideology of digital capitalism, the scale of these asset "bubbles" increases due to the lack of constraints on the expansion of fiat currency.

§9.4.c

Understanding the special circumstances created in digital capitalism where the fiat currency is simultaneously divorced from the universal equivalent commodity *and* generated as a debt requires a consideration of how the Ponzi scheme can function as a model for the development of this system. Capital scarcity is a constant feature of this arrangement as there is always a greater outstanding debt than there is currency to repay it; the Ponzi scheme demonstrates this accelerating process of circulation.

The Ponzi scheme is a special variety of investment fraud where the normal conditions of investment and rent paid on capital invested becomes an explicit formulation of "robbing Paul to pay Paul." As in all capital investments, the earlier the investor, the greater their profit; however, even though a Ponzi scheme produces initial "profits," all investors ultimately lose all of their "investment" because the structure itself does not allow their repayment—a portion of their "investment" has already been repaid to them as their "profits." Thus, the Ponzi scheme has a continual need for expansion ("economic growth") to maintain its equilibrium: there is no production of new values, only the recycling and expansion of claims against future production.

The rentier/fiat currency issued by the Federal Reserve Bank mirrors the Ponzi scheme's repayment of investors using their own investment (generation of claims against future production): only it is the Federal Reserve bank that is in the position of investor in the scheme—the rentier currency issued by the bank (as with the commodities sold by the Ponzi scheme) must be repaid to the bank with interest. The more rentier currency there is in circulation, the greater the debt to the bank; thus, the digital capitalist economy will inevitably produce a 'crash' when the limits of productive capacity (labor) cannot keep pace with the demands of virtualized value via rentier currency; this is the inherent scarcity of capital within digital capitalism itself.

Two conditions enable the Ponzi scheme to continue functioning: the recycling of "profits" as new investments (which the Federal Reserve does when it purchases Treasury bonds issued by the United States government, essentially buying its own debt[16]); and through the introduction of new sources of investment via derivatives and the financial markets themselves.

The Ponzi structure makes itself visible through cycles of asset inflation—so called "bubbles" of which the "Housing Bubble" of 2008 is simply a highly visible example, followed by periods of deleveraging—in which the investments lose their value, thus the amount required to be repaid for them—that return the system to equilibrium. The contradiction between the futurity of currency and the reality of labor, called the "unwinding of debt," are inherent features of how digital capitalism maintains equilibrium through/as a virtualization of values. In the process, it forces a continual process of valorization as the need to identify new, unfinancialized domains that do not require repayment steadily increases. The agnotistic dimension of digital capitalism is essential for it continues to function only so long as there are new investors (i.e. sources of value entering the system), thus maintaining equilibrium through/as the stream of "profit" payments. To meet the rentier/fiat currency's claims on future labor, there have been a variety of effects imposed by the need for equilibrium: the addition of new sources of labor (women enter the labor force); the reduction in the value of labor itself

[16] Craig Torres, "Fed to Buy $300 Billion of Longer-Term Treasuries," *Bloomberg News,* March 18, 2009, http://www.bloomberg.com/apps/news?pid=20601068&sid=aPlq8GB5FWSc.

("offshoring" and "globalization"); the expansion of capital formulation into previously unvalorized domains (securitization and other innovative forms of investment, and the invention of new "markets" for goods such as "children"); through automation, the immaterial production characteristic of the digital; and increased efficiency (or increased labor) without increased wage. The emergence of affective labor is both an example of this extension, and an enabler for the valorization process within the social.

However, the paradox of immaterial value and futurity makes the revaluation of the rentier/fiat currency inevitable because the expansion needed to continue making rentier payments continually increases directly in proportion to the already-existing commitments, and eventually confronts the limits imposed by physicality in the scarcity of capital. It is such a collision that created the "Housing Bubble" as mortgage holders could no longer (or were no longer willing to) meet the obligations posed by their debt. Considered in such terms the obvious solution to the problem posed lies with the debt; however, as the debts are systemic, the nature of digital capitalism itself makes addressing the causes of asset bubbles impossible.

§9.5

The distinction between the valuation of immaterial and physical capital determines the generation of 'capital' within digital capitalism. As the nature of exchange value is reified in the form of currency, the relations between currency and commodity have significance for the nature of capital; as fiat currency exists as a pure social value, and the aura of the digital masks a systemic myopia derived from the absolute incommunicabilty between virtuality and physicality: it reiterates the divide that is the scarcity of material production in physical real-world fabrication (the so-called productive economy) as the scarcity of capital in digital reproduction (emergent in the inability to contain the contradiction between immaterial value and futurity in fiat currency).

Within the rentier/fiat currency system is the action of the digital aura both as expansive procedure and as immaterial 'production' via the commodification of virtual "assets" without relationship to physical commodities; it makes the capitalist paradox of escalating value reveal the systemic paradox of rentier/fiat currency through the inability to meet the fiscal demands imposed through the twin forms of interest on investment (ground rent) and the need to produce profit on capital expenditures to provide social reproduction. The scarcity of capital within this construction becomes apparent via the inherent imbalance between the number of potential future claims (*infinite*) and the quantity of immanent labor (physical, automated and immaterial) available (*finite*). This contradiction manifests itself as a systemic failure in the system of exchange: what is called a "freeze on credit" precisely because the rentier/fiat currency's expansion of value depends on generating greater numbers of debits against future production, (i.e. the extension of "credits"). As the claims on labor exceed the ability to meet those claims, rentier/fiat currency reveals itself as *futurity,* rendered visible by the cessation of exchange: no exchange is possible when *all* labor is already allocated. Only the (re)payment of existing debits over time or their wholesale forgiveness (via a "jubilee") will enable credit to resume circulation.

Chapter Ten

On Immaterialism

The emergence of digital capitalism as a dominant ideology is a reflection not of an escape from physicality but of a systematic attempt to deny physicality. This development is the effect of the underlying apparatus—figured through the aura of the digital and the agnotology::surveillance dynamic—coming to dominate the political economy as the ideology of automation replaces human agency and labor with autonomous facture. The full transition, however, depends on an interlocking set of structural changes to the historical nature of *both* use value *and* exchange value (currency) in relation to their foundations as a reservoir of already-produced value identified through the relative value of commodities and emergent from human labor. The immaterialism apparent in digitally deployed financialization as a vehicle for the semiotic development of wealth and accumulation without physical production; the process known as "financialization" is an epiphenomenon, a symptom, of how the 'aura of the digital' strips concerns and the ability to recognize the distinction between immaterial and physical production. It is this immaterialist production (validated by the ideology of automation) that dominates the political economy through the substitution of immaterial values for physical production and semiosis for manufacturing, while maintaining its dominance through the security apparatus. It is the logical terminus of the transition to a "digital economy" where all commodities that can be delivered with digital technology will be, with the ultimate goal of eliminating most manufacturing entirely through the digital fabrication of physical objects (already apparent in on-demand publishing and the 3D printer); the replacement of physical currency by an immaterial one (exemplified by Bitcoin, as well as the use of both debit and credit cards) is part of this shift towards an economy based upon digital technology.

The changed nature of the digital economy, most visible in how the financial institutions receiving bailouts in 2008 and 2009 became stronger as a result, shows the new relationship between the physical commodity-form and the immaterial value (and increasingly immaterial nature) of currency. The emergence of immaterialism does not represent a rupture with physicality: the immaterialism that is the defining feature of digital capitalism is intricately and innately tied to physicality. The "rupture" posed by the changed relationship between physical and immaterial production is an ideological claim made by immaterialism following the "aura of the digital"; much of the pathological and self-destructive aspects of digital capitalism develop from the ideology of the digital's rupture with physicality being false.

The development of immaterial labor and its consequent deployment of financialization necessarily generates asset bubbles, followed by crashes, precisely because the denial of physicality that is the aura of the digital is an illusion (this, in fact, is the meaning of the *aura of the digital*—it is an illusion that *denies the constraints imposed by physical materiality*). However, the problem posed by immaterial value in digital capitalism does not suggest a dialectic opposition of immaterial and physical, so much as a spectrum of dominance where physical and immaterial value exist dynamically with interpenetrating positions of greater and lesser significance all maintained through agnotology::surveillance. The shift from coincident values to this variable dynamic spectrum is essential for the immaterial generation of value through semiosis.

The immaterial values identified within digital capitalism present a logical development that follows from a shift in Marx's fundamental assumptions about the structure and relationship of the commodity-form, exchange value, relative value, labor and their relationship/role in/as currency. It is precisely because currency is coincident with commodity-form that Marx has no need to address the situation emergent in digital capitalism. For his theory, currency is a dynamic inseparable from the concept of commodity-form.

The contradiction between the futurity of currency and the reality of labor, called the "unwinding of debt," is an inherent feature of how digital capitalism employs a virtualization of values. As digital capitalism expanded, the US Dollar assumed the role of universal equivalent between both commodities and currencies. Its exchange value is the relative value of *all* exchanges within the global political economy; that the US Dollar also happens to be a fiat currency led to the emergence and current dominance of immaterial production. The immaterial force of digital capitalism develops from the breach in the duality of currency and commodity-form; thus, in digital capitalism there is, necessarily, no "saving" of past labor value. Following the Ponzi model, it forces a continual process of valorization as the need to identify new, unfinancialized domains that do not require repayment steadily increases. Historically this has meant the expansion of labor, or the invention of new markets; in digital capitalism, it develops a specifically novel form of valorization through automation that enables the transformation of social actions and activities to commodity-form in ways that were previously (historically) impossible.

Yet, what digital capitalism poses for Marxist analysis is not a hard break with the established interpretations so much as a fundamental modification to address immaterialism. Such a modification does not mean that all existing interpretations are necessarily no longer applicable, but rather that their application should not be assumed to function in precisely the same fashion. What I have termed "digital capitalism" is less a rupture with the past than the heightening of key elements present at all times within capitalism itself; immaterial production's shift into positions of dominance does not entail a disappearance of physicality, but rather its stripping from consciousness.

§10.1

As digital technologies developed in the 1960s, expanded throughout our culture in the 1970s, 1980s, and most visibly in the 1990s, there was a general reordering of industrial culture and production around this new technology. Automation of both physical and immaterial production, globalized offshoring of labor, and the networking of shipping, communication, and immaterial trade all depend on these digital technologies; without them, the reduction of latency in communication essential to immaterial production would be impossible. The speed of many of these transactions is striking: trades lasting only a fraction of a second using High Frequency Trading "bots"—automated digital systems—have become the dominant productive force in immaterial value generation.

Within the digital we have a technology that appears to be essentially a matter of immateriality—of course this is not true; however, what is of interest is that we seem to behave as if it were true, and it this behavior that is significant.

Immaterial production is possible because the digital is a semiotic realm where the meaning of a work is separated from the physical representation of that work; the "aura of the digital" describes an ideology that claims a transformation of objects into a semiotically-based immateriality, which is linked to the actual conditions of digital technology, most obvious in the relationship of a digital "copy" to the digital "original." Both are identical (not merely equivalent, but the same); based in implementations of code, they do not decay when copied, used, or reproduced—making it possible to sell a digital work and retain it at the same time. This final factor enables the ideology of accumulation without production that is specific to digital capitalism.

§10.2

The paradox of immaterial value and futurity in fiat currency can be recognized in the non-physical basis of exchange value: the relationship between currency and commodity is not automatic; Marx recognized this fact by defining "currency" as a pure social relation. Thus the contrast between the virtualized currency of digital capitalism and traditional currency is stark: traditional currency was a physical commodity with a clearly defined value. Its symbolic value was directly connected to its commodity nature, and its relative value to other commodities was limited by physical production.

Changing the traditional relationship of commodity to currency also changes the relationship between that currency and labor; immaterial value emerges as a labor-debt. While currency maintains its exchange basis through the social relationship at the heart of the universal exchange commodity, the shift to the production of immaterial values independent of physical production necessarily sets labor against value.

The virtualized (digital) value produced by semiosis replaces the physical commodity form, and immaterial labor replaces physical production, revealing the process of reification that legitimates immateriality as a vehicle for wealth production. Market-based semiosis generates wealth without expenditure via the spontaneous creation of exchange value *sans* labor or consumption of resources, because semiosis is transactional, not productive. This change appears as/ through financialization; the accumulation it enables also distances all other exchanges from their connections to physical commodities. The distancing is a function of the digital immaterialism, and is the basis of financialization; *it is the reason why the current financialization is merely a symptom of immaterial values gaining a dominant position.*

§10.3

Digital capitalism is a global phenomenon, and not simply a symptom of hegemonic decline, for several, interlocking reasons: (1) the US Dollar functions as *the* global reserve currency, meaning that all other currencies' value and conversion is in relation to the US Dollar, and (2) that in spite of deep systemic shifts in American industrialization via offshoring and globalism that have resulted in the United States becoming a net exporter of raw materials for manufacturing in China, Japan, and elsewhere (in effect resembling a developing nation in its dependency on foreign manufacture), it remains in a position of global economic dominance.

While (2) almost certainly is a function of (1)—that the economic dominance is a function of the role the US Dollar plays in global economics, David Harvey's crisis of over accumulation of capital where the local market is no longer capable of providing sufficiently profitable investments in production and infrastructure driving a move to financialization cannot be reconciled with the reality that (3) China, like Japan in the 1980s before it, invests its trade surplus not in developing and expanding its domestic infrastructure and market, but instead in US Treasury bonds and other immaterial assets. The Japanese- and now Chinese-led Asian investment in US Treasury securities and US Dollar-based investments, including subprime mortgage-backed derivatives, reveals the global scope of this immaterialist process in action where immaterial values dominate over physical commodities and production.

This discrepancy between Harvey's model (much as with those posed by Giovanni Arrighi and Immauel Wallerstein) and actual market behavior finds a resolution or explanation in factor (3). The international basis of digital capitalism is logically predicted (and required) by the ascendancy of immaterialism. That it serves the dominant economic interests of the United States follows from the central position that the US Dollar plays as global reserve currency and the relationship between the US Dollar and the Chinese Yuan. The global economy in the first decades of the twenty-first century is intricately tied to that of the United States.

Because there is no commodity equivalent, fiat currency is not an embodiment of productive action, or a repository of already-generated-value precisely because it has no commodity-basis, and thus cannot be translated into a commodity; it undoes the preservation of values generated by past labor through/as currency. This foundation requires the emergence of internal asset bubbles in China (credit, real estate, etc.); however, these should not develop, given Harvey's model where the financialization producing bubbles is a symptom of decline in hegemonic dominance and the over accumulation of capital without productive sites for investment. Similar bubbles developed in Japan in the 1980s, and are present throughout the global market: consider the construction/debt bubble in Dubai, and the various problems of the so-called "PIIGS" in Europe in 2011 and later that were aided/enabled by investment banks during the 2008 Housing Bubble's expansion. Consider too, the discrepancies in labor value in the form of the minimum wage between the United States and those sites where offshore production occurs, including China; and that China's currency is directly "pegged" to the US Dollar in the way the US Dollar was "pegged" to specific quantities of gold prior to its transition to fiat currency status (1 oz. = US$35, set by the Bretton Woods Agreements in 1946). These facts are the key distinction between his concept of over accumulation of capital and my suggestion of the scarcity of capital. It is not that there is too much capital in this global system, but that there is too little to meet the obligations posed by the production of immaterial values on a global scale, with the US securities markets and investment firms in a central position.

Thus, the contemporary shift to financialization is not driven by a lack of physically productive sites for investment in these developing markets, but rather by (1) an ideology of rupture between physical and immaterialist value, recognizable as the aura of the digital, and (2) the use of fiat currency as the globally dominant reserve currency; the possible transition to a currency created by the IMF's SDR, or Special Drawing Rights, would be the substitution of one social reification (fiat currency) for another. In this respect, the scarcity of capital may be a negative reflection (or logical inversion) of Harvey's over accumulation of capital, with consequently both homologous effects, and significant differences.

§10.4

The ascent of the *aura of the digital* is the dominance of immaterial concerns over and against physicality. It is this dominance of an immaterial ideology, *not* a disconnection from physicality, that produces digital capitalism. The aura of the digital is apparent in this immaterial production because digital technology enables an illusion of production without consumption. This shift from a basis in limiting factors and scarcity is inherent to the immateriality posed by the digital; at the same time, it denies how scarcity of capital is imposed by the dual forms of interest and profit on capital expenditures. How this dynamic plays out creates both asset bubbles and their collapse; however, the issue of immaterial asset bubbles is *not* that they eventually collapse, but rather the belief in structures which *produce* them: it is a question of behavior and ideology.

The cyclical boom-bust character of capitalism has been a continuous feature of its history stretching into the nineteenth century. What has changed is not that these cycles continue to happen—they are unavoidable. As attempts to hoard physical assets to hedge against currency fears follow one asset bubble and crisis, a new asset bubble (followed by another crisis) appears instead. The cyclic nature of these expansions and collapses intensifies the conflict between labor and value as the responses of digital capitalism tend to reinforce the immaterial bias already in effect, making the divisions between social classes greater with each new conflict.

Dramatic increases in currency-in-circulation are an essential feature of the immaterially-based accumulative procedure. The value of fiat currency only exists as a result of social action and trust in the fiat currency. The generation of new value without production is only possible when currency (universal equivalency) is separated from a basis in commodities—it is a virtual economy where values cannot be brought into question without placing the entire system of value into question. Dangers posed to this immaterial system necessarily force agents within that system to conserve immaterial values via a bailout and suspension of normal trading rules, or else risk losing the social trust necessary for the fiat currency to continue to function.

However, because of the unique role of the US Dollar in the global system of exchange, digital capitalism poses a special situation for this traditional resolution to the asymmetry of value and labor. Since digital capitalism develops from (1) fiat currency replacing the universal equivalent, (2) its global deployment as mediator of all exchanges, *and* from (3) a transition to the semiotic value generation of financialization means that the traditional solutions cannot be employed without threatening to collapse the trust that is the social basis of fiat currency. As the Ponzi model suggests, digital capitalism is threatened with immanent collapse when this circulation ceases. Asset "bubbles" are not only required by this system, they are a function of digital capitalism in action; thus the necessity for bailouts when asset bubbles burst.

Scarcity of capital within this construct becomes apparent via the inherent imbalance between existing values and the number of potential future claims posed by a derivatives market whose value is significantly larger than the quantity of immanent labor (physical, automated, and immaterial) available to produce new physical values to match those claims; however, it is not a question of commodity values vs. speculative values, but between *rentier claims* and *production capacity*. Within this fiat currency system the action of the digital aura is both an expansive procedure and an immaterial "production" via the commodification of virtual "assets" without relationship to physical commodities. Scarcity of capital is a constant feature of this arrangement. There is always a greater outstanding debt than currency to repay it; it is modeled by the Ponzi scheme, which demonstrates this accelerating process of circulation and the inevitable collapse that follows it.

The biopolitical paradigm of distraction that has been termed "affective labor" is a symptom of agnotology that affects *all* participants, even those charged with "managing" digital capitalism. The limited horizons produced within this social network of agents and immaterial assets constrains the awareness of potential solutions to those that reinforce the established dynamic precisely because it is the enabling factor for the perpetuation of the cycle of bubbles and the escalation of values they create. The ideology reified in the aura of the digital suggests the problem posed by this inherent instability and potentially immanent collapse can be resolved via the shift from physical production to semiotic (immaterial) production. It appears in digital capitalism as a reflection of the desire to transcend these cycles; the claim that these cycles had been surmounted was commonly in circulation throughout the run-up in asset values, most apparent in the claim (by Alan Greenspan among others) that there was no "Housing Bubble."

The instability of digital capitalism that creates collapse (and the movement towards necrosis) is fundamentally the imbalance predicted by the Ponzi model of accumulation: the inability of production to meet the demands posed by capital. Semiotic manipulation characterizes this immaterial production. Values are generated through cycles of exchange, creating asset bubbles; they are a function of the semiotic reassembly and transfer of derivative (secondary and tertiary) immaterial commodities. This is a system haunted by the attempt to expand towards infinity inherent to capitalism in general. The shift to fiat currency (as much as the use of rentier currency) appear, much as the aura of the digital does, as solutions to this inherent paradox. It is ironic that these "solutions" are exaggerations of the underlying problematic itself; yet this factor is the ideological blindness, as much as the emergence of agnotology, that enables the shift towards immaterialism through the aura of the digital and the rise of digital capitalism.

References

There are many sources and materials that contributed to the development of this critique of digital capitalism. This bibliography lists a selection that contributed to the primary form of this analysis.

Abbing, Hans. 2004. *Why are Artists Poor? The Exceptional Economy of the Arts.* Amsterdam: Amsterdam University Press.

Abraham, Ralph, Peter Broadwell, and Ami Radunskaya. 1996. "MIMI and the Illuminati: Notes." *Pomona College* (Faculty Pages*)*, December 17, pages.pomona.edu/~aer 04747/mimi/miminotes.html.

Adorno, Theodor W. 2000. *Aesthetic Theory*, trans. Robert Hullot-Kentor. Minneapolis: University of Minnesota Press.

Agambien, Giorgio. 2009. *What is an Apparatus?* trans. David Kishik and Stefan Pedatella. Stanford: Stanford University Press.

Akerlof, George A., Paul M. Romer, Robert E. Hall, and N. Gregory Mankiw. 1993. "Looting: The Economic Underworld of Bankruptcy for Profit." *Brookings Papers on Economic Activity* 2: 1–73.

Albert, David Z. 1992. *Quantum Mechanics and Experience.* Cambridge: Harvard University Press.

"Anonymity." 2015. *Bitcoin Wiki!*, February 22: http://en. bitcoinwiki.org/Anonymity.

Arrighi, Giovanni, Terrence Hopkins, and Immanuel Waller-stein. 1989. *Anti-Systemic Movements.* New York: Verso.

Baker, James A., III, and Lee H. Hamilton, co-chairs. 2006. *The Iraq Study Group Report.* New York: Vintage.

Barber, Simon, Xavier Boyen, Elaine Shi, and Ersin Uzun. 2012. "Bitter to Better — How to Make Bitcoin a Better Currency." In *Financial Cryptography and Data Security,* ed. Angelos D. Keromytis, 399–414. Berlin: Springer.

Barthes, Roland. 1977. *Image — Music — Text,* trans. Stephen Heath. New York: Hill and Wang.

---. 1985. *The Responsibility of Forms: Critical Essays on Music, Art, and Representation,* trans. Richard Howard. Berkeley: The University of California Press.

Baudrillard, Jean. 1987. *The Ecstasy of Communication,* trans. Bernard and Carolyn Schutze. New York: Semiotext(e).

---. 2000. *Impossible Exchange,* trans. Chris Turner. New York: Verso.

---. 2005. *The Intelligence of Evil, or the Lucidity Pact,* trans. Chris Turner. New York: Berg.

---. 1990. *Seduction,* trans. Brian Singer. New York: St. Martin's Press.

---. 1983. *Simulations,* trans. Phil Beitchman, Paul Foss, and Paul Patton. New York: Semiotext(e).

Beardsley, Monroe C. 1958. *Aesthetics: Problems in the Philosophy of Criticism.* New York: Harcourt, Brace and World.

Benjamin, Walter. 1969. "The Work of Art in the Age of Mechanical Reproduction." In *Illuminations: Essays and Reflections,* ed. Hannah Arendt, trans. Harry Zohn, 217–251. New York: Schocken Books.

Bernanke, Benjamin. 2009. "Four Questions about the Financial Crisis." Speech given at Morehouse College, Atlanta, Georgia, April 14. *Federal Reserve System,* www.federal reserve.gov/newsevents/speech/bernanke20090414a.htm.

Bertelsen, Lance. 1992. "Journalism, Carnival, and *Jubilate Agno.*" ELH 59.2 (Summer): 357–384.

Bey, Hakim. 1991. *T.A.Z.: The Temporary Autonomous Zone.* Brooklyn: Autonomedia.

Biddle, Peter, Paul England, Marcus Peinado, and Bryan Willman. 2002. "The Darknet and the Future of Content Distribution." Paper presented at ACM Workshop on Digital Rights Management, Washington DC, November 18. *Applied Cryptography Group* (Stanford University), crypto.stanford.edu/DRM2002/darknet5.doc.

"Bitcoin History." 2015. *Bitcoin Wiki!*, June 15: http://en.bitcoinwiki.org/Bitcoin_history.

Bleuler, Eugen. 1950. *Dementia Praecox, or the Group of Schizophrenias.* New York: International Universities Press.

---. 1912. *The Theory of Schizophrenic Negativism*, trans. William A. White. New York: Journal of Nervous and Mental Disease.

Bridle, James. "The New Aesthetic." *Tumblr.com*, http://new-aesthetic.tumblr.com/.

---. "The Meaning of the New Aesthetic." 2012. *Tumblr.com*, March 15: http://booktwo.org/notebook/sxaesthetic/.

---. "Waving At The Machines." 2011. *Booktwo.org*, December 5: http://booktwo.org/notebook/waving-at-machines/.

Brooks, David. 2001. *Bobos in Paradise.* New York: Simon and Schuster.

Calvete de Estrella, Juan Christobal. 1930. *El Felicísimo Viaje del Muy Alto y Muy Poderoso Príncipe Don Felipe.* Madrid: La Sociedad de Bibliofilos Espanoles.

Cassirer, Ernst. 1953. *Langauge and Myth.* New York: Dover.

Chapman, Bob. 2008. "Liquidity Injection Won't Cure Wall Street Disease." *The International Forecaster*, October 15, theinternationalforecaster.com/International_Forecaster_Weekly/Liquidity_Injection_Wont_Cure_Wall_Street_Disease.

Chossudovsky, Michel and Andrew Gavin, eds. 2010. *The Global Economic Crisis: The Great Depression of the XXI Century.* Montreal: Center for Research on Globalization.

Christin, Nicholas. 2013. "Travelling the Silk Road: A Measurement Analysis of a Large Anonymous Online Marketplace." Paper presented at the 22nd International World Wide Web Conference, May 13–17, Rio de Janeiro, Brazil.

Cole, David. 2014. "We Kill People Based on Metadata." *New York Review of Books,* May 10, www.nybooks.com/blogs/nyrblog/2014/may/10/we-kill-people-based-metadata/.

Crimp, Douglas. 1995. *On the Museum's Ruins.* Cambridge: The MIT Press.

Critical Art Ensemble. 2001. *Digital Resistance: Explorations in Tactical Media.* Brooklyn: Autonomedia.

---. 1996. *Electronic Civil Disobedience.* Brooklyn: Autonomedia.

---. 1994. *The Electronic Disturbance.* Brooklyn: Autonomedia.

---. 1998. *Flesh Machine.* Brooklyn: Autonomedia.

---. 2006. *Marching Plague.* Brooklyn: Autonomedia.

---. 2002. *The Molecular Invasion.* Brooklyn: Autonomedia.

Culler, Jonathan. 2006. *The Literary in Theory.* Stanford: Stanford University Press.

Davies, Katie. 2013. "The Monster Machines Mining Bitcoins in Cyberspace that Could Make Techies a Small Fortune (but cost $160,000 a day to power)." *Daily Mail,* April 15, www.dailymail.co.uk/news/article-2309673/Techies-building-powerful-computers-Bitcoins-new-digital-currency-make-millions.html.

Debord, Guy. 1995. *The Society of the Spectacle,* trans. Donald Nicholson-Smith. New York: Zone Books.

Deleuze, Gilles and Félix Guattari. 1983. *Anti-Oedipus,* trans. Robert Hurley, Mark Seem, and Helen R. Lane. Minneapolis: University of Minnesota Press.

Dennis, Dion. 2003. "The Digital Death Rattle of the American Middle Class: A Cautionary Tale." *CTheory,* November 18, www.ctheory.net/articles.aspx?id=402.

Disch, Thomas. 1998. *The Dreams Our Stuff Is Made Of.* New York: Touchstone.

Döpfner, Mathias. 2014. "Open Letter to Eric Schmidt: Why We Fear Google." *Frankfurter Allgemeine,* April 14, www.faz.net/-gsf-7oid8.

Druckrey, Timothy. 1999. *Ars Electronica: Facing the Future.* Cambridge: The MIT Press.

Dyson, Freeman. 1985. *Infinite in All Directions.* New York: Harper and Row.

Eco, Umberto. 1979. *A Theory of Semiotics.* Bloomington: University of Indiana Press.

---. 1992. *Interpretation and Overinterpretation,* ed. Stefan Collini. Cambridge: Cambridge University press.

---. 1994. *The Limits of Interpretation.* Bloomington: University of Indiana Press.

Eggertsson, Gauti. 2010. "The Paradox of Toil." Federal Reserve Bank of New York Staff Reports 433 (March), www.newyorkfed.org/research/staff_reports/sr433.html.

Einhäuser, Wolfgang, Kevan A.C. Martin, and Peter König. 2004. "Are Switches in Perception of the Necker Cube Related to Eye Position?" *European Journal of Neuroscience* 20.10: 2811–2818.

Eno, Brian and Peter Schmidt. 1975. *Oblique Strategies: Over One Hundred Worthwhile Dilemmas.* London.

Farrell, Stephen. 2014. "BCP 188: Pervasive Monitoring Is an Attack." *Internet Engineering Task Force Datatracker,* May 12, https://datatracker.ietf.org/doc/rfc7258/.

Feynman, Richard. 1998. *The Meaning of It All.* Reading: Helix Books.

Ford, Martin R. 2009. *The Lights in the Tunnel: Automation, Accelerating Technology and the Economy of the Future.* New York: Acculant Publishing.

Foucault, Michel. 1972. *The Archaeology of Knowledge,* trans. A.M. Sheridan Smith. New York: Pantheon.

---. 2003. *The Birth of the Clinic: An Archaeology of Medical Perception.* London: Routledge.

---. 1995. *Discipline and Punish: The Birth of the Prison,* trans. A.M Sheridan Smith. New York: Vintage.

---. 1977. *Language, Counter-Memory, Practice,* trans. Donald F. Bouchard and Sherry Simon, ed. Donald F. Bouchard. Ithaca: Cornell University Press, 1977.

---. 1988. *Madness and Civilization,* trans. Richard Howard. New York: Vintage.

---. 1991. *Remarks on Marx*, trans. R. James Goldstein and James Cascaito. New York: Semiotext(e).

Frey, Carl Benedikt and Michael A. Osborne. 2013. "The Future of Employment: How Susceptible are Jobs to Computerization?" *Oxford Martin School*, September 17, http://www.oxfordmartin.ox.ac.uk/publications/view/1314.

Friedman, Milton. 2002. *Capitalism and Freedom*. Chicago: University of Chicago Press.

Garreau, Joel. 1992. *Edge City*. New York: Anchor.

Garrison, Mark. 1982. "The Poetics of Ambivalence." *Spring: An Annual of Archetypal Psychology and Jungian Thought*: 213–232.

Goodman, Cynthia. 1987. *Digital Visions*. New York: Abrams.

Greenberg, Clement. 1955-1993. *The Collected Essays and Criticism*, ed. John O'Brian, Vols. 1-4. Chicago: University of Chicago Press.

Greenspan, Alan. 1990. "Letter to SEC Chairman Richard C. Breeden," November 1, http://economyblog.ncpa.org/wp-content/plugins/uploads/Greenspan%20letter%20to%20SEC%20November%201990.pdf.

Hallock-Greenewalt, Mary. 1946. *Nourathar: The Fine Art of Light-Color Playing*. Philadelphia: Westbrook.

Hankins, Thomas L. and Robert J. Silverman. 1995. *Instruments and the Imagination*. Princeton: Princeton University Press.

Harding, Luke. "How Edward Snowden went from loyal NSA contractor to whistleblower." *The Guardian*, January 31, www.theguardian.com/world/2014/feb/01/edward-snowden-intelligence-leak-nsa-contractor-extract.

Heidegger, Martin. 1996. *Being and Time*, trans. Joan Stambaugh. New York: State University of New York Press.

Hesse, Carla. 2002. "The Rise of Intellectual Property, 700 b.c.–a.d. 2000: An Idea in the Balance." *Daedalus* 131.2 (Spring): 26–45.

Hofstadter, Douglas R. *Gödel, Escher, Bach: An Eternal Golden Braid*. New York: Basic Books, 1979.

Holland, John. 1995. *Hidden Order: How Adaptation Builds Complexity*. Reading: Perseus. Books.

Houston, Joe. 2002. *Post-Digital Painting.* Bloomfield Hills: Cranbrook.

Hungerford, Thomas L. 2013. "Changes in Income Inequality Among U.S. Tax Filers Between 1991 and 2006: The Role of Wages, Capital Income, and Taxes." *Social Science Research Network,* January 23, ssrn.com/abstract=2207372.

Jameson, Frederic. 1995. *Postmodernism or the Cultural Logic of Late Capitalism.* Durham: Duke University Press.

---. 1992. *Signatures of the Visible.* New York: Routledge.

Kaplan, Wendy. 1988. *The Art that is Life: The Arts and Crafts Movement in America, 1857-1920.* Boston: Bulfinch.

Katyal, Sonia K. 2006. "Semiotic Disobedience." *Washington University Law Review* 84.3: http://openscholarship.wustl.edu/law_lawreview/vol84/iss3/1/.

Keiser, Max. 2010. "Some Other Alternatives to Fiat Currencies." *Max Keiser,* December 13, www.maxkeiser.com/2010/12/some-other-alternatives-to-fiat-currencies/.

Klein, Naomi. 2008. *The Shock Doctrine.* New York: Picador.

---. 2005. "The Rise of Disaster Capitalism." *The Nation,* April 14, http://www.thenation.com/article/rise-disaster-capitalism/.

Kuhn, Thomas S. 1996. *The Structure of Scientific Revolutions.* Chicago: University of Chicago Press.

Latour, Bruno. 2014. "On Some of the Affects of Capitalism." Lecture given at the Royal Academy, Copenhagen, February 26. *Bruno Latour* (website), http://www.bruno-latour.fr/sites/default/files/136-AFFECTS-OF-K-COPENHAGUE.pdf.

Lears, T.J. Jackson. 1981. *No Place of Grace: Anti-Modernism and the Transformation of American Culture, 1880-1920.* New York: Pantheon.

Levin, Thomas Y., Ursula Frohne, and Peter Weibel. 2002. *CRTL Space.* Cambridge: The MIT Press.

Levine, Yasha. 2013. "The Psychological Dark Side of Gmail." *Alternet,* December 31, www.alternet.org/media/google-using-gmail-build-psychological-profiles-hundreds-millions-people.

Loos, Adolph. 2002. "Crime and Ornament," in *The Arts and Popular Culture in the Shadow of Adolph Loos*, eds. Bernie Miller and Melony Ward, 29–36, New York: XYZ Books.

Lovink, Gert and Sabine Niederer. 2008. *Video Vortex Reader: Responses to Youtube.* Amsterdam: Institute of Network Cultures.

Marazzi, Christian. 2011. *The Violence of Financial Capitalism.* Los Angeles: Semiotext(e).

Marcuse, Herbert. 1954. *Reason and Revolution.* New York: Humanities Press.

---. 1968. "The Affirmative Characters of Culture." In *Negations*, trans. Jeremy Shapiro. Boston: Beacon.

Marx, Karl. 1992. *Capital,* Vol. 1, trans. Ben Fowkes. New York, Penguin Classics.

---. 1999. *Capital,* Vol. 3, ed. Friedrich Engels. New York: International Publishers.

---. 1993. *The Grundrisse.* London: Penguin Classics.

McDonough, Tom. 2004. *Guy Debord and the Situationalist International: Texts and Documents.* Cambridge: The MIT Press.

McLuhan, Marshall and Bruce R. Powers. 1989. *The Global Village.* New York: Oxford University Press.

Menger, Carl. 1950. *Principles of Economics,* trans. James Dingwall and Bert F. Hoselitz. New York: The Free Press.

Mihm, Stephen. 2009. "Why Capitalism Fails." *The Boston Globe*, September 13, www.boston.com/bostonglobe/ideas/ articles/2009/09/13/why_capitalism_fails.

Mumford, Lewis. 1962. *The City in History.* New York: Harcourt, Brace and World.

Nagel, Ernest and James R. Newman. 1958. *Gödel's Theorem.* New York: New York University Press.

Nakamoto, Satoshi. [n.d.] "Bitcoin: A Peer-to-Peer Electronic Cash System," *Bitcoin* (website), http://www.bitcoin.org/ bitcoin.pdf.

Nanex Flash Crash Summary Report. 2010. *Nanex.net*, September 27, http://www.nanex.net/FlashCrashFinal/ Flash CrashSummary.html.

Navas, Eduardo. 2012. *Remix Theory: The Aesthetics of Sampling.* New York: Springer.

Necker, Louis Albert. 1832. *The London & Edinburgh Philosophical Magazine and Journal of Science* 1: 329–337.

Nunn, Samuel. 2006. "Tell Us What's Going to Happen: Information Feeds to the War on Terror." *CTheory*, September 1, http://www.ctheory.net/articles.aspx?id=518.

O'Doherty, Biran. 2000. *Inside the White Cube: The Ideology of the Gallery Space,* rev. edn. Berkeley: The University of California Press.

Palihapitiya, Chamath. 2013. "Why I Invested in Bitcoin." *Bloomberg View*, May 30, http://www.bloombergview.com/articles/2013-05-30/bitcoin-the-perfect-schmuck-insurance.

Pally, Marcia. 1994. *Sex and Sensibility.* Hopewell: Ecco Press.

Parlá, Rey. 2008. "Interview with José Parlá." *Skin* 2.17 (August): 38–39.

---. "Organic Harmonies." In *Wreckless Abandon.* Miami: O.H.W.O.W.

Perelman, Michael. 2000. *The Invention of Capitalism.* Durham: Duke University Press.

Petric, Vlada. 1987. *Constructivism in Films: The Man with a Movie Camera.* Cambridge: Cambridge University Press.

Pevsner, Nickolaus. 2011. *Pioneers of Modern Design: From William Morris to Walter Gropius.* Bath: Palazzo Editions.

Polleit, Thorsten. 2011. "Fiat Money and Collective Corruption." *QJAE: Quarterly Journal of Austrian Economics* 14.4: 397–414; https://mises.org/library/fiat-money-and-collective-corruption-0.

Prada, Juan Martin. 2010. "Economies of Affectivity." *Caring Labor: An Archive,* July 29, 2010, https://caringlabor.wordpress.com/2010/07/29/juan-martin-prada-economies-of-affectivity/.

Proctor, Robert N. and Londa Schiebinger, eds. 2008. *Agnotology: The Making and Unmaking of Ignorance.* Stanford: Stanford University Press.

Reich, Robert B. 2008. *Supercapitalism: The Transformation of Business, Democracy, and Everyday Life*. New York: Vintage.

Reid, Fergal and Martin Harrigan. 2013. "An Analysis of Anonymity in the Bitcoin System," in *Security and Privacy in Social Networks*, eds. Yaniv Altshuler et al. (New York: Springer), 197–223.

Richards, Robert. 1998. "Rhapsodies on a Cat Piano." *Critical Inquiry* 24.3: 700–736.

Rombes, Nicholas. 2005. "The Rebirth of the Author." *CTheory*, October 5, www.ctheory.net/articles.aspx?id=480.

"Satoshi Nakamoto." 2014. *Bitcoin Wiki!*, August 14: http://en.bitcoinwiki.org/Satoshi_Nakamoto.

Schott, Gaspar. 1657. *Magia Universalis natura et artis*. Herbipoli: Henric Pigrin.

Schwartz, Lillian. 1992. *The Computer Artist's Handbook*. New York: Simon and Schuster.

"The Silk Road." Wikipedia, en.wikipedia.org/wiki/Silk_Road_(marketplace).

Smith, Patrick. 1986. *Andy Warhol's Art and Films*. Ann Arbor: UMI Research Press.

Sokal, Alan and Jean Bricmont. 2004. *Intellectual Impostures*. New Delhi: Profile Books.

Stutz, Dave. 2004. "Some Implications of Software Commodification." *Synthesist*, March 2, www.synthesist.net/writing/commodity_software.html.

Sutzl, Wolfgang. 2007. "Tragic Extremes." *CTheory*, September 20, http://www.ctheory.net/articles.aspx?id=582

Tencer, Daniel. 2009. "Spitzer: Federal Reserve is 'a Ponzi scheme, an inside job'." *Global Research*, July 28, http://www.globalresearch.ca/index.php?context=va&aid=14559.

Thompson, Derek. 2010. "Google's CEO: 'The Laws are Written by Lobbyists'." *The Atlantic*, October 1, http://www.theatlantic.com/technology/archive/2010/10/googles-ceo-the-laws-are-written-by-lobbyists/63908/#video.

Timberg, Craig. 2014. "Research in India Suggests Google Search Results Can Influence an Election." *The Washington Post*, May 12, https://www.washingtonpost.com/blogs

/the-switch/wp/2014/05/12/research-in-India-suggests-google-search-results-can-influence-an-election.

Torres, Craig. 2009. "Fed to Buy $300 Billion of Longer-Term Treasuries." *Bloomberg News,* March 18, www.bloomberg.com/apps/news?pid=20601068&sid=aPlq8GB5FWSc.

"Total Information Awareness." *The Center for Media and Democracy*, www.sourcewatch.org/index.php?title=Total_Information_Awareness.

Tully, James. 2006. "Communication and Imperialism." *CTheory*, February 22, http://www.ctheory.net/articles.aspx?id=508.

"Un Orchestre de Chats et un concert d'ânes." In *La Nature* 541 (1883): 319-320.

US Census Bureau. 2003. "Educational Attainment," www.census.gov/population/www/socdemo/education/cps2003.html.

Van Vechten, Carl. 1920. "The Cat in Music." *The Musical Quarterly* 6.4: 573–585.

Veblen, Thorstein. 1994. *The Theory of The Leisure Class.* New York: Dover.

Vertov, Dziga. 1984. *Kino-Eye: The Writings of Dziga Vertov*, ed. Annette Michselson, trans. Kevin O'Brien. Berkeley: University of California Press.

Virilio, Paul. 1986. *Speed and Politics*, trans. Mark Polizzotti. New York: Semiotext(e).

---. 1989. *War and Cinema: The Logistics of Perception*, trans. Patrick Camiller. New York: Verso.

---. 2003. *Art and Fear*, trans. Julie Rose. New York: Continuum.

Weckerlin, Jean-Baptiste. 1877. *Nouveau Musiciana: extraits d'ouvrages rares ou bizarres.* Paris: Garnier Freres.

Weschler, Lawrence. 1999. *Boggs: A Comedy of Values.* Chicago: University of Chicago Press.

Wieser, Friedrich von. 1927. *Social Economics.* New York: Adelphi Company.

Wittgenstein, Ludwig. 1972. *On Certainty*, trans. G.E.M. Anscombe. New York: Harper and Row.

---. 2000. *Philosophical Investigations*, trans. G.E.M. Anscombe. London: Blackwell Publishers.

Woolf, Nancy J and Stuart Hameroff. 2001. "A Quantum Approach to Visual Consciousness." *Trends in Cognitive Science* 5.11 (November): 472–478.

Woolf, Nicky. 2015. "Silk Road's Dread Pirate Roberts Convicted of Running an Online Drug Marketplace." *The Guardian*, February 4, http://www.theguardian.com/technology/2015/feb/04/silk-road-ross-ulbricht-convicted-drug-charges.

Wu, Chin-Tao. 2002. *Privatizing Culture*. New York: Verso.